CAMBRIDGE TEXTS IN THE
HISTORY OF PHILOSOPHY

———

NICOLAS MALEBRANCHE
Dialogues on Metaphysics and on Religion

CAMBRIDGE TEXTS IN THE
HISTORY OF PHILOSOPHY

Series editors
KARL AMERIKS
Professor of Philosophy at the University of Notre Dame
DESMOND M. CLARKE
Professor of Philosophy at University College Cork

The main objective of Cambridge Texts in the History of Philosophy is to expand the range, variety and quality of texts in the history of philosophy which are available in English. The series includes texts by familiar names (such as Descartes and Kant) and also by less well-known authors. Wherever possible, texts are published in complete and unabridged form, and translations are specially commissioned for the series. Each volume contains a critical introduction together with a guide to further reading and any necessary glossaries and textual apparatus. The volumes are designed for student use at undergraduate and postgraduate level and will be of interest, not only to students of philosophy, but also to a wider audience of readers in the history of science, the history of theology and the history of ideas.

For a list of titles published in the series, please see end of book.

NICOLAS MALEBRANCHE

Dialogues on Metaphysics and on Religion

EDITED BY

NICHOLAS JOLLEY

University of California, San Diego

TRANSLATED BY

DAVID SCOTT

Gonzaga University, Spokane

CAMBRIDGE
UNIVERSITY PRESS

Published by the Press Syndicate of the University of Cambridge
The Pitt Building, Trumpington Street, Cambridge CB2 1RP
40 West 20th Street, New York, NY 10011–4211, USA
10 Stamford Road, Oakleigh, Melbourne 3166, Australia

First published 1997

Printed in the United Kingdom at the University Press, Cambridge

A catalogue record for this book is available from the British Library

Library of Congress cataloguing in publication data
Malebranche, Nicolas, 1638–1715.
[Entretiens sur la métaphysique & sur la religion. English]
Dialogues on metaphysics and on religion / Nicolas Malebranche : edited by Nicholas Jolley,
translated by David Scott.
p.   cm. – (Cambridge texts in the history of philosophy)
Includes bibliographical references and index.
1. Metaphysics – Early works to 1800.
2. Religion – Philosophy – Early works to 1800.
3. God – Early works to 1800.
4. Occasionalism – Early works to 1800.
5. Imaginary conversations – Early works to 1800.
I. Jolley, Nicholas.   II Scott, David (David James Frederick).
III. Title.   IV. Series.
B1893.E63E5   1997
110–dc20   96–19806   CIP

ISBN 0 521 57402 1 hardback
ISBN 0 521 57435 8 paperback

CE

Contents

Acknowledgments

Nicholas Jolley is grateful to Desmond Clarke, Tad Schmaltz, and David Scott for helpful comments on a previous draft of the Introduction.

David Scott is especially grateful to Desmond Clarke for his editorial comments and for his suggestions for translation. Professors F. E. Andrews and James Doull also offered useful translation suggestions, as did Professor Nicholas Jolley. He is grateful to Drs. Catherine and Michael Tkacz for their assistance with the translation of some of the text's Latin passages, and to Dr. Lindeth Vasey for her editorial comments. Finally, he would also like to acknowledge having had the benefit of the translations of the *Dialogues on Metaphysics and on Religion* by Morris Ginsberg (London, George Allen & Unwin Ltd., 1923) and by Willis Doney (New York, Abaris Books, 1980).

Abbreviations

AT   C. Adam and P. Tannery (eds.), *Œuvres de Descartes* (12 vols., Paris, Cerf, 1897–1913; reprint Paris, Vrin/CNRS, 1964–76)

CSM   J. Cottingham, R. Stoothoff, and D. Murdoch (eds.), *The Philosophical Writings of Descartes* (3 vols., Cambridge, Cambridge University Press, 1985–91). Vol. III (*The Correspondence*) incorporates a revised version of Anthony Kenny's translation of Descartes' letters and is abbreviated as "CSMK"

G   C. I. Gerhardt (ed.), *Die Philosophischen Schriften von G. W. Leibniz*, (7 vols., Berlin, Weidmann, 1875–90)

LO   T. M. Lennon and P. J. Olscamp (trans.), *Nicolas Malebranche: The Search after Truth* (Columbus, Ohio, Ohio State University Press, 1980); republished with a new Introduction by T. Lennon, in Cambridge Texts in the History of Philosophy, 1997

OC   A. Robinet (ed.), *Œuvres complètes de Malebranche* (20 vols., Paris, Vrin, 1958–76)

Introduction

At Christmas 1686 Malebranche wrote to a correspondent, Pierre Berrand:

> I am pressed to compose a metaphysics. I believe that indeed that's very necessary, and that I should have more facility for the task than many people. Good metaphysics must govern everything and I shall try to establish in it the principal truths which are the foundations of religion and ethics. It seems to me that what I shall do will be better than what I have done previously.[1]

Malebranche was surely justified in his confidence that the work he envisaged would be better than anything he had previously written. Although it is less famous and narrower in scope than the earlier *Search after Truth*, the *Dialogues on Metaphysics and on Religion*, first published in 1688, is Malebranche's masterpiece; certainly, from a strictly literary point of view it is a far better work than the notoriously rambling *Search*. But the literary quality of the *Dialogues* is not the only reason why it provides a more accessible introduction to Malebranche's philosophy than the earlier book; another is the difference in conception between the two works. In *The Search after Truth* Malebranche is chiefly concerned to analyze the nature and sources of error, and to propose strategies for avoiding it; the *Search* is to a large extent a treatise on method. By contrast, the *Dialogues* is a work on metaphysics in the broad sense which includes not only ontology but also the theory of knowledge. It is in these terms that we must understand the fact that Malebranche's most famous doctrines, such as occasionalism and vision

[1] Malebranche to Berrand, 26 December 1686, *OC* XII–XIII vi.

in God, are accorded the prominent place in the *Dialogues* which they are denied in the *Search*.

The *Dialogues* and the characters

By the time of writing the *Dialogues* Malebranche's philosophy had been embroiled in controversy for a number of years, and as Willis Doney has observed, Malebranche thus had the benefit of knowing which of his doctrines caused most difficulties for his readers.[2] Malebranche's awareness of these areas of difficulty may help to explain his decision to cast his major work on metaphysics in the form of a series of dialogues. For Malebranche the dialogue offered a way of vividly presenting the objections which he had encountered and of responding to them; Malebranche was able to show that he understood how counterintuitive his doctrines appeared to many readers. In the *Dialogues* the role of presenting objections to Malebranche's philosophy is chiefly assigned to Aristes who is opposed by the Malebranchian spokesman, the "meditator" Theodore. But it is a sign of Malebranche's literary skill that Aristes's speeches are not simply a random collection of objections; on the contrary, Malebranche has taken some pains to invest his character with a distinctive philosophical personality of his own. Aristes is presented as a rather worldly figure who is intrigued by what he has heard of the Malebranchian philosophy and is eager to know more, but he is initially skeptical because of a temperamental inclination towards empiricism; as he says, he has had a lifelong tendency to trust the testimony of the senses in the search for truth (Dialogue IV xvi) and in a rather Lockean way he is inclined to believe that ideas are the workmanship of the understanding (II vii). Although Aristes is a willing disciple, and can even at times serve as a spokesman for Malebranchian views, he also shows a marked tendency to backslide into the empiricism which is natural to him and, as Malebranche suggests, to all human minds (VII xvi).

[2] See W. Doney (trans.), *Nicolas Malebranche: Entretiens sur la Métaphysique/Dialogues on Metaphysics* (New York, Abaris, 1980), p. 8. Between the publication of the *Search* and the composition of the *Dialogues*, Malebranche had been engaged in controversy with Simon Foucher and Antoine Arnauld. The exchange with the latter, which was initiated by the publication of Arnauld's *Des vraies et des fausses Idées* [*On True and False Ideas*] (1683), was particularly important and long-lived; it centered chiefly on Malebranche's theory of ideas, but it also involved such issues as the nature of self-knowledge and our knowledge of the external world.

The first few dialogues are a straightforward duologue between the Malebranchian spokesman and the empiricist objector, but the work does not continue in this fashion; in Dialogue VII Malebranche surprises the reader by introducing a new speaker, Theotimus. At least in retrospect we can see that Malebranche has prepared the ground for his entrance in earlier dialogues; at the end of Dialogue IV, for instance, we learn that, in conversations that have taken place offstage, Theotimus has defended the honor of reason against the assaults of Aristes (IV xxii). Although Theotimus sometimes proposes difficulties for Theodore and echoes Aristes's objections, he describes himself as having long been convinced of Malebranche's principles (VII xii). We may thus be prompted to wonder why Malebranche felt the need to introduce a third speaker into the dialogues. Two answers suggest themselves. Most obviously, the introduction of the third person serves a dramatic purpose by breaking the monotony of the straightforward duologue. More importantly, Theotimus's support helps to dispel the impression that Theodore is the lonely advocate of a rather eccentric philosophical position. On the contrary, Theotimus's role as a long-standing disciple of Theodore tends to convey the idea that Malebranche's doctrines have started to gain a foothold in the philosophical community. The Malebranchian philosophy is, as it were, the wave of the future.

Philosophy and theology

Aristes speaks for many readers when he objects to Theodore's recourse to truths of faith to solve philosophical problems (IX v). Certainly, those who think of Malebranche as a devoted, if unorthodox, disciple of Descartes may not be prepared for Malebranche's peculiar way of blending metaphysical and religious themes. It is true of course that there is a kind of theology even in Descartes; he uses reason to prove the existence of God and, notoriously, he appeals to God's existence to solve philosophical problems such as skepticism about the external world. But although Descartes is an exponent of philosophical theology, as a matter of policy he seeks to stay clear of revealed theology; when asked for his views about issues such as grace and transubstantiation, he characteristically says that he prefers to leave theology to the theologians.[3] Malebranche, by contrast, belongs to the Augustinian tradition which shows no such inclination to place philosophy and theology in separate compartments. It is unfair to accuse Malebranche, as is sometimes done, of simply confusing or identifying the two disciplines; even in the *Dialogues* there are passages where the speakers reveal an awareness of the difference between the methods and assumptions of the two areas of inquiry (see, for example, I, VI i, and XIV xiii). It would be more accurate to say that, in line with Augustine and Anselm, Malebranche believes that philosophy and theology may be serviceable to each other in their common endeavor of seeking truth. Philosophy can serve theology by affording rational insight into the mysteries of the Christian faith; faith should ultimately give way to rational understanding.[4] Theology can serve philosophy by providing answers to problems which can in principle be solved in no other way. The *Dialogues on Metaphysics and on Religion* offers some striking examples of the second strategy in particular. Thus Malebranche appeals to revelation, for instance, for assurance of the existence of bodies. More remarkably, he cites the effects of the biblical Fall to explain why we are inclined to believe that the senses are reliable guides to the true nature of bodies. Here the contrast with Descartes is revealing. What Descartes had explained in terms of the effects of youthful education,[5] Malebranche explains in terms of a Christian dogma.

There is, however, a much deeper sense in which Malebranche seeks to harness philosophy and theology. Malebranche's whole philosophical system is informed by a profound theological intuition; it is the intuition expressed in Paul's words in Acts that in God we live, move, and have our being (Acts 17:28). It is in a systematic attempt to do justice to this intuition that Malebranche argues for the total dependence of creatures on the Creator in all their operations; in the special case of human beings he adduces ingenious and sometimes subtle arguments to show that we are wholly lacking in causal and cognitive resources of our own.

---

[3] See, for example, Descartes to Mersenne, 6 and 27 May 1630, AT I 150, 153; CSMK 25, 26. Cf. Descartes to Mesland, 2 May 1644 and 9 February 1645, AT IV 117, 165; CSMK 234, 242.

[4] For statements of this idea, see, for example, IV xvii; VI i; and XIV iv. Here Malebranche is alluding to the traditional Anselmian formula of *fides quaerens intellectum* (faith seeking understanding). For helpful accounts of Malebranche's view of the relationship between faith and reason, see Martial Gueroult, *Malebranche* (3 vols., Paris, Aubier, 1955–9), vol. 1, ch. 1; and Geneviève Rodis-Lewis, *Nicolas Malebranche* (Paris, Presses Universitaires de France, 1963), pp. 25–33.

[5] Descartes, Meditation I, AT VII 18; CSM II 12. The *Meditations* is published in this series.

In the *Dialogues*, in contrast to the *Search*, Malebranche never loses sight of this central intuition; it gives to the work a profound and satisfying thematic unity.

One might further characterize Malebranche's project in the *Dialogues* by saying that it seeks to reinterpret the Cartesian system in the light of the Pauline doctrine. Sometimes the reader will find that Malebranche is able to take over Cartesian theses without serious modification. This tendency is apparent early on in the *Dialogues*. In the first dialogue Malebranche's spokesman Theodore expounds familiar Cartesian arguments for the mind–body dualism which officially at least provides the metaphysical framework for the created universe. Again, the reader soon encounters echoes of the familiar insistence in the *Meditations* on the need to turn away from the senses in the search for truth. But at other times the attempt to do philosophical justice to the Pauline doctrine leads Malebranche to depart quite radically from Cartesian teaching. Either he pushes Descartes' ideas much further than he himself was prepared to do, as in the case of occasionalism, or he combines these teachings with a return to Platonic–Augustinian themes, as in the case of vision in God. In what follows we shall concentrate on the doctrines and arguments which are most distinctive of Malebranche, although we shall indicate some points of contact with Cartesian teaching.

Ideas and vision in God

In *The Search after Truth* the doctrine of vision in God is tucked away in the middle of the work.[6] An attractive feature of the *Dialogues*, by contrast, is that Malebranche introduces the doctrine early on; the claim that "we can see all things in God" appears explicitly in the title of Dialogue II, and the ground is at least prepared for it in the first by a discussion of the nature of ideas. But although it soon becomes clear that Malebranche here is breaking with the Cartesian theory of ideas by taking them out of the mind and locating them in God, the reader of the first two dialogues may well be puzzled about the scope of the doctrine. Although Malebranche speaks of seeing things in God, it is natural to wonder whether he is advancing a theory of visual perception at all; in

---

[6] III.2.vi, *OC* 437–47; LO 230–5.

view of his emphasis on the "intelligible world," it appears that his real concern is to offer a theory of abstract thought. It may seem, then, that the term "vision" is being used in a merely Pickwickian sense.

In reality there can be no real doubt about the intended scope of the doctrine. The famous thesis that we see all things in God is designed as a theory of the truly perceptual element in sense perception and as a theory of abstract thought. For Malebranche, whether we see the sun by day or think of it by night, the immediate objects of the mind are ideas in God. Indeed, for all his talk of the intelligible world, the case of abstract thought is not Malebranche's real interest in the early dialogues; his main concern is with the theory of sense perception. Through Theodore, Malebranche adopts the following strategy to argue for his distinctive doctrine. First, he argues for a version of the representative theory: the immediate objects of perception are never bodies but always nonmaterial ideas. Second, he argues that such ideas must be located in God. It will be seen, then, that in order to make the case for vision in God Malebranche must persuade the reader of the need to make two separate distinctions; not only must the immediate objects of the mind be distinguished from bodies but they must be further distinguished from mental states or modifications.

In the *Dialogues* Theodore offers a version of a familiar argument for the representative theory of perception. According to Malebranche, a perception is always the perception of some object; as he often puts it, to perceive nothing is not to perceive, and to see nothing is not to see.[7] As we might say, perception is inherently intentional. Now if the physical universe were destroyed, I could still have exactly the same immediate objects of perception as I do now; this claim is presumably buttressed by the evidence of dreams and hallucinations. But by hypothesis such objects could not be material in this case; they must, then, be immaterial items or ideas. From this rather modest conclusion Malebranche seeks to move to the general thesis that the immediate objects of perception are always ideas, and this move seems to involve him in a non-sequitur. From the fact that in cases of hallucination I do not directly perceive bodies it does not follow that I do not directly perceive them in cases of veridical perception. But Steven Nadler has come to Malebranche's rescue here. Malebranche seems to be com-

---

[7] See, for example, *Search* IV.11, *OC* II 99; LO 320. Cf. *OC* VI 202.

mitted to the principle that all the immediate objects of perception are homogeneous; they all have the same ontological status.[8] When this principle is introduced as an extra premise, the logical gap in the argument is plugged.

So far Malebranche has not sought to establish anything with which an orthodox Cartesian need disagree. If successful, the argument establishes that ideas are the immediate objects of perception, but it does not show that such ideas cannot be in the human mind. Thus Malebranche must now argue that ideas have properties which make it impossible for them to be located anywhere but in God. Unfortunately, the argument which Malebranche chiefly parades for this purpose in the *Dialogues* is not one of his clearest and may involve some distracting side issues; it turns on considerations about infinity (I VIII–IX).[9] Theodore claims that in perceiving the physical world we perceive the idea of extension (or what Malebranche also calls intelligible extension); this idea is infinite by virtue of the fact that infinitely many possible objects fall within its extension in the logical sense of the term. But every mental state is finite. The idea of extension thus cannot be a mental state and must exist in an infinite being, namely God.

Malebranche's case for the infinity of ideas was savagely attacked by Antoine Arnauld from the orthodox Cartesian standpoint that ideas are mental events.[10] Arnauld observes that Malebranche fails to engage with the Cartesian distinction between two irreducibly different aspects of ideas. On the one hand, ideas can be considered in terms of their "formal" or intrinsic reality as mental states; in this respect they are indeed finite modifications of the human mind. But on the other hand they can be considered in terms of their objective or representative reality, and when they are regarded in this light, in terms of content, there is no reason why they should not be infinite. Thus, as an orthodox Cartesian, Arnauld concedes to Malebranche that an idea may be infinite *in repraesentando* (representatively), but he still insists that it must be

---

[8] *Malebranche and Ideas* (Oxford, Oxford University Press, 1992), p. 83.

[9] A difficulty is that Malebranche seems to invoke infinity in two quite different contexts without clearly distinguishing them. He speaks of the idea of infinite extension, meaning thereby the idea of physically unlimited space, but he also speaks of the idea as infinite in the sense of applying to infinitely possible objects.

[10] Arnauld to Malebranche, 22 May 1694, *Œuvres de M. Arnauld* (Paris, 1780), vol. 40, pp. 88–9; quoted in Nadler, *Malebranche and Ideas*, p. 40. As Nadler observes, Arnauld is emphasizing a point that had earlier been made by Pierre-Sylvain Régis in his *Système général*.

finite *in essendo* (intrinsically). By means of this distinction Arnauld seeks to block Malebranche's argument for locating ideas in God.

At first sight Arnauld's critique can seem devastating, but further reflection suggests some doubts about its adequacy. Arnauld seems to suppose that Malebranche is arguing from our idea of infinity (or infinite extension) to the infinity of the idea as part of a general strategy for taking ideas out of the mind. But though Malebranche may sometimes appear to argue in this way, it is not clear that this is his main case for denying that ideas are mental entities. Malebranche is not so much appealing to the content of a given idea (the idea of infinity) as to the very nature of ideas themselves; ideas – for example, the idea of extension – apply to infinitely many possible objects, and no mere finite modification can do this. Whether Malebranche has a non-question-begging argument for this last thesis is perhaps doubtful, but at least it seems that he is not simply ignoring the distinction between what is true of ideas *in essendo* and what is true of ideas *in repraesentando*.[11] Even if we concede to Arnauld that ideas may have properties under one description which they do not have under another, he has not undermined Malebranche's basic strategy for taking ideas out of the mind.

Perhaps we can best see the strength of Malebranche's case if we focus, not on infinity, but on some of the other properties of ideas which he cites in order to make his case for putting ideas in God. Malebranche says, for example, that ideas are "common to all intellects" (I IX); in other words, when you and I think of a circle, we think of a numerically identical object. But the orthodox Cartesian must acknowledge that mental states are private to individual minds; to say that you and I think of the same thing can be no more than a manner of speaking. Again, Malebranche observes that ideas are eternal, and in partial support of this, it can at least be pointed out that the idea of a circle did not come into existence when I first started to think of a circle, and it will not cease to exist when I stop thinking of a circle. But the orthodox Cartesian must admit that mental states are fleeting or transitory. Considerations like these at least lend some plausibility to Malebranche's central contentions: ideas are not mental states or events; rather, they are logical or abstract entities which inhabit a Platonic "third realm" which Malebranche identifies with God.

---

[11] In reply to Régis Malebranche at least denied that he was ignoring this distinction: see *OC* XVII–1 302–3.

Despite the unclarity of his argument from infinity, then, Malebranche makes some rather persuasive points about the nature of ideas. But here an obvious objection must be faced. It may seem that in arguing for the location of ideas in God, Malebranche has simply switched the subject; it appears that he is now talking about concepts or objects of thought rather than about objects of perception. We could put the objection in another way. Let us suppose, for the sake of argument, that Malebranche succeeds in establishing his case for the representative theory of perception; in other words, the objects that we immediately perceive are always ideas. It is not clear why such objects must have the characteristics of eternity, infinity, and publicity, etc., to which Malebranche draws our attention; such properties may indeed belong to concepts, but it is a further question whether they are also predicable of the immediate objects of sense perception. Thus, even if Malebranche can make a plausible case for locating concepts in God, it does not follow that the immediate objects of perception are likewise in God.

The answer to this objection reveals just how far Malebranche is from holding a standard version of the representative theory of perception. In Malebranche's view, not merely do the objects which we immediately perceive share properties with concepts; they *are* concepts. Indeed, they are concepts of geometrical properties which, for Malebranche as a Cartesian in this respect, are the only properties which bodies truly possess. To perceive a body thus involves a relation to geometrical concepts in God. It is true of course that such concepts cannot be sensed; they must be apprehended in acts of intellectual awareness. But it is a mistake to suppose that Malebranche has simply overlooked this philosophical truth; rather, he can accommodate it by taking over Descartes' epistemological thesis that bodies are perceived through the intellect, not through the senses. As Malebranche says in the *Dialogues*, perceiving a square is a matter of judgment (V viii); we might say that, for him, all seeing is a case of seeing *that*. Descartes had been led to recognize an intellectual element in visual perception through reflecting on size and distance perception. In the Sixth Replies he recognizes a third, and highest, grade of sensory response to bodies which essentially involves judgment:

> ... suppose that, as a result of being affected by this sensation of colour, I judge that a stick, located outside me, is coloured; and

suppose that on the basis of the extension of the colour and its
boundaries together with its position in relation to the parts of the
brain, I make a rational calculation about the size, shape and distance
of the stick: although such reasoning is commonly assigned to the
senses ... it is clear that it depends solely on the intellect.[12]

Malebranche too is impressed by the element of rational calculation
here, and he has interesting things to say on the topic, though, as we
shall see, his account is not free from difficulties.

In the *Dialogues*, as in the Elucidations to *The Search after Truth*,
Malebranche takes the opportunity to clarify the doctrine of vision in
God in order to forestall possible misunderstandings. In his earliest
presentations of the doctrine Malebranche had tended to write of a
multiplicity or plurality of ideas in God; he had seemed to suggest that
there was a one-to-one correspondence between ideas and bodies, or
perhaps at least between ideas and kinds of bodies. Although Malebranche continues to speak on occasion of ideas in God, he indicates
that, where the physical world is concerned, this is really only a manner
of speaking; strictly, such ideas are only portions of intelligible extension
which God displays to our minds. We must not of course be deceived
by such language into supposing that physical parts or portions are in
question; for intelligible extension is clearly an ideal entity. Nonetheless,
Malebranche's talk of the parts of intelligible extension in God exposed
him to the charge that he had fallen victim to the Spinozistic thesis that
God is formally or intrinsically extended.[13]

Malebranche also seeks to defend his doctrine against the objection
that it runs counter to the scriptural assertion that no one has ever seen
God; according to Christian orthodoxy, of course, such vision will be
deferred to the life to come. It is to this objection that Malebranche is
responding when he emphasizes that he is not committed to the thesis
that we see God's essence absolutely; when we perceive ideas in God,
we see the divine essence only insofar as it is representative of bodies (II
11). There is thus an important distinction to be drawn between vision in
God and vision of God. Ironically, it might be more appropriate here to
suggest that Malebranche makes use of a Spinozistic maneuver in order
to counter an objection; he is distinguishing for epistemological

---

[12] Sixth Replies to the Objections to the *Meditations*, AT VII 437; CSM II 295.
[13] De Mairan to Malebranche, 6 May 1714, *OC* XIX 877–9. Cf. Arnauld, *Des vraies et des fausses Idées*, *Œuvres de M. Arnauld* (Paris, 1780; reprint Brussels, 1967), vol. 38, p. 255.

purposes between different descriptions of God. Spinoza had insisted that God can be known by human beings only under the two attributes of thought and extension; in a structurally similar way, Malebranche emphasizes that God can be perceived only in a certain respect – that is, only in so far as he is representative of bodies.

Ideas and sensations

We have seen, then, that Malebranche offers a highly unorthodox version of the representative theory of perception. According to his version of the doctrine, the immediate objects of perception are not sense-data or the like as they are in more standard versions of the doctrine; they are logical concepts located in God. Such a revision of the representative theory is not without striking advantages; it allows Malebranche to do justice, rather ingeniously, to the intuition that two different people can directly perceive numerically the same object. But it may seem that Malebranche has paid a high price for this advantage, for at first sight he appears to offer a theory of sense perception which wholly leaves out the sensory element. Even if Malebranche agrees with Descartes that our perception of bodies is in some sense intellectual, he ought to recognize that there is a difference between seeing the sun by day and thinking of the sun by night. But we may wonder whether Malebranche has the philosophical resources to offer an account of the difference.

In fact he is well aware of the problem, and offers an interesting solution, but he believes that it cannot be answered in terms of the theory of ideas alone. Although, as we shall see below, there are certain tensions in Malebranche's account, what we might call his official position is fairly clear: what distinguishes sense perception from thinking is the role played by *sentiments* or sensations. For Malebranche, any case of sense perception is a complex of heterogeneous elements; a geometrical idea or concept is joined to – or perceived in combination with – various sensations (see V II–III).[14] To see the sun by day is to perceive a geometrical concept of a circle in conjunction with various color sensations which are in some sense projected on to the idea.[15] To say that it is in terms of sensations that Malebranche explains the difference

---

[14] Cf. *Search* III.2.vi, *OC* I 445; LO 234.
[15] See Elucidation X, *Search*, *OC* III 152; LO 626. It is not clear how sensations can be projected on to logical concepts. For criticism of this kind, see Nadler, *Malebranche and Ideas*, pp. 64–6.

between perceiving and thinking is not of course to deny that, even in thinking, I may have some sensations; it is only to say that I cannot have qualitatively identical sensations when I see the sun and when I merely think of it.

In his theory of sensations Malebranche partly follows and partly goes beyond Cartesian teaching. Malebranche of course agrees with his great predecessor that there is nothing in bodies which remotely resembles our sensations, for bodies possess only geometrical properties. But whereas Descartes had sometimes anticipated the Lockean thesis that color and the secondary qualities in general are dispositional properties of bodies,[16] Malebranche consistently adheres to the thesis that such qualities are purely mind-dependent sensations. Further, he agrees with Descartes about the fundamental purpose of sensations; they assist us in our quest for biological survival. The heat and color of the fire serve to warn us that we must withdraw our hand if we wish to avoid damage to our body. As we saw at the beginning, Malebranche gives a theological twist to this doctrine by adding that our natural tendency to mistake the purpose of sensations is one of the unfortunate effects of the Fall. Unlike us, Adam was under no illusion about their lack of cognitive value.

In one philosophically interesting way, Malebranche seems to pioneer a distinctly non-Cartesian theory of sensations. Although Descartes characteristically speaks of them as confused, he nonetheless assigns sensations to the category of ideas. The fact that for Descartes sensations are ideas implies that they have representational content; by this he at least sometimes seems to mean that to have a sensation of color, for example, is to have a confused representation of the surface textures of bodies. Malebranche, by contrast, seems to anticipate the modern adverbial theory of sensations: to have a color sensation is not to have a certain content before the mind; it is simply to sense in a particular way. Thus when I perceive the setting sun the only immediate object of my mind is a geometrical idea or concept, but insofar as I am having a sensation of red, I may be said to be sensing redly. In the *Dialogues* Malebranche's commitment to the adverbial theory is not very evident; it is somewhat obscured by his tendency to follow Descartes in speaking of the confusion of sensations. But it is at least adumbrated in Malebranche's sharp distinction between sensation and ideas.

---

[16] Descartes, *Principles of Philosophy*, AT VIIIA 22–3: CSM I 285.

Ideas and self-knowledge

Although it may not illuminate every aspect of the subject, the *Dialogues on Metaphysics and on Religion* is remarkable among Malebranche's writings for its stress on the centrality of sensations in the theory of the mind. We may appreciate the significance of the *Dialogues* in this respect if we consider Malebranche's repeated claim that the mind is not a light to itself. In his earlier writings such as the *Search* Malebranche takes this patristic thesis to mean simply that the mind needs to be illuminated by divine ideas in order to achieve genuine propositional knowledge of the world; such an interpretation of the doctrine is of course consistent with recognizing a Cartesian faculty of pure intellect. But in the *Dialogues* Malebranche interprets the patristic doctrine in a stronger sense; the only intrinsic properties of the mind are dark and confused sensations which are of no cognitive value at all. Thus on this account the doctrine of the Church Fathers is intended to exclude the mind's possession of a purely intellectual faculty. It is in terms of this strong thesis that Malebranche understands the further patristic claim that the mind is a *lumen illuminatum* (illuminated light), not a *lumen illuminans* (illuminating light).[17]

In the *Dialogues* the claim that I am not a light to myself appears in close conjunction with the thesis that we have no idea of the soul. Versions of both these claims are found in Malebranche's earlier writings, but in the present work his treatment of them is somewhat puzzling; for he appears to deduce the second thesis from the first, and this deduction is problematic. Typically, when Malebranche says that we have no idea of the soul, he means that we are not related to the archetypal idea in God; here the contrast is with our relationship to the idea of body which makes possible an a priori science of geometry. But the fact that I have no idea of the soul in this sense clearly does not follow from the claim that I am not a light to myself, even when this is interpreted in the strong sense explained above.[18] It is true of course

---

[17] Elucidation X, *Search*, *OC* III 157–8; LO 630. Malebranche cites the Church Fathers Cyril of Alexandria, Augustine, and Gregory for the distinction.

[18] Nor of course does the entailment hold in the opposite direction. From the fact that I have no idea of the soul it does not follow that the soul is not a light to itself. It is consistent to maintain both that God has not revealed his archetypal idea of the soul to us and that our mind has cognitive resources of its own which allow it to achieve genuine knowledge of the properties of bodies.

that if the mind has no intrinsic capacity for genuine knowledge at all, then *a fortiori* it has no such capacity for self-knowledge. Thus from the fact that my mind has no real cognitive resources of its own, it does indeed follow that it cannot achieve knowledge of its modifications or the laws to which it is subject either by introspection or by attending to innate ideas. But the denial of the possibility of self-knowledge in this sense is not what Malebranche normally means by saying that we have no idea of the soul; on the contrary, as we have seen, he takes this to mean that we have no access to God's archetypal idea of the mind. And when it is understood in this sense the conclusion does not follow.

The structure of Theodore's argument in Dialogue III is not entirely clear (III vii), but perhaps it should be interpreted in the following way. If we were able to achieve genuine self-knowledge, then one of two things must be the case: either our mind can achieve such knowledge through its native cognitive resources or it can achieve it with the assistance of divine illumination. But neither of these disjuncts is true. Against the Cartesians Malebranche holds that the mind does not, and cannot, supply us with knowledge of the nature of its modifications either through introspection or through attending to an innate idea of itself; Descartes is wrong to assert the existence of innate ideas. In this sense, then, the mind is not a light to itself. But neither can we achieve such knowledge through divine illumination, for God has not disclosed his archetypal idea of the soul to us. If this is Malebranche's argument, then it is certainly valid; the claim that I am not a light to myself plays some role, but does not bear the whole weight of the deduction. However, the thesis that we are not related to God's archetypal idea of the mind stands in need of defense. Perhaps Malebranche would simply appeal to the fact that we have no science of psychology comparable to the sciences of physics and geometry. But it would still need to be shown that our lack of such a science is not a historical accident which will be remedied in the course of time.

Occasionalism

Through his theory of vision in God Malebranche seeks to establish the cognitive impotence of the human mind unassisted by divine illumination. In later dialogues he switches his attention from the theory of knowledge to ontology, and argues for a more general thesis which points the same moral. Through his theory of occasionalism Malebranche seeks to establish that all creatures are causally impotent. Here too then Malebranche is doing justice to the Pauline idea that in God we live, move, and have our being. Yet it would be wrong to emphasize only the theological dimensions of the doctrine, for occasionalism may also be seen as an acute philosophical response to Cartesian problems; indeed, in some ways it is an attempt to complete the Cartesian revolution in metaphysics. For Malebranche saw more clearly than Descartes that the conception of created substances as endowed with genuine causal powers is a relic of the Aristotelian ontology which has no real place in the Cartesian metaphysics of matter in motion; rather, to explain the behavior of bodies all that is needed is a set of mathematical equations plus a specification of the initial conditions. Although Malebranche retains the concept of causality in the case of God, he nevertheless sees something very important with regard to the physical world at least: the traditional idea of causal powers needs to be replaced by the more modern notion of law.[19]

Malebranche's most famous and influential argument for occasionalism turns on the nature of the causal relation. As Malebranche expresses it in the *Search*, "a true cause is one such that there is necessary connection between it and its effect."[20] Malebranche employs this definition to show that God is a true cause, for it is logically impossible that an omnipotent being should will a state of affairs and that state of affairs not obtain. By contrast, no creature is a genuine cause, for there is no necessary connection between the states of any two creatures. It is not logically necessary, for example, that the second billiard ball should move off along the surface of the table when it is struck by the first. The principle of course applies with equal force to the case of human beings. It is not logically necessary that my arm should go up when I will to raise it. No creature, then, is a true cause; events in the created world are rather occasional causes in the sense that they are the occasions on which God's genuine causal activity is exercised.[21]

---

[19] Cf. the remark by Lévy-Bruhl: "Natural causality is the last of the 'occult qualities'; it must disappear like the others. God has linked his works together, but he has not created any linking entities between them. In short, as a worthy successor of Descartes, Malebranche replaces the confused scholastic notion of cause by the clear scientific notion of law." (quoted in Charles J. McCracken, *Malebranche and British Philosophy* [Oxford, Clarendon Press, 1983], p. 102).

[20] VI.2.iii, *OC* II 316; LO 450.   [21] Ibid., *OC* II 315; LO 449.

This argument from necessary connection has fascinated commentators, for its negative component was developed by Hume and taken over for his own very different purposes. Moreover, Malebranche's notion of an occasional cause is a close relation of Hume's notion of constant conjunction. Curiously, however, in the *Dialogues* Malebranche rather plays down this powerful argument; he sketches it in places, but he does not present it as fully as he does in the *Search*. Although the *Dialogues* is a little disappointing in this respect, it has some compensating features, for the work contains fascinating hints of other, related Humean themes. To prepare us for the thesis that finite substances do not genuinely interact, Malebranche appeals to the data of experience; we are told to "assume only just what experience teaches you" (VII IV). And the moral we are supposed to draw is precisely the Humean one that we have no experience of causal, i.e. necessary, connection. Thus Malebranche can sound like an empiricist when it suits his purposes.

The argument which Malebranche chooses to highlight in the *Dialogues* employs a theological premise accepted by both Descartes and the Scholastics: God conserves the world by continuously creating it. According to Malebranche, when the doctrine of continuous creation is properly understood, we shall see that it rules out the existence of secondary causes. When God conserves a body, he does not simply will that it continue to exist at some place or other; rather, his volitions are fully specific with respect to location and velocity. In the case of a collision between two billiard balls, for example, God wills all their determinate states both before and after the collision. Thus God is the true cause of all events in the physical world. It is natural to respond that this argument for occasionalism is unsatisfactory as it stands; to make it valid we need a further premise to the effect that there is no causal overdetermination. Without the addition of this premise the argument is vulnerable to the objection that both God and the first billiard ball, say, are genuine causally sufficient conditions of the states of the second ball following the collision. A theologically minded philosopher such as Malebranche should, it seems, have no difficulty in justifying the exclusion of causal overdetermination; he could appeal to simplicity of the divine ways in order to fill the lacuna in the argument.

In the *Dialogues* Malebranche seems to agree that, as it stands, the argument stops short of fully proving occasionalism. But instead of appealing to the simplicity of God's ways, he adopts a more controversial strategy; he makes a stronger claim to the same end of ruling out genuine secondary causes altogether. Malebranche argues that on the assumption of God's continuous creation the causality of creatures is not just redundant but actually a contradiction. The claim is intriguing, but it seems to rest on a modal fallacy. We can see this by first noting that Malebranche is of course entitled to affirm the following principle:

> (1) Necessarily, if God wills that a body b be at place p at time t, then b is at p at t.

This principle is simply an application of the more general thesis that the efficacy of the divine volitions is entailed by God's omnipotence. But in trying to show that a contradiction results from ascribing genuine causal powers to creatures Malebranche seems to have in mind the following principle:

> (2) If God wills that a body b be at place p at time t, then necessarily, b is at p at t.

Acceptance of this principle will indeed lead to a contradiction, for it is obviously inconsistent to affirm both that b is necessarily at p at t and that another body, a, has the power to move body b out of p at t. But Malebranche has no grounds for making the stronger claim (2). Thus it seems that Malebranche may have conflated the (harmless) necessity of the consequence with the (harmful) necessity of the consequent. Interestingly enough, the same fallacy is often diagnosed in attempts to show the incompatibility of free will and divine foreknowledge.

Although it is the argument from continuous creation which is most prominent in the *Dialogues*, Malebranche also makes some use of a third strategy for proving occasionalism; this is what we may call the argument from knowledge. This argument employs the principle that if A is the cause of B, then A knows how to bring about B; it then seeks to show that no creature knows how to bring about its alleged effects. The argument is not original with Malebranche; it is associated above all with Arnold Geulincx, who stated the principle: "*Quod nescis quomodo fiat, id non facis*" (You do not cause that which you do not know how to cause).[22] Like the more powerful argument from necessary connection, this one is only sketched in the *Dialogues*. But in the present case

---

[22] *Sämtliche Schriften*, ed. H. J. de Vleeschauwer (5 vols., Bad-Cannstatt/Stuttgart, Frommann-Holzboog, 1968), vol. 2, p. 150.

Malebranche's reticence is a virtue, not a weakness; for the key principle seems to have little intuitive plausibility. It appears to rest on a wild generalization from a few cases of causal agency.

Although his occasionalist thesis is clear in outline, it raises two problems of interpretation. The first concerns the nature of God's causal activity. Malebranche constantly emphasizes that God acts through general laws, not through particular volitions, and even his otherwise hostile critic Arnauld cited this fact in his defense against Leibniz's strictures.[23] Some scholars, however, have argued that all Malebranche means by this claim is that the divine plans for the universe are regular; aside from the miracles acknowledged by the Christian faith, God does not make exceptions to the laws that he has ordained. But, according to this view, Malebranche does not mean to deny that in addition to willing physical laws, for instance, God must will that bodies behave in accordance with the laws that he has laid down; in this sense, then, God acts through particular volitions. Such a view does not entail that divine volitions themselves occur in time – a claim that would be inconsistent with God's atemporal manner of existence; but it does imply that God (timelessly) wills particular events in time, and not just general laws. One argument for this interpretation relies on a doctrine on which, as we have seen, Malebranche lays great stress in the *Dialogues*: God sustains the universe by continuously creating it. To some readers this doctrine suggests that Malebranche's God is constantly active in the world, insuring through particular volitions that bodies behave in conformity to law.

In fact, however, the *Dialogues* itself can be invoked to show that this interpretation is misguided. In Dialogue XII Malebranche indicates that God's general laws are efficacious by their very nature; with regard to the laws of soul–body union, for instance, Theodore observes that they are simply the constant and invariably efficacious volitions of the Creator (XII I). It is true, it seems, that in addition to willing the laws, God must will the initial conditions; otherwise no determinate universe will come into existence (see X XVII). But it is a mistake to suppose that any further divine volitions are needed in order to insure conformity to law. Once this point is firmly grasped, we can see that the doctrine of continuous creation poses no real difficulty. To say that God continu-

---

[23]   See Arnauld to Leibniz, 4 March 1687, G II 84.

ously creates a billiard ball, for example, just is to say that all its states can be genuinely explained in terms of the laws of physics and the initial specifications which God has willed.

The second problem of interpretation concerns the consistency of Malebranche's commitment to occasionalism in the *Dialogues*. As we have seen, occasionalism maintains that since God alone is a true cause, creatures have no genuine causal power at all. But in places Malebranche may seem to retreat to the weaker thesis that creatures have no genuine causal power of their own. In Dialogue XII, for instance, Aristes (who here has Theodore's approval) speaks of God as communicating his power to creatures. Now, on the face of it, to say that God has communicated his power to me is not to deny that I have power; on the contrary, it is to assert that I do have power, while adding that I am not its source. We can underline the difficulty for Malebranche here by considering a parallel issue in his theory of knowledge. If Malebranche said that God communicated his ideas to me, he would appear to be advocating a position more like Descartes' theory of innate ideas than his own doctrine of vision in God. For the latter doctrine maintains, not simply that minds have no ideas of their own, but that they have no ideas at all. And in the *Dialogues on Metaphysics and on Religion*, Malebranche is careful to uphold the strong epistemological thesis.

This problem can be solved in the same spirit as the preceding one; indeed, if anything, the textual warrant for the solution is stronger in the present case. Malebranche is not really retreating at all from the occasionalist thesis; rather, he is offering a reductive analysis of the traditional idea that God communicates his power to creatures. In Dialogue VII, for instance, Theodore claims that "God communicates His power to creatures and unites them with one another, only because He establishes their modalities, occasional causes of the effects which He produces Himself" (VII x). Thus the language of communicated power is not in conflict with the occasionalist thesis that God alone is a true cause.

The human mind, vision in God, and occasionalism

In traditional textbook accounts the doctrine of occasionalism is sometimes presented simply as an *ad hoc* solution to the mind–body problem. Descartes supposedly had difficulty explaining how two heterogeneous substances could causally interact, and the occasionalists came to the rescue by appealing to God to bridge the troublesome causal gap. Fortunately, this picture of occasionalism cannot survive a reading of Malebranche's *Dialogues*. It is clear from this work that occasionalism is a general and principled thesis about causal relations; indeed, as we have argued, it is fuelled by the realization that on the new Cartesian metaphysic of matter the traditional Aristotelian idea of causal powers needs to be replaced by the idea of law. Yet the textbook thesis is right in one respect: the doctrine of occasionalism does at least address the mind–body problem which Descartes arguably introduced into philosophy. In the *Dialogues on Metaphysics and on Religion*, as elsewhere, Malebranche maintains that human acts of willing are merely occasional causes of voluntary physical movements, and that motions in the brain are merely occasional causes of acts of sensation and imagination.

The fact that he does appeal to occasionalism to solve the mind–body problem raises an interesting question. As we have seen, the doctrine of vision in God also addresses issues about mental states, and it is natural to ask how the two doctrines are related to each other. Unfortunately, the question is not easy to answer. The *Dialogues* is especially rich in statements relevant to this issue, but it is not clear that it offers a single satisfactory theory.

Let us begin by noting that Malebranche's earlier writings, such as the *Search*, suggest the following picture of the relation between the two doctrines. The vision in God is a theory of thinking and of the perceptual element in sense perception; it says that to perceive or think of a circle is to be related to the idea or concept of a circle located in God. Occasionalism, if we abstract from the "action" of mind on body, is a theory of sensation and imagination; it says that when I have a sensation of red, for example, I am sensing redly, and that this act of sensation is occasionally caused by states of the brain. To say that the two theories divide the field in this way is not of course to deny that both of them bear on the philosophical analysis of sense perception. As we have seen, sense perception, for Malebranche, is a compound of two heterogeneous mental states: the intentional act of perceiving ideas and the non-intentional act of having a sensation. Thus on this account vision in God and occasionalism have distinct but overlapping provinces.

In the *Dialogues* Malebranche seems dissatisfied with this account, but in trying to replace it he appears to be pulled in two different directions.

His most explicit and important statement on the issue (in Dialogue XIII) exhibits a tendency to extend the doctrine of occasionalism to cover the intentional acts of perceiving and thinking; thus even the theory of vision in God is interpreted in occasionalist terms. This development seems to be motivated by a desire to offer a more symmetrical account of perception and sensation. In contrast to earlier works such as the *Search* Malebranche appears to be guided by the intuition that the perception of ideas, no less than the having of sensations, is governed by laws; there are laws of soul–God union, no less than psycho-physical laws of soul–body union (XIII ix). But by interpreting the theory of vision in God in nomological terms Malebranche thereby introduces occasionalism in its train; for Malebranche, wherever there are laws governing created substances, there are also occasional causes. Thus to satisfy the demands of the nomological account of vision in God Malebranche is driven to hunt around for occasional causes; and, rather desperately perhaps, he fastens on "acts of attention" as the best candidate to fill the bill. The problem with this move lies in specifying the objects of such acts of attention; obviously, Malebranche cannot say that when I think of a triangle, the occasional cause of my thought is an act of attention to the idea of a triangle, for then the explanation is circular.

Elsewhere in the *Dialogues* Malebranche tends to move in the opposite direction; he seeks to extend the doctrine of vision in God to all mental phenomena (and thus *a fortiori* to mental phenomena which were formerly the exclusive province of occasionalism). Malebranche again introduces a claim that was missing from his earliest writings; in this case it is the claim that in addition to their other properties, such as infinity and eternity, ideas in God are efficacious; that is to say, they have the power of causing perceptions in finite minds. In the *Dialogues* Malebranche argues that all mental states are caused by the action of God's efficacious ideas (see, for example, V v). The difference between thinking and seeing is actually constituted, it seems, by the different ways in which one and the same idea in God affects the human mind. It is important to note that though Malebranche here uses the theory of efficacious ideas to extend the doctrine of vision in God in this way, there is nothing in the theory which compels him to do so; it would be possible to claim that divine ideas are efficacious, while restricting their sphere of application to the causation of thought and perception.

In one place in the *Dialogues*, then, Malebranche claims that all mental phenomena fall within the purview of occasionalism; in another place he claims that they all fall within the purview of vision in God. It may be objected that though these two claims are both inconsistent with the position of the *Search*, they are not clearly inconsistent with each other. The fact that the two claims are found in the same work makes it natural to look for a way of reconciling them. One might try to exhibit their fundamental consistency by saying that they are concerned with different levels. At the level of divine action, all mental states are genuinely caused by God's efficacious ideas; the efficacy of ideas now takes the place of the efficacy of the divine will. At the level of creatures, however, who of course are lacking in real power, all mental states have occasional causes, the nature of which depends on the kind of state that is in question: sensations are occasionally caused by states of the brain; perceptions and thoughts are occasionally caused by acts of attention. It is tempting to argue, then, that when Malebranche's attempts to extend the spheres of the two doctrines are understood in this way, there is no inconsistency between them.

This is an attractive approach, and it may be that he does have some such strategy of reconciliation in mind. But it seems to run into difficulties. According to the extended version of vision in God, all mental states essentially involve a relation to the divine ideas; according to the extended version of occasionalism, however, such a relation holds only with respect to thoughts and perceptions. Indeed, the extended version of vision in God tends to suggest that all mental states are on a continuum; it implies that they are all intentional states by virtue of their relation to divine ideas. By contrast, the extended version of occasionalism seems to retain the recognition that mental states are fundamentally heterogeneous in character, and that only a subset of them are intentional. The latter doctrine thus preserves an attractive feature of Malebranche's earlier philosophy which sets him apart from Descartes and Leibniz.

Before we conclude this section, it is worth noting that some mental phenomena seem to place a strain on the taxonomic scheme that he outlines in Dialogue XIII. Under the rubric of the laws of the union of soul and body Malebranche classifies some mental states which do not clearly belong there. Consider, for instance, Malebranche's discussion of perceiving the sun in Dialogue XII ii–iv. Malebranche refers such a mental state to the laws of the union of soul and body, and this classification is open to question. It is true that Malebranche opens the discussion here by talking about our sensations of colors, and such sensations are indeed clearly governed by the laws of soul–body union; they have occasional causes which are physical states of the brain. But Malebranche's real concern in this discussion is with the visual perception of size and distance; he wants to explain why the sun appears to us larger at the horizon than at the zenith. Such perceptions of the primary qualities of bodies, to borrow Locke's terminology, involve the mind's relation to ideas, and hence the union of the soul and God.

In fact, as one scholar has noted, there appears to be a serious tension in Malebranche's account of size and distance perception.[24] On the one hand, Malebranche is struck by the reflex, automatic nature of such "compound sensations" as he calls them in the *Search*;[25] their reflex character, in addition to the fact that they occur on the occasion of physical changes in the brain and retina, may lead him to refer such "sensations" to "the laws of the union of soul and body." On the other hand, Malebranche is struck by the element of computation in our perception of the size of a body such as the sun. On his account, we make judgments or inferences about size on the basis of apparent distance; thus we come to perceive the sun as larger at the horizon than at the zenith. The intellectual, cognitive element in such perception makes it inappropriate for Malebranche to speak here of sensations, and to classify such judgments under the rubric of the laws of soul–body union.

Knowledge of the existence of bodies

Seventeenth-century philosophers who hold that the immediate objects of perception are ideas tend to find the existence of the physical world problematic. Despite his distinctive theory of ideas, Malebranche is no exception to this tendency; like Descartes and Locke, at least as they are traditionally understood, he agrees that there is a logical gap between the immediate objects of perception and the external physical world.

---

[24] T. Meyering, "Fodor's Modularity: A New Name for an Old Dilemma," *Philosophical Psychology*, 7 (1994), 39–62.

[25] Malebranche employs the term "compound sensation" in the *Search* I.7; he also speaks of them, famously, as "natural judgments" (*OC* I 97; LO 34). The two labels point to the ambiguity in his position.

But Malebranche differs from them in his attitude to this logical gap. Locke, for example, appears to try to bridge it by means of causal inference; the existence of bodies is a hypothesis which offers the best causal explanation of our experiences. But this strategy of course is not open to Malebranche; for if by "cause" we mean genuine cause, then causal inference of this sort cannot lead us to the existence of bodies.

In the *Dialogues*, however, Malebranche is chiefly concerned to emphasize the existence of a different logical gap. As Theodore puts it, bodies are not necessary emanations of the Deity (VI v). In other words, the existence of God does not logically imply the existence of bodies. Although the official target sounds like neoplatonism, it seems that, unofficially at least, Malebranche may also have Descartes in his sights. Descartes of course, no more than Malebranche, believes that bodies are necessary emanations of God, but he does seek to offer a theological proof of their existence; that is, he presents an argument for the existence of bodies which crucially rests on the principle that God is not a deceiver. In the *Dialogues*, Malebranche argues not merely that Descartes' proof is flawed, but that all proofs of the existence of bodies must fail.

Although Descartes is one of his prime targets, in one way Malebranche agrees with him; like Descartes he adopts a theological approach to the problem of the existence of the external world. But this very similarity underlines a difference between the two philosophers which is equally characteristic and revealing. Descartes tries to solve the problem through the methods of natural or philosophical theology; Malebranche, by contrast, appeals to the data of the Christian faith: revelation speaks of bodies, and it is revelation which provides our sole warrant of their existence. According to Malebranche, the appeal to revealed religion does not beg the question here by assuming the existence, for example, of sacred books and prophets; for even if we regard these as mere appearances, as we must if the question is not to be begged, we can still have grounds for believing the claims that are made by their means about the existence of bodies.

The Christian faith thus assures us of the existence of bodies, and it is clear from the doctrine of occasionalism that God's relationship to the physical world is in some sense a causal one. But reflection on this fact may lead us to wonder whether Malebranche was entitled to the earlier claim that God's existence does not logically imply the existence of bodies. Malebranche's assimilation of the causal relation to logical implication may seem to involve him in difficulties here. In particular, the following propositions may appear to form an inconsistent triad:

(1) The existence of God does not logically imply the existence of bodies.
(2) There is a necessary connection between a true cause and its effect.
(3) God is the true cause of bodies.

It may seem that (2) and (3) jointly imply: Necessarily, if God exists, then bodies exist; and this would flatly contradict (1). But in fact the appearance of inconsistency can be removed, for (2) and (3) should be read in such a way that they commit Malebranche only to the principle: Necessarily, if God wills that bodies exist, then bodies exist. And this of course is consistent with Malebranche's denial that bodies are necessary emanations of the deity.

No one is likely to be attracted today by his positive approach to the problem of the external world. But his emphasis on the indemonstrability of the existence of bodies is at least historically significant. Berkeley, who read the *Search* if not the *Dialogues*, may be seen to be engaged in a dialogue with Malebranche on this issue. Berkeley in effect concedes that there would be an unbridgeable logical gap between ideas and the existence of bodies if bodies are taken to be mind-independent entities. But it is just the assumption that forms the antecedent of this conditional that Berkeley denies. He famously argues for a phenomenalist interpretation of bodies in terms of mind-dependent ideas. Once he has made the move to phenomenalism, he is in a position to close the logical gap which impressed Malebranche and perhaps Locke.

Theodicy

The full title of the work is *Dialogues on Metaphysics and on Religion*, and it is fair to say that it is religion, rather than metaphysics, which predominates in the later dialogues. Of course, even in the early dialogues, theological assumptions are often invoked; and the metaphysics itself is of essentially theological inspiration. Yet the early dialogues are nonetheless rich in philosophical argument. By contrast, in the later dialogues (especially perhaps the last two), the proportion of philosophical argument is less, and the *Dialogues* ends with an unappealing excursus into Catholic apologetics.

Perhaps what is of most interest in the later *Dialogues* is Malebranche's intriguing sketch of a theodicy; this is his attempt to answer the question of how the various types of imperfection in the world are consistent with the existence of a just God. Malebranche's venture into theodicy is thoroughly continuous with the themes of the earlier discussions, for it emphasizes, as they do, that God's activity in the world is governed by covering laws. Indeed, the nomological nature of God's activity is central to Malebranche's defense of the divine character. He holds that God seeks to create a universe that is worthy of him, but he claims that God does not create the best world absolutely; rather he creates the best world subject to the "side-constraint" that his ways must honor him. What this means is that God must create a world that is governed by simple, general laws, and the need to satisfy this condition involves a loss of overall value. God could have created more perfection by intervening frequently to suspend the laws of nature; he could have done this, for example, by insuring that rain falls only where it can make land fertile. But the price of such an intervention on God's part would be a violation of the simplicity and generality of his ways; hence the side-constraint that God's ways must honor him would be violated. With his characteristic willingness to venture into revealed theology Malebranche ingeniously extends this principle to the sphere of grace in a way that shocked critics such as Arnauld.[26] The distribution of divine grace is similarly subject to simple, general laws which in a sense tie God's hands. Thus God could have intervened to suspend the laws of grace to insure that it is granted only to those who need it and can profit by it. But again the price of such intervention would be a violation of the side-constraint that God's ways must honor him.

Readers of this material will be struck by remarkable echoes of Leibnizian themes – it is of course Leibniz who coined the term "theodicy" – and these echoes are no accident. Leibniz's own theodicy

---

[26] Arnauld's response is found in *Réflexions philosophiques et théologiques sur le nouveau système de la nature et de la grâce* (Paris, 1685). As the title indicates, the work is a response to Malebranche's *Treatise on Nature and Grace* (1680). See S. Nadler, *Arnauld and the Cartesian Philosophy of Ideas* (Manchester, Manchester University Press, 1989), Appendix, for a helpful account of Arnauld's reactions.

was developed as a response to the Malebranchian project. It is indeed Malebranche who is the target of a section in Leibniz's *Discourse on Metaphysics* entitled "Against those who believe that God might have made things better."[27] But though the title correctly points to a real difference between their positions, it is misleading in that it suggests a greater opposition than really exists. Indeed, it is not too much to say that Leibniz's theodicy is really a minor variation on a theme by Malebranche. What Leibniz does is to abandon Malebranche's conception of simplicity of means as a constraint on God's attempt to maximize perfection; instead, he proposes that simplicity should be incorporated into the criteria for the evaluation of possible worlds. For Leibniz, the best possible world is the one which is at the same time the simplest in hypotheses and the richest in phenomena.[28] In this way he is able to defend the thesis that God creates the best possible world absolutely, while agreeing with Malebranche that God sets a high value on economy of means.

The fact that Malebranche is one of the leading targets of Leibniz's theodicy is a valuable reminder of his stature in the seventeenth century. And of course it is not merely Malebranche's theodicy but his other doctrines, such as occasionalism and vision in God, which were the target of Leibnizian attack. Indeed, we know that the *Dialogues on Metaphysics and on Religion* itself is a work which Leibniz took very seriously; for one of his best short works takes the form of an elegant continuation of the *Dialogues* in which Malebranchian doctrines are subjected to often searching criticism.[29] The attention which Leibniz paid to the *Dialogues* is understandable, for it articulates a coherent and compelling metaphysics which is in many ways a powerful and worthy rival to Leibniz's own system. In none of his other works does Malebranche succeed as well in synthesizing the new Cartesian philosophy with the themes of Pauline and Augustinian theology, and this synthesis stands as one of the great achievements of seventeenth-century philosophy.

---

[27] Leibniz, *Discourse on Metaphysics* 3, G II 12. It was composed in part as a response to Malebranche's *Treatise on Nature and Grace*, his most systematic statement of his theodicy.

[28] G IV 431.

[29] "Entretien de Philarete et d'Ariste, suite du premier entretien d'Ariste et de Theodore," G VI 579–94.

Chronology

1638 Born in Paris on 5 August
1654 Enters Collège de la Marche in Paris
1656 Graduates as Maître ès Arts from Collège de la Marche
1656–9 Studies theology at the Sorbonne
1660 Enters the Oratory, a Catholic order founded in 1611 by Cardinal de Bérulle
1661 Attends the Oratorian house in Saumur (April to October)
1664 First encounters works of Descartes (*Treatise on Man*); ordained priest on 14 September
1674–5 *The Search after Truth* published
1677 *Christian Conversations* published
1678 *Elucidations* published as a supplement to the third edition of the *Search*
1680 *Treatise on Nature and Grace* published
1683 *Christian and Metaphysical Meditations*; publication of Arnauld's *On True and False Ideas* initiates long controversy with Malebranche on philosophical and theological issues (which continues until Arnauld's death in 1694 and beyond)
1684 *Treatise on Ethics* published
1685 Undertakes mission to Normandy to the *nouveaux convertis* – new converts to Catholicism from Calvinism (Autumn)
1688 *Dialogues on Metaphysics and on Religion* published
1690 *Treatise on Nature and Grace* placed on the Index of Forbidden Books in Rome
1692 *Laws of the Communication of Motions* published

Further reading

The standard French edition of Malebranche's writings, prepared by the Centre National de la Recherche Scientifique (CNRS) under the direction of André Robinet, is the *Œuvres complètes de Malebranche* (Paris, J. Vrin, 1958–84[*OC*]). Shortly after Malebranche's death a biography was written by his friend Y. M. André, *La Vie du R. P. Malebranche* (published by P. Ingold in Paris, 1886; reprint Geneva, Slatkin Reprints, 1970). The authoritative bibliography on Malebranche is *Bibliographia Malebranchiana: A Critical Guide to the Malebranche Literature into 1989*, by P. Easton, T. M. Lennon and G. Sebba (Carbondale and Edwardsville, Southern Illinois Press, 1992). This supersedes the bibliography in volume 20 of the standard edition of Malebranche's works, which in its turn superseded *Nicolas Malebranche, 1638–1715: A Preliminary Bibliography*, by Gregor Sebba (Athens, University of Georgia Press, 1959).

Older general works on Malebranche's philosophy include Francisque Bouillier, *Histoire de la philosophie cartésienne* (Paris, Durand, 1868), Victor Delbos, *Étude de la philosophie de Malebranche* (Paris, Bloud & Gay, 1924), and Léon Ollé-Laprune, *La philosophie de Malebranche* (2 vols., Paris, Ladrange, 1870). One of the best recent introductions to Malebranche's thought is *Nicolas Malebranche* (Paris, Presses Universitaires de France, 1963), by Geneviève Rodis-Lewis. More advanced, technical francophone studies are by Martial Gueroult, *Malebranche* (3 vols., Paris, Aubier, 1955–9); and by André Robinet, *Système et existence dans l'œuvre de Malebranche* (Paris, J. Vrin, 1965). In English, an introduction to the wider context of Malebranche's writings is *The Rise of Modern Philosophy*, ed. Tom Sorell (Oxford, Clarendon Press,

1993), which includes J. Cottingham's "A New Start? Cartesian Metaphysics and the Emergence of Modern Philosophy" (pp. 145–66). Short, general introductions to Malebranche's thought can be found in Willis Doney's article on Malebranche in *The Encyclopedia of Philosophy* (New York, Collier-Macmillan, 1967), and in Thomas Lennon's highly recommendable "Philosophical Commentary", in *The Search after Truth* (Columbus, Ohio State University Press, 1980, pp. 759–848). Full-length studies also exist, in particular by Ralph W. Church, *A Study in the Philosophy of Malebranche* (London, George Allen & Unwin, 1931), Beatrice K. Rome, *The Philosophy of Malebranche* (Chicago, Henry Regnery, 1963), and Daisie Radner, *Malebranche: A Study of a Cartesian System* (Assen and Amsterdam, Van Gorcum, 1978).

Several collections of articles provide comprehensive discussions of Malebranche's philosophy. French scholarship in the first half of this century is well represented in the *Revue de métaphysique et de morale*, 23 (1916), the *Revue internationale de philosophie*, 1 (1938–9), and the *Revue philosophique de la France et de l'étranger*, 125 (1938), which features discussions by such noted scholars of seventeenth-century thought as Paul Schrecker, A. A. Luce, Henri Gouhier, and Émile Bréhier. Many other important anglophone and francophone articles are reprinted in volume 11 of *Essays on Early Modern Philosophers*, ed. Vere Chappell (New York, Garland Publishing, Inc., 1992).

The above full-length monographs or collections of articles deal extensively with Malebranche's occasionalism and theory of knowledge. More targeted discussions of occasionalism are by Joseph Prost, *Essai sur l'atomisme et l'occasionalisme dans la philosophie cartésienne* (Paris, Henry Paulin, 1907) and Steven Nadler, "Occasionalism and the General Will in Malebranche," *Journal of the History of Philosophy*, 31 (1993), 31–47. As for more specific epistemological studies, see L. Bridet, *La Théorie de la connaissance dans la philosophie de Malebranche* (Paris, Marcel Rivière, 1929) and Desmond Connell, *The Vision in God: Malebranche's Scholastic Sources* (Louvain, Éditions Nauwelaerts, 1967). More recently, Steven Nadler's *Malebranche and Ideas* (Oxford, Oxford University Press, 1992) reassesses the traditional indirect realist, representationalist understanding of Malebranche's doctrine of ideas. A critical reply to this is D. Scott, "Malebranche's Indirect Realism: A Reply to Steven Nadler," *British Journal for the History of Philosophy*, 4 (1996), 53–78. Nadler's study complements his earlier *Arnauld and the Cartesian Philosophy of Ideas* (Manchester, Manchester University Press, 1989), and both are part of a large body of literature on seventeenth-century theory of knowledge, a broad study of which is Nicholas Jolley, *The Light of the Soul* (Oxford, Clarendon Press, 1990). Jolley's "Sensation, Intentionality, and Animal Consciousness: Malebranche's Theory of Mind," *Ratio*, 8 (1995), 28–42 is a more directed examination, while *Perceptual Acquaintance From Descartes to Reid* (Oxford, Blackwell, 1984) by John W. Yolton involves a full-length treatment of many of the issues involved.

An important study of Malebranche's ethical thought is by Ginette Dreyfus, *La volonté selon Malebranche* (Paris, J. Vrin, 1958). In English, the only full-length study of Malebranche's ethical theory is Craig Walton, *De la recherche du bien: A Study of Malebranche's Science of Ethics* (The Hague, Martinus Nijhoff, 1972), and Walton has recently supplemented this in the introduction to his translation of Malebranche's *Treatise on Ethics* (Dordrecht, Kluwer Academic Publishers, 1993, 1–41). For shorter recent discussions, see T. M. Schmaltz, "Human Freedom and Divine Creation in Malebranche, Descartes and the Cartesians," *British Journal for the History of Philosophy*, 2 (1994), 3–50 and D. Scott, "Malebranche and the Soul's Power," *Studia Leibnitiana*, 28 (1996), 1–21.

Few general works on Malebranche fail to note the religious tenor of his thought, and the premier studies in this respect are *La vocation de Malebranche* (Paris, J. Vrin, 1926) and *La philosophie de Malebranche et son expérience religieuse*, 2nd edn. (Paris, J. Vrin, 1948), both by Henri Gouhier. Also note Joseph Vidgrain, *Le Christianisme dans la philosophie de Malebranche* (Paris, Alcan, 1923) and Michael E. Hobart, *Science and Religion in the Thought of Nicholas Malebranche* (Chapel Hill, University of North Carolina Press, 1982). For an understanding of Malebranche's physics, see Paul Mouy, *Le Développement de la physique cartésienne, 1646–1712* (Paris, J. Vrin, 1934), and a shorter discussion by Thomas L. Hankins, "The Influence of Malebranche on the Science of Mechanics During the Eighteenth Century," *Journal of the History of Ideas*, 28 (1967), 193–211.

Malebranche's main philosophical debt is to Descartes, and Ferdinand Alquié's *Le cartésianisme de Malebranche* (Paris, J. Vrin, 1974) is the most detailed examination of the relation between these two philosophers. A general discussion of the reception of Malebranche's philosophy is found in the collection *Nicholas Malebranche: His Philosophical Critics and Successors*, ed. Stuart Brown (Assen and Maastricht, Van Gorcum, 1991). As for the reception of Malebranche by his contemporaries, one of the most important works is Antoine Arnauld's *Des vraies et des fausses idées*, which has been translated by Stephen Gaukroger as *On True and False Ideas* (Manchester, Manchester University Press, 1990). Again in the critical vein Simon Foucher's *Critique de la Recherche de la Verité* of 1675 is worth mentioning (New York, Reprint Corp., 1969; intro. R. A. Watson). Richard A. Watson provides a philosophical commentary to Foucher's criticism in his *The Downfall of Cartesianism 1673–1712* (The Hague, Martinus Nijhoff, 1966).

The chief tenets of Malebranche's philosophy are discussed by Leibniz in his "Conversation Between Philarète and Aristes, After a Conversation Between Aristes and Theodore" (vol. 6 of *Philosophischen Schriften*, ed. C. I. Gerhardt [Berlin, 1875–90, pp. 579–90]), although for a wider study of Malebranche's philosophical relation to Leibniz, see André Robinet's collection of primary source material, *Malebranche et Leibniz: Relations personnelles* (Paris, J. Vrin, 1955). Shorter studies are by Jacques Jalabert, "Leibniz et Malebranche," *Les Etudes philosophiques*, 3 (1981), 279–92; Nicholas Jolley, "Leibniz and Malebranche on Innate Ideas," *Philosophical Review*, 97 (1988), 71–91; and Roger Woolhouse, "Leibniz and Occasionalism," in *Metaphysics and Philosophy of Science in the Seventeenth and Eighteenth Centuries* (Dordrecht, Kluwer Academic Publishers, 1988, pp. 165–83). Further useful discussion is found in C. Wilson's excellent *Leibniz's Metaphysics: A Historical and Comparative Study* (Princeton, Princeton University Press, 1989). The philosophical relation between Malebranche and Spinoza is the subject of Joseph Moreau's "Malebranche et le spinozisme," in *Malebranche: Correspondance avec J.-J. Dortous de Mairan* (Paris, J. Vrin, 1947). A shorter discussion of this issue is Daisie Radner, "Malebranche's Refutation of Spinoza," in *Spinoza: New Perspectives*, ed. R. W. Shahan and J. I. Biro (University of Oklahoma, Norman, 1978, pp. 113–28). For a comparative study of Malebranche extending beyond the seventeenth century, see Maurice Merleau-Ponty, *L'Union de l'âme et du corps chez Malebranche, Biran et Bergson* (Paris, J. Vrin, 1968).

The main treatment of Malebranche's reception by and influence upon British philosophy is found in Charles J. McCracken, *Malebranche and British Philosophy* (Oxford, Clarendon Press, 1983). Malebranche's epistemology was attacked by John Locke in "An Examination of P. Malebranche's Opinion of Seeing All Things in God" (*Philosophical Works*, ed. J. A. St. John [London, 1872]). Because of their doctrinal similarities Malebranche and Berkeley have been frequently compared: see A. A. Luce, *Berkeley and Malebranche: A Study in the Origins of Berkeley's Thought* (London, Oxford University Press, 1934). Shorter discussions on Malebranche's relation to Berkeley are: Harry Bracken, "Berkeley and Malebranche on Ideas," *Modern Schoolman*, 41 (1963), 1–16 and Anita Fritz, "Berkeley's Self – Its Origin in Malebranche," *Journal of the History of Ideas*, 15 (1954), 554–72.

Note on the text

The *Dialogues on Metaphysics and on Religion* (*Entretiens sur la métaphysique et sur la religion*) was first published in 1688 and went through four editions in Malebranche's lifetime. In the third edition of 1696 Malebranche added a preface and *Dialogues on Death* (*Entretiens sur la mort*), both of which were included in the subsequent editions of the *Dialogues*. The second, third and fourth editions all incorporated minor stylistic and doctrinal revisions and corrections. The present translation is based almost exclusively on the text of the fourth edition of 1711 (as it appears in vol. 12 of *OC*), and the Preface and the *Dialogues on Death*, which are of minor philosophical interest, have not been included in this edition. The biblical passages are from the Latin Vulgate, and the editors have relied on the Douay Rheims version of the Bible for the translation of these passages.

In the original French Malebranche capitalized many nouns which would not be capitalized in standard English today, and consequently we have dispensed with most of them. However, there are two important exceptions. Partly because they are philosophical terms of art upon which Malebranche lays great emphasis, and partly in order to preserve something of the original flavor of the text, we have retained the capitalization of "Reason" and "Being." On the few occasions when Malebranche fails to capitalize these terms, we are faithful to his practice. The ellipses (e.g. 2:20) are in the original.

Dialogues on Metaphysics and on Religion

Dialogue I

The soul, and its distinction from the body. The nature of ideas. The world in which our bodies live and which we look at is very different from the one we see.

THEODORE. Well then, my dear Aristes, since you wish it, I must tell you about my metaphysical visions. But to do so I must leave these enchanted places which delight our senses and which, by their variety, distract a mind like mine. Because I am extremely afraid of taking, for the immediate deliverances of inner truth, some of my prejudices or those obscure principles which owe their birth to the laws of the union of the soul and body; and because in these surroundings I cannot, as perhaps you can, silence a certain disturbing noise which throws confusion and turmoil into all my ideas; please, let us leave here. Let us withdraw to your study, in order to retreat into ourselves more easily. Let us attempt to have nothing prevent us each from consulting our common master, universal Reason. For it is inner truth that must govern our discussion. This is what must dictate to me what I should tell you and what you are to learn through me. In a word, it belongs to inner truth alone to judge and pronounce upon our differences. For today we think only of philosophizing: and although you submit perfectly to the authority of the church, you wish me to speak from the outset as if you refused to accept the truths of faith as principles of our knowledge. In effect, faith must regulate our mind's path; but it is only sovereign Reason which fills it with understanding.

ARISTES. Let us go, Theodore, wherever you wish. I am disgusted with everything I see in this material and sensible world, since hearing you speak of another world completely full of intelligible beauties. Remove me to that happy and enchanted region. Make me contemplate all those wonders of which you spoke to me the other day in so magnificent a manner and with so pleased an air. Let us go; I am ready to follow you to this country which you consider inaccessible to those who heed only their senses.

THEODORE. You are enjoying yourself, Aristes, and I am not angered by it. You mock me in so delicate and fair a manner that I understand that you wish to amuse yourself, but that you do not wish to offend me. I forgive you this. You are following the secret urgings of your ever playful imagination. However, allow me to tell you that you are speaking about what you do not understand. No, I shall not lead you to foreign soil; but perhaps I shall teach you that you are yourself a foreigner in your own country. I shall teach you that the world you live in is not as you believe it to be, because actually it is not the way you see or sense it. You judge on the basis of the relation of your senses to all the objects surrounding you, and your senses beguile you infinitely more than you can imagine. They are faithful witnesses only in respect of what concerns the good of the body and the preservation of life. As for everything else, there is no precision, no truth in their testimony. This you will see, Aristes, without leaving yourself, without me "removing you to that enchanted region" which your imagination represents to you. The imagination is a fool who is pleased to play the fool. Its jests, its unexpected movements distract you, and me too. However, if you please, Reason must always remain in charge in our discussion. It must decide and pronounce. Yet it remains silent and constantly eludes us whenever the imagination appears, and we listen to its pleasantries and fix upon the various phantoms it presents to us, instead of silencing it. Thus, be respectful in the presence of Reason. Be silent, if you wish to understand the deliverances of inner truth clearly and distinctly.

ARISTES. Theodore, you are taking very seriously what I said to you without much reflection. I beg your forgiveness for my small liberty. I assure you that . . .

THEODORE. You have not angered me, Aristes, you have entertained me. For, once again, you possess so lively and pleasant an imagination, and I am so assured of your heart that you will never anger me and will always please me, at least as long as you only mock me to

4

my face; and what I have just told you is simply to make you understand that you have a terrible resistance to the truth. That quality which makes you shine in the eyes of others, which wins hearts for you, which draws esteem, which makes all those who know you desire to possess you, is the most irreconcilable enemy of Reason. I shall pose you a paradox whose truth I cannot presently demonstrate.* However, you will soon recognize it through your own experience, and perhaps you will see the reasons for it in the course of our discussion. For that there is still much ground to cover. But believe me, both the dull and the sharp mind are equally closed to the truth. The only difference is that ordinarily the dull mind respects it, and the sharp one despises it. Nonetheless, if you really are resolved to reprimand your imagination, you will enter unhindered into that place where Reason delivers its responses. And after you have listened to it for a while, you will have only scorn for all that has until now captivated you and, if God touches your heart, you will have only disgust for it.

ARISTES. Let us go quickly, then, Theodore. Your promises imbue me with a zeal I cannot express to you. Certainly I shall do all you prescribe for me. Let us double our step ... With God's help we shall at last arrive at the place destined for our discussion. Let us go in ... Sit down ... What is there here to prevent us from entering into ourselves to consult Reason? Do you want me to block all the light passages, so that darkness eclipses everything that is visible in this room and can strike our senses?

THEODORE. No, my dear man. The darkness strikes our senses as much as the light. It erases the glare of the colors. But at this time of day it can give rise to some confusion or slight unease in our imagination. Simply draw the curtains. This bright day may inconvenience us a little and may perhaps give too much glare to certain objects ... So be it. Sit down.

Reject, Aristes, everything that has entered your mind through the senses. Silence your imagination. Let everything be in a perfect silence in you. Even forget, if you can, that you have a body, and think only about what I am going to say to you. In a word, pay attention and do not quibble about my preamble. Your attention is the only thing I ask of you. Without this effort or mental struggle against the impressions of the body there will be no conquests in the land of truth.

* *Traité de morale* [I], Ch. 12 [*OC* XI, 135–45].

ARISTES. So I believe, Theodore. Speak. But allow me to interrupt you whenever I cannot follow.

THEODORE. That is fair. Listen.

I. Nothingness has no properties. I think. Therefore I am. But what am I, I who think, at the time when I think? Am I a body, a mind, a human being? As yet I know nothing of all this. I know only that, at the time I think, I am something that thinks.[1] However, let us see. Can a body think? Can a thing extended in length, width, and depth reason, desire, sense? Undoubtedly not, for all the ways of being of such an extended thing consist only in relations of distance; and it is evident that these relations are not perceptions, reasonings, pleasures, desires, sensations – in a word, thoughts. Therefore this *I* that thinks, my own substance, is not a body, since my perceptions, which surely belong to me, are something entirely different from relations of distance.

ARISTES. It seems clear to me that all the modifications of extension can be only relations of distance; and that thus extension cannot know, will, or sense. However, perhaps my body is something other than extension. For it seems to me that it is my finger which feels the pain of a prick, that it is my heart which desires, that it is my brain which reasons. The inner feeling that I have of what happens in me teaches me what I am telling you. Prove to me that my body is simply extension, and I shall grant you that my mind, or whatever it is in me that thinks, wills, and reasons, is neither material nor corporeal.

II. THEODORE. What, Aristes! Do you believe that your body is composed of some substance other than extension? Do you not understand that extension is sufficient for the mind to form a brain, a heart, arms, and hands, and all the veins, arteries, nerves, and so on, of which your body is composed? If God destroyed the extension of your body, would you still have a brain, arteries, veins, etc.? Do you think a body can be reduced to a mathematical point? For I do not doubt that God can form everything in the universe with the extension of a grain of sand. Certainly, where there is no extension – I say none – there is no corporeal substance. Think about this seriously; and to convince yourself of it, pay attention to this.

---

[1]   The wording of this passage is strongly reminiscent of Descartes' *Meditations* II. As for the principle that "Nothingness has no properties," cf. Descartes' *Principles of Philosophy* I 52 (AT VIII-I 24–5).

Everything that exists either can be conceived to exist on its own, or it cannot be conceived on its own. There is no middle ground, for these two propositions are contradictory. Now, everything that can be conceived on its own without the thought of anything else – everything, I say, that can be conceived by itself as existing independently of any other thing or without the idea of it representing anything else – is certainly a being or a substance; and everything that cannot be conceived by itself or without the thought of any other thing, is a way of being or a modification of substance.

For example, we cannot think of roundness without thinking of extension. Roundness, therefore, is not a being or a substance, but a way of being. We can think of extension without thinking of anything else in particular. Thus, extension is not a way of being; it is a being itself. As the modification of a substance is but the substance itself in a particular way, it is obvious that the idea of a modification necessarily contains the idea of the substance of which it is the modification. And as a substance is a being which subsists in itself, the idea of a substance does not necessarily contain the idea of another being. We have no other way of distinguishing substances or beings from modifications or ways of being, except through the various ways in which we perceive these things.

Now, return into yourself. Is it not true that you can think of extension without thinking of another thing? Is it not true that you can perceive extension entirely by itself? Thus, extension is a substance, and in no sense a way or manner of being. Hence extension and matter are but a single substance. Yet I can perceive my thought, my desire, my joy, my sadness, without thinking of extension, and even without supposing that there is any extension. Therefore all these things are not modifications of extension, but modifications of a substance which thinks, senses, desires, and is quite different from extension.

All the modifications of extension consist simply in relations of distance. Yet it is obvious that my pleasure, my desire, and all my thoughts are not relations of distance. For all relations of distance can be compared, measured, and exactly determined by the principles of geometry, and our perceptions and sensations can be neither compared nor measured in this way. Thus my soul is not material. It is not the modification of my body. It is a substance which thinks and has no resemblance to the extended substance of which my body is composed.

ARISTES. That seems to me to be demonstrated. But what can you conclude from it?

III. THEODORE. I can derive an infinity of truths from it. For the distinction between the soul and the body is the foundation of the principal tenets of philosophy, and among others of the immortality of our being.[*] For, to mention it in passing, if the soul is a substance distinguished from the body, if it is not its modification, it is evident that even if death annihilated the substance of which our body is composed, which does not happen, it would not thereby follow that our soul would be annihilated. However, it is not yet time to deal thoroughly with this important question. First I must prove many other truths to you. Try to be attentive to what I am about to tell you.

ARISTES. Proceed. I shall follow you as attentively as I can.

IV. THEODORE. I am thinking of a variety of things: of a number, of a circle, of a house, of such and such beings, of being. Thus, all these things exist, at least while I think of them. Certainly, when I think of a circle, of a number, of being or of infinity, of a particular finite being, I perceive realities. For if the circle I perceived were nothing, in thinking of it I would be thinking of nothing. Thus, I would be thinking and not thinking at the same time. Yet the circle I perceive has properties that no other figure has. Therefore this circle exists while I am thinking of it, because nothingness has no properties and one nothingness cannot be different from another nothingness.

ARISTES. What, Theodore! Everything you think of exists? Does your mind give being to this room, this desk, these chairs, because you think of them?

THEODORE. Slowly. I am saying that everything I think of is or, if you prefer, exists. The room, the desk, the chairs which I see, all these things exist, at least while I see them. But you are confusing what I see with a piece of furniture which I do not see. There is a greater difference between the desk I see and the one you believe you see, than there is between your mind and your body.

ARISTES. I understand you partly, Theodore, and I am ashamed at

[*] Cf. *De la Recherche de la vérité*, Bk. 4, Ch. 2, §IV [*OC* II,22ff.]. Cf. *infra*, Dialogue III, §§ X, XII. The distinction between the soul and the body is the foundation of all knowledge relating to human beings.

having interrupted you. I am convinced that everything we see, or everything we think of, contains some reality. You are not speaking of objects, but of their ideas. Yes, undoubtedly, the ideas we have of objects exist while they are present to our minds. However, I thought you were talking about objects themselves.

V. THEODORE. "About objects themselves!" Oh, we are not there yet. I am trying to conduct my reflections in an orderly way. Many more principles than you think are required to demonstrate what no one doubts. For where are those who doubt that they have a body, that they are walking on solid ground, that they live in a material world? However, soon you will know what few people understand, namely that while our body walks in a material world, our mind for its part is ceaselessly transported into an intelligible world which touches it and thereby becomes sensible to it.

Because people regard as nothing the ideas that they have of things, they give the created world much more reality than it has. They do not doubt the existence of objects, and they attribute many qualities to them which they do not have. But they do not even think of the reality of their ideas. This is because they listen to their senses and do not sufficiently consult inner truth. For, once again, it is much easier to demonstrate the reality of ideas or, in your terms, "the reality of that other world entirely full of intelligible beauties," than to demonstrate the existence of this material world. Here is the reason for this.

Ideas have an eternal and necessary existence, and the corporeal world exists only because it pleased God to create it. Thus, to see the intelligible world, it suffices to consult Reason which contains intelligible, eternal, and necessary ideas, the archetype of the visible world. This is something that all minds which are rational or are united to Reason can do. However, to see the material world, or rather to judge that this world exists, for this world is invisible by itself, God must necessarily reveal it to us, for we cannot see His arbitrary volitions in necessary Reason.

Now, God reveals the existence of His creatures to us in two ways: through the authority of the holy Scripture, and through the mediation of our senses. Assuming the first authority – and it cannot be rejected – the existence of bodies can be rigorously demonstrated.[*] By the second

[*] Cf. *infra*, Dialogue VI.

9

way, we can be sufficiently assured of the existence of particular bodies. However, this second way is not presently infallible. For some think they see their enemy before them, while they are quite far away. Others, who have only two legs, think they have four paws. Still others feel pain in an arm amputated long ago. Hence, natural revelation,* which is consequent upon the general laws of the union of the soul and body, is now subject to error. I shall tell you the reasons for this. However, particular revelation can never lead directly to error, because God cannot will to deceive us. This, then, was a little aside, to allow you to glimpse some truths I shall prove to you in the following, to spark your curiosity in them, and to revive your attention a little. I return to where I was. Listen.

I am thinking of a number, of a circle, of a room, of your chairs, in a word, of particular beings. I am also thinking of being or of the infinite, of undetermined being. All these ideas have some reality while I think them. You do not doubt this, because nothingness has no properties, and they do. For they enlighten the mind or make themselves known to it; some even strike it and make themselves sensed by it, and this in a thousand different ways. At least it is certain that the properties of one are very different from those of another. If, then, the reality of our ideas is genuine and, even more, if it is necessary, eternal, and immutable, it is clear that we are together removed to a world other than the one our bodies inhabit; there we are "in a world entirely full of intelligible beauties."

Let us suppose, Aristes, that God annihilated all the beings He created, except you and me, your body and mine. (I speak to you as to one who already believes and knows many things, and in this I am certain that I am not deceived. I would annoy you were I to talk to you with too scrupulous a precision, and as if you knew nothing at all yet.) Let us suppose further that God impresses on our brains all the same traces, or rather that He presents to our minds all the same ideas we have now. On this supposition, Aristes, in which world would we spend the day? Would it not be in an intelligible world? Now, take note, it is in that world that we exist and live, although the bodies we animate live and walk in another. It is that world which we contemplate, admire, and sense. But the world which we look at or consider in turning our head in all directions, is simply matter, which is invisible by itself and has

* Dialogues IV and VI.

none of all those beauties we admire and sense in looking at it. Please reflect closely on this. Nothingness has no properties. Thus, if the world were destroyed it would have no beauty. Now, on the supposition that the world is destroyed and that God nonetheless produces the same traces in our brain, or rather that He presents to our mind the same ideas that are produced in the presence of objects, we would see the same beauties. Hence, the beauties we see are not material beauties, but intelligible beauties rendered sensible as a consequence of the laws of the union of the soul and body, since the assumed annihilation of matter does not carry with it the annihilation of those beauties we see in looking at the objects surrounding us.

ARISTES. I fear, Theodore, you are assuming something false. For if God had destroyed this room, certainly it would no longer be visible, because nothingness has no properties.

VI. THEODORE. You are not following me, Aristes. By itself your room is absolutely invisible. If God had destroyed it, you say, it would no longer be visible, since nothingness has no properties. That would be true were the visibility of your room a property that belonged to it. Were it destroyed it would no longer be visible. I grant this, for in a sense it is true. However, what I see in looking at your room, that is, in turning my eyes in all directions to consider it, would always be visible even if your room were destroyed – what am I saying? – even if it had never been built! I contend that Chinese people who have never been here can see in their country everything I see when I look at your room, assuming – what is not at all impossible – that their brains are agitated in the same way as mine when I consider it. Do not those who have a high fever or who are sleeping see chimeras of all kinds that never existed? What they see exists, at least at the time they see it. But what they believe they see does not exist; that to which they refer what they see is not real at all.

I repeat, Aristes: speaking precisely, your room is not visible. It is not actually your room that I see when I look at it, because I could certainly see everything I see now even if God had destroyed it. The dimensions I see are immutable, eternal, and necessary. These intelligible dimensions which represent to me all these spaces occupy no space. The dimensions of your room are, on the contrary, changing and corruptible; they fill a certain space. However, in telling you too many truths, I fear I am now multiplying your difficulties. For you seem to me to have trouble enough distinguishing ideas, which alone are visible by themselves, from the objects they represent, which are invisible to the mind because they can neither act on it nor represent themselves to it.

ARISTES. It is true I am a little bewildered. For I have trouble following you in this land of ideas, to which you ascribe a genuine reality. I find nothing to hold on to in anything that does not have a body. And this reality of your ideas that I cannot prevent myself from believing to be true for the reasons you have given me, appears to me not to have much solidity. For, I ask you, what becomes of our ideas once we no longer think of them? It seems to me that they return to nothingness. And if this is so, then your intelligible world is destroyed. If, in closing my eyes, I annihilate the intelligible room I now see, then the reality of this room is quite meagre, hardly anything at all. If it suffices for me to open my eyes in order to create an intelligible world, surely this world counts for less than the one in which our bodies live.

VII. THEODORE. True, Aristes. If you give being to your ideas, if an idea requires but a blink of the eye to annihilate it, it is indeed a slight thing. However, if they are eternal, immutable, necessary, in a word, divine – I mean the intelligible extension from which they are formed – surely they will be more considerable than that matter which is inefficacious and absolutely invisible by itself. What, Aristes, can you really believe that by willing to think of, for example, a circle, you give being to the substance, as it were, of which your idea is formed, and that when you cease willing to think of it, you annihilate it? Be careful. If it is you who give being to your ideas, it is by willing to think of them. Now, pray tell, how can you will to think of a circle, if you do not already have some idea of it, from which to form and complete it? Can something be willed without being known? Can you make something from nothing? Certainly, you cannot will to think of a circle, unless you already have the idea of it, or at least the idea of the extension of which you can consider certain parts without thinking of others. You cannot see it closely or distinctly unless you already see it confusedly and from afar. Your attention brings you nearer to it, makes it present to you, even forms it. This I grant. But it is clear that it does not produce it from nothing. Your inattention distances you from it, but it does not annihilate it altogether. For if it annihilated it how could you form the desire to produce it, and on what model would you make it anew, so similar to itself? Is it not clear that this would be impossible?

ARISTES. Still not too clear to me, Theodore. You are convincing me, but not persuading me. This ground is real. I really feel it. When I strike it with my foot, it resists me. There is something solid here. But that my ideas have a certain reality independent of my thought, that they exist even when I am not thinking of them, of this I cannot be persuaded.

VIII. THEODORE. This is because you are unable to enter into yourself to examine Reason and because, wearied by the labor of attention, you listen to your imagination and your senses which speak to you without your taking pains to consult them. You have not reflected enough on the proofs I have given you that their testimony is deceptive. Not long ago there was a man, otherwise quite sensible, who believed he was always in water up to his waist, and who constantly feared it would rise and drown him. He felt it as you feel the earth. He found it cold, and he always moved quite slowly because the water, he said, prevented him from going any faster. Yet when one spoke to him and he listened attentively, he was disabused of the idea. But straight away he would fall back again into his error. When a man believes himself to be transformed into a cock, a hare, a wolf, or an ox like Nebuchadnezzar,[2] he feels in himself, in place of his legs, the feet of the cock; in place of his arms, the hocks of an ox; and in place of his hair, a crest or horns. Why do you not grasp that the resistance you feel in pressing your foot on the floor is simply a sensation that strikes your soul, and that, absolutely speaking, we can have all our sensations independently of objects? In sleep have you never felt a very heavy body on your chest prevent you from breathing; or have you never believed you were struck, and even injured, or believed you struck others, that you were walking, dancing, or jumping on solid ground?

You believe this floor exists because you feel it resist you. What then? Has the air less reality than your floor because it has less solidity? Has ice more reality than water because it is harder? But besides you are mistaken: no body can resist a mind. This floor resists your foot. I grant that. But it is something entirely different from your floor or your body

---

[2] Daniel 4: 22ff.

which resists your mind or gives it the sensation you have of resistance or solidity.

Nevertheless, I still agree with you that your floor resists you. But do you think your ideas do not resist you? Find me then two unequal diameters in a circle, or three equal ones in an ellipse. Find me the square root of eight and the cube root of nine. Make it just to do unto others what is unacceptable to ourselves; or, to take an example more suited to you, make two feet of intelligible extension equal no more than one. Certainly the nature of this extension cannot countenance that. It resists your mind. Do not, therefore, doubt its reality. Your floor is impenetrable to your foot; your senses teach you this in a confused and deceptive way. Intelligible extension is also impenetrable in its own way; it makes you see this clearly through its own evidence and light.

Listen to me, Aristes. You have the idea of space or extension, a space, that is, which has no limits. This idea is necessary, eternal, immutable, and common to all minds, to people, to angels, and to God Himself. This idea, take note, is indelibly in your mind, like that of being or the infinite, of indeterminate being. It is always present to you. You cannot separate yourself from it or completely lose sight of it. Now, it is from this vast idea that not only the idea of a circle and of all purely intelligible figures is formed, but also the idea of all the sensible figures we see in looking at the created world. All of this occurs according to the various applications to our mind of the intelligible parts of this ideal, immaterial, intelligible extension; it occurs sometimes as a result of our attention, when we know these figures, and sometimes as a result of the traces and agitations of our brain, when we imagine or sense them. At present I need not explain all this to you more precisely.[*] Simply consider that this idea of an infinite extension must have a great deal of reality, since you cannot comprehend it, and whatever effort of mind you make, you cannot exhaust it. Consider that it is impossible for it to be simply a modification of your mind, for the infinite cannot actually be the modification of something finite. Say to yourself: my mind cannot comprehend this vast idea. It cannot measure it. Thus it infinitely surpasses my mind. And if it surpasses it, it is clearly not its modification. For the modifications of beings cannot extend beyond those beings themselves, because the modifications of beings are simply

---

[*] Cf. the *Conversations chrétiennes*, pp. 123f. of the 1702 edition [*OC* IV 75f.]; *Réponse à Monsieur Regis*, pp. 27ff. [*OC* XVII–1 281ff.]; *Entretiens sur la Mort* II [*OC* XIII 385–415].

those same beings existing in a particular way. My mind cannot measure this idea, for it is finite, and the idea is infinite. For the finite, however great it may be, applied or repeated as we might, can never equal the infinite.

ARISTES. How subtle and quick you are! Go slowly, if you please. I deny that the mind perceives the infinite. The mind, I admit, perceives an extension whose limits it does not see, but it does not see an infinite extension. A finite mind can see nothing infinite.

IX. THEODORE. No, Aristes, the mind does not see an infinite extension, in the sense that its thought or perception is adequate to an infinite extension. If that were so, it would comprehend it and would itself be infinite. For an infinite thought is required to measure an infinite idea, in order actually to be joined to everything the infinite encompasses. But the mind actually sees that its immediate object is infinite; it actually sees that intelligible extension is infinite. And this is not, as you believe, because it does not see its limit, for if that were so it could then expect to find it or could at least doubt whether or not it had one. Rather, this is because it sees clearly that it has none.

Let us suppose that a man, fallen from the clouds, walks the earth continuously in a straight line, I mean, in one of those great circles by which geographers divide it, and that nothing prevents him from traveling. Could he, after several days' journey, decide that the earth is infinite, because he did not find its end? If he were wise and reserved in judgment, he would believe it to be quite large, but he would not judge it to be infinite. And as a result of walking, finding himself at the same place from which he had departed, he would realise he had actually gone around it. However, when the mind thinks of intelligible extension, when it seeks to measure the idea of space, it sees clearly that it is infinite. It cannot doubt that this idea is inexhaustible. Let the mind take from it enough to represent the place of a hundred thousand worlds and at each instant again a hundred thousand more, this idea will never cease to furnish it with everything it requires. But this is not how it discovers it to be infinite. On the contrary, it is because it sees it as actually infinite, because it knows very well it will never exhaust it.

Geometers are the most exact of those who engage in reasoning. Now, all agree that there is no fraction which, multiplied by itself, yields a product of eight, although in increasing the terms of the fraction this number can be approached to infinity. All agree that if the hyperbola and its asymptotes and many other similar lines are continued to infinity, they will continually approach each other without ever meeting. Do you think that they discover these truths by trial and error, and that they judge of things they do not see by some small thing they have discovered? No, Aristes. Imagination and the senses, or those who follow their teaching, judge in that way. But true philosophers judge precisely only on what they see. And yet they are not afraid to affirm, without ever having tested it, that no part of the diagonal of a square, be it a million times smaller than the smallest grain of dust, can equal exactly and without remainder this diagonal of a square and any one of its sides. It is likewise true that the mind sees the infinite as much in the small as in the great, not through the repeated division or multiplication of its finite ideas, but through the infinity itself which it discovers in its ideas and which belongs to them; ideas which at once teach it that on the one hand there is no unity, and on the other hand there are no limits to intelligible extension.

ARISTES. I give in, Theodore. Ideas have more reality than I thought, and their reality is immutable, necessary, eternal, common to all intellects and in no way modifications of the being of the intellect which, because it is finite, cannot actually receive infinite modifications. The perception I have of intelligible extension belongs to me, it is a modification of my mind. It is I who perceive this extension. But the extension I perceive is not a modification of my mind. For I am well aware that it is not myself I see when I think of infinite spaces, of a circle, of a square, of a cube, when I look at this room or turn my eyes to the sky. The perception of this extension is mine. But as for this extension and all the figures I discover in it, I would certainly like to know how all that is not mine. The perception I have of extension cannot exist without me. It is therefore a modification of my mind. But the extension I see subsists without me. For you can think of it without my thinking of it, you and everyone else.

X. THEODORE. You might add, without worry, "and God Himself." For in terms of their intelligible reality all our clear ideas are in God. It is only in Him that we see them. Do not imagine that what I am saying to you is new: it is the opinion of St. Augustine.[*] If our ideas

[*] Cf. the *Réponse au Livre des vrayes & fausses Idées* 7 & 21 [*OC* VI 63–9; 143–50].

are eternal, immutable, and necessary, you can readily see that they can be found only in an immutable nature. Yes, Aristes, in Himself God sees intelligible extension, the archetype of the matter from which the world is formed and in which our bodies live; and, once again, it is only in Him that we see it. For our minds live solely in universal Reason, in that intelligible substance which contains the ideas of all the truths we discover, whether as a consequence of the general laws of the union of our mind with this same Reason,* or as a consequence of the general laws of the union of our soul with our body, the occasional or natural cause of which is simply traces impressed on the brain through the action of objects or the flow of animal spirits.

The order of exposition does not at present permit me to explain all this in detail. However, in order to satisfy partially the desire you have to know how the mind can discover all kinds of figures and see the sensible world in intelligible extension, note the three ways you perceive a circle, for example. You conceive it, you imagine it, you sense or see it. When you conceive it, intelligible extension is applied to your mind with indeterminate limits in respect of size, but equally distant from a determinate point, and all on a single plane; and then you conceive a circle in general. When you imagine it, a determinate part of this extension, the limits of which are equally distant from a point, lightly touches your mind. And when you sense or see it, a determinate part of this extension sensibly touches your soul and modifies it by the sensation of some color. For intelligible extension becomes visible and represents a certain body in particular only by means of color, because it is only by the variety of colors that we judge the difference between the objects we see. All the intelligible parts of intelligible extension are of the same nature insofar as they are ideas, just as all the parts of local or material extension have the same nature as a substance. But as the sensations of color are essentially different, by means of them we judge the variety of bodies. If I distinguish your hand from your coat and both from the air surrounding them, this is because the sensations of light or color that I have of them are very different. That is evident. For if I had the same sensation of color for everything in your room, I would see no diversity in objects with my sense of sight. Therefore you judge rightly that intelligible extension, applied diversely to our mind,** can provide

---

* Cf. *infra*, Dialogue XII.
** On this matter, cf. *De la Recherche de la vérite*, Bk. 3, Pt. 2 [*OC* I 413ff.], & Elucidation X [of *De*

us with all the ideas we have of mathematical figures and of all the objects we admire in the universe, and finally of everything our imagination represents to us. For just as one can sculpt all kinds of figures from a block of marble by using a chisel, so God can represent all material beings to us through various applications of intelligible extension to our mind. But how this happens, and why God does it this way, we can examine in what follows.

This will do, Aristes, for a first discussion. Try to accustom yourself to metaphysical ideas and to raise yourself above your senses. You will find yourself, if I am not mistaken, transported to an intelligible world. Contemplate its beauties. Go over in your mind everything I have said to you. Nourish yourself on the substance of truth, and get ready to enter further into this unknown land which you have as yet only approached. Tomorrow I shall attempt to lead you to the throne of the sovereign majesty, to whom belongs from all eternity this happy and unchanging land in which our minds reside.

ARISTES. I am still thoroughly amazed and startled. My body dulls my mind, and I am at pains to grasp firmly those truths you have revealed to me. And still you propose to lift me even higher. My head will reel, Theodore; and if tomorrow I feel as I do today, I shall not have the confidence to follow you.

THEODORE. Meditate on what I have told you, Aristes, and tomorrow I promise you will be ready for anything. Meditation will strengthen your mind and give you the ardor and wings to surpass creatures and elevate yourself to the presence of the creator. Farewell, my friend. Be brave.

ARISTES. Goodbye, Theodore. I shall do as you have instructed.

la Recherche de la vérité, OC III 127ff]. Cf. further my *Réponse au Livre des vrayes & fausses Idées* by Mr. Arnauld [*OC* VI 11–189], and my *I. Lettre* concerning his *Défense* [*OC* VI 193–274]. Or my *Réponse à la III. Lettre posthume de Monsieur Arnauld* [*OC* IX 897–989].

Dialogue II
The Existence of God

We can see all things in Him, and nothing finite can represent Him. Thus, it is sufficient to think of Him to know that He exists.[1]

THEODORE. Well, Aristes, what do you think of that intelligible world to which I led you yesterday? Is your imagination no longer frightened by it? Does your mind proceed with a firm and confident gait in that land of meditators, in that region inaccessible to those who listen only to their senses?

ARISTES. What a beautiful spectacle the archetype of the universe is, Theodore! I have contemplated it with extreme satisfaction. What a pleasant surprise it is that the soul, without suffering death, is transported to the land of truth where it discovers an abundance to nourish it. It is true that I am still not quite accustomed to this celestial manna, to this entirely spiritual nourishment. At certain moments it seems very thin and light to me. But when I savor it attentively I find it has so much flavor and solidity that I can no longer bring myself to go to graze with the beasts on material ground.

THEODORE. Oh, my dear Aristes, what are you saying to me? Are you speaking seriously?

ARISTES. Quite seriously. No, I no longer want to listen to my senses. I wish always to enter into the most secret part of myself, and to live on the abundance I find there. My senses are meant to lead my body to its usual pasture, and I allow it to follow them. But that I myself should follow them! That I shall do no more. I desire to follow Reason

---

[1] Here I follow the first edition. In the second, third, and fourth editions Malebranche writes: "Thus, it is sufficient to think of Him to know what He is."

alone, and by means of my attention to proceed into that land of truth where I discover those delicious foods which alone can nourish intellects.[2]

THEODORE. That is because you have momentarily forgotten that you have a body. But you will not go long without thinking of it, or rather without thinking in relation to it. This body you presently neglect will soon require you yourself to lead it to pasture and to occupy yourself with its needs. For now the mind is not so easily disengaged from matter. However, while you are this pure mind, tell me, I ask you, what have you discovered in the land of ideas? Do you now know what that Reason is, about which so much is said in this material and terrestrial world, but of which so little is known there? Yesterday I promised to elevate you above all creatures, and to conduct you into the very presence of the creator. Have you not flown there yourself, without thinking of Theodore?

I. ARISTES. I confess I believed – without lacking the respect I owe you – that I could go alone on the path you showed me. I have followed it and have, it seems to me, clearly understood what you told me yesterday, namely that universal Reason is an immutable nature and is found only in God. Here, in a few words, are all the steps I followed. Judge them and tell me if I have gone astray. After you left me I remained for a time quite startled and taken aback. However, an inner drive urged me on and it seemed to me as if I were saying to myself – I do not know how – "Reason is common to me and Theodore: why then can I not consult and follow it without him?" I consulted and followed it, and unless I am mistaken it led me to Him who possesses it as His own and by the necessity of His being. For it seems to me to lead there quite naturally. Here, then, quite simply and without embellishment, is my reasoning.

Infinite intelligible extension is not a modification of my mind. It is immutable, eternal, and necessary. I can doubt neither its reality nor its immensity. Now, everything immutable, eternal, necessary, and above all infinite is not a creature and cannot belong to a creature. Thus it belongs to the creator and can be found only in God. Therefore there is a God and a Reason; a God in whom is found the archetype I

---

[2] Here I treat *"mon attention"* as a specific faculty.

contemplate of the created world in which I live; a God in whom is found the Reason that enlightens me by the purely intelligible ideas which it abundantly furnishes to my mind and to the minds of all people. For I am sure that all people are united to the same Reason as I; because I am certain they see or can see what I see when I enter into myself and discover there the truths or necessary relations contained in the intelligible substance of the universal Reason which lives in me, or, rather, in which all intellects live.

II. THEODORE. You have not gone astray, my dear Aristes. You have followed Reason and it has led you to Him who engenders it from His own substance and possesses it eternally. However, do not imagine you have discovered the nature of the supreme Being to whom it has led you. When you contemplate intelligible extension you still see only the archetype both of the material world in which we live, and of an infinity of other possible worlds. You are then actually seeing the divine substance, for that alone is visible or capable of enlightening the mind. But you do not see it in itself or as it really is. You see it only in its relation to material creatures, only as it is participable by or representative of them. Consequently it is not strictly speaking God whom you see, but only the matter He can produce.

Certainly, by infinite intelligible extension you see that God exists. For it is only He who contains what you see, because nothing finite can contain an infinite reality. But you do not see what God is. For the divinity has no limits in His perfections, and what you see when you think of immense spaces lacks an infinity of perfections. I say "what you see," and not "the substance which represents to you what you see." For that substance, which you do not see in itself, has infinite perfections.

Surely, the substance containing intelligible extension is all-powerful. It is infinitely wise. It contains an infinity of perfections and realities. For example, it contains an infinity of intelligible numbers. But this intelligible extension has nothing in common with any of these things. There is no wisdom, no power, no unity in that extension you contemplate. For you know that all numbers are commensurable among themselves, because they have unity as a common measure. If, then, the parts of this extension, which are divided and subdivided by the mind, could be reduced to unity, they would always be commensurable among themselves in virtue of this unity; which you certainly know to be false. Hence, the divine substance in its simplicity, to which we cannot attain, contains an infinity of entirely different intelligible perfections by which God enlightens us without making Himself visible to us such as He is or according to His specific and absolute reality, but according to His general reality and relative to His possible works. Nevertheless, try to follow me; I shall conduct you as close to the divinity as I can.

III. Infinite intelligible extension is simply the archetype of an infinity of possible worlds resembling ours. By it I see only particular beings, only material beings. When I think of this extension I see the divine substance only insofar as it is representative of bodies, and participable by them. Note, however, when I think of being and not of particular beings, when I think of the infinite and not of a particular infinite, it is certain, in the first place, that I do not see so vast a reality in the modifications of my mind. For if I cannot find sufficient reality in them to represent the infinite in extension, that is all the more reason why I shall not find enough there to represent the infinite in all ways. Thus it is only God, the infinite, indeterminate being, or the infinitely infinite infinite, who can contain the infinitely infinite reality I see when I think of being, and not of particular beings or of particular infinites.

IV. In the second place, it is certain that the idea of being, of reality, of indeterminate perfection, or of the infinite in every way, is not the divine substance insofar as it is representative of or participable by a particular creature. For every creature is necessarily a particular being. It is contradictory for God to make or engender a being in general or infinite in every way, which is not God Himself or equal to His principle. The Son and Holy Spirit do not participate in the divine Being, they receive it in its entirety. Or, to speak of things more proportioned to our mind, it is clear that the idea of a circle in general is not intelligible extension insofar as it is representative of a particular circle or participable by a particular circle. For the idea of a circle in general or the essence of a circle represents or applies to an infinite number of circles. This idea contains that of the infinite. For to think of a circle in general is to perceive an infinite number of circles as a single circle. I do not know whether you are grasping what I want you to understand. Here it is in a couple of words. The idea of being without restriction, of the infinite, of generality, is not the idea of creatures or the essence that applies to them, but the idea that represents the divinity or the essence that applies to it. All particular beings participate in being; but no particular being equals it. Being contains all things but all beings, both created and possible, in all their multiplicity, cannot fill the vast extension of being.

ARISTES. It seems to me that I do see your meaning. You define God as He defines Himself in speaking to Moses: "I am who am."* Intelligible extension is the idea or archetype of bodies. But being without restriction, in a word Being, is the idea of God; this is what represents Him to our mind as we see Him in this life.

V. THEODORE. Very well. But above all take note that God or the infinite is not visible by an idea that represents Him. The infinite is its own idea. It has no archetype. It can be known, but it cannot be made. It is only creatures, only particular beings which can be created, which are visible by the ideas representing them even before they are produced. We can see a circle, a house, a sun, without there being any such thing. For everything finite can be seen in the infinite which contains their intelligible ideas. But the infinite can be seen only in itself. For nothing finite can represent the infinite. If we think of God, He must exist. A particular being, although known, is able not to exist. Its essence can be seen without its existence, its idea without the thing itself. However, the essence of the infinite cannot be seen without its existence, the idea of being without being. For being has no idea that represents it. It has no archetype containing all its intelligible reality. It is its own archetype and it contains in itself the archetype of all beings.

Thus, you can easily see that this proposition 'There is a God' is by itself the clearest of all the propositions affirming the existence of something, and that it is even as certain as 'I think therefore I am.' Moreover, you see what God is since God and being or the infinite are but the same thing.

VI. However, once again, do not be deceived. You see what God is only very confusedly and as from afar. You do not see Him as He is because, although you see the infinite or being without restriction, you see it only very imperfectly. You do not see it as a simple being. You see

* Exodus 3: 14.

the multiplicity of creatures in the infinity of uncreated being, but you do not distinctly see its unity there. For you do not see it so much according to its absolute reality as according to what it is in relation to possible creatures, whose number can be increased to infinity without their ever equalling the reality that represents them. This is because you see it as universal Reason, which illumines intellects according to the degree of light now required for them to be led and to reveal its perfections insofar as they are participable by limited beings. But you do not discover that property,* which is essential to the infinite, of being at once one and all things, composed, so to speak, of an infinity of different perfections, and so simple that each perfection in it contains all the others without any real distinction.

God does not communicate His substance to creatures. He communicates only His perfections, not as they are in His substance but as His substance represents them and as the limitation of creatures can bear them. Intelligible extension, for example, represents bodies: it is their archetype or idea. But although this extension occupies no place, bodies are extended locally and can only be extended locally because of the essential limitation of creatures and because no finite substance can have that property, incomprehensible to the human mind, of being at once one and all things, perfectly simple and possessing all kinds of perfections.

Thus, intelligible extension represents infinite spaces but fills none, and although it so to speak fills all minds and is revealed to them, it does not at all follow that our mind occupies space. It would have to occupy space infinitely to see infinite spaces, were it to see them by means of a local union to locally extended spaces.**

The divine substance exists everywhere without being locally extended. It has no limits. It is not contained in the universe. But it is not that substance spread out everywhere that we see when we think of spaces.† For if that were so we would never be able to think of infinite spaces, because our mind is finite. But the intelligible extension we see in the divine substance containing it is simply that substance itself insofar as it is representative of material beings and is participable by them. That is all I can tell you. However, take note that unrestricted

---

  * Cf. *I. Lettre touchant la Défense de M. Arnauld*, remark 18 [*OC* VI 249–53].

  ** Cf. *I. Lettre touchant la Défense de M. Arnauld*, remark 2, §XIff. [*OC* VI 210ff.].

  † *Ibid.* Cf. *infra*, Dialogue VIII.

being, or the infinite that we perceive in every way, is not simply the divine substance insofar as it is representative of all possible beings. For although we do not have particular ideas of all these beings, we are assured they cannot equal the intelligible reality of the infinite. Thus, in one sense it is the very substance of God that we see. But in this life we see it only in a manner so confused and remote that we see that it is rather than what it is; we see that it is the source and exemplar of all beings rather than its own nature or its perfections in themselves.

ARISTES. Is there not a contradiction in what you are telling me? If nothing finite can have enough reality to represent the infinite – which seems evident to me – must we not necessarily see the substance of God in itself?

VII. THEODORE. I do not deny that we see the substance of God in itself. We see it in itself in the sense that we do not see it by means of something finite that represents it. But we do not see it in itself in the sense that we grasp its simplicity and discover therein its perfections.

As you agree that nothing finite can represent the infinite reality, it is clear that if you see the infinite you see it only in itself. Yet it is certain that you see it. For, otherwise, in asking me whether God or an infinite being exists you would be asking me a ridiculous question, by means of a proposition whose terms you did not understand. It is as if you asked me if a Blictri exists,* that is to say, a particular thing, without knowing what it is.

Surely everyone has the idea of God or thinks of the infinite, when they ask whether such a being exists. However, they believe they can think of it without its existing because they do not reflect that nothing finite can represent it. Since they are able to think of many things that do not exist because creatures can be seen without existing, for we do not see them in themselves but in the ideas representing them, they imagine it is the same with the infinite and that they can think of it without its existing. This is what makes them seek, without recognizing, that which they encounter at every moment and which they would soon recognize if they turned into themselves and reflected on their ideas.

ARISTES. You are convincing me, Theodore, but I still have some doubt. For it seems to me that the idea I have of being in general or of the infinite, is an idea of my own making. It appears that the mind can

---

* This is a term which evokes no idea.

fashion general ideas out of several particular ideas. When we have seen several trees, an apple tree, a pear tree, a plum tree, etc., we make a general idea of a tree from them. Just as when we have seen several beings, we form the general idea of being. Thus, this general idea of being is perhaps nothing but a confused assemblage of all the others. This is how I was taught it, and how I have always understood it.

VIII. THEODORE. Your mind, Aristes, is a wonderful craftsman. It knows how to derive the infinite from the finite, the idea of being without restriction from the ideas of particular beings. Perhaps this is because it discovers sufficient reality in its own resources to give finite ideas what they lack in order to be infinite. I do not know whether this is what you have been taught, but I believe I know you have never understood the matter well.

ARISTES. If our ideas were infinite, surely they would be neither our creation nor modifications of our mind. That is beyond dispute. However, perhaps they are finite, though we are able to perceive the infinite by them. Or perhaps the infinite we see is not really this way. It is, as I have just said, simply the confused assemblage of several finite things. Perhaps the general idea of being is but a confused cluster of the ideas of particular beings. I have trouble ridding my mind of this thought.

IX. THEODORE. Yes, Aristes, our ideas are finite, if by "our ideas" you mean our perceptions or the modifications of our mind. But if by the idea of the infinite you mean what the mind sees when it thinks of it, or what is then the immediate object of the mind, surely that is infinite, for we see it as such. Take note, I say: we see it as such. The impression the infinite makes on the mind is finite. There is even more perception in the mind, more impression of an idea, in a word, more thought, when we know a small object clearly and distinctly than when we think confusedly of a large object, or even of infinity. However, although the mind is almost always more touched, more penetrated, more modified by a finite idea than by an infinite one, nonetheless there is more reality in the idea of the infinite than in the finite, in being without restriction than in particular beings.

You cannot rid yourself of the idea that general ideas are simply a confused assemblage of certain particular ideas, or at least that you have the power to form them out of that assemblage. Let us see what is true and what is false in this thought to which you are so strongly predisposed. You think, Aristes, of a circle, one foot in diameter, then of one of two feet, of one three feet, of one four feet, etc., and finally you do not determine the size of the diameter, and you think of a circle in general. The idea of that circle in general, you say, is therefore simply the confused assemblage of the circles of which I have thought. Certainly, this conclusion is false, for the idea of the general circle represents infinite circles and applies to them all, whereas you have thought only of a finite number of circles.

Perhaps it is rather the case that you have found the secret of forming the idea of a circle in general from five or six circles you have seen. And this is true in one sense, false in another. It is false in the sense that there is sufficient reality in the idea of five or six circles to form the idea of a circle in general from them. But it is true in the sense that, having recognized that the size of circles does not change their properties, you have perhaps stopped considering them one after the other according to their determinate size, in order to consider them in general according to an indeterminate size. Thus, you have, as it were, formed the idea of circle in general, by spreading the idea of generality over the confused ideas of circles you have imagined. However, I maintain you could form general ideas only because you find enough reality in the idea of the infinite to give the idea of generality to your ideas. You can think of an indeterminate diameter only because you see the infinite in extension and can increase or decrease extension to infinity. I hold that you could never think of these abstract forms of genera and species were the idea of infinity, which is inseparable from your mind, not entirely naturally joined to the particular ideas you perceive. You could think of a particular circle, but never of the circle. You could perceive a particular equality of radii, but never a general equality between indeterminate radii. The reason is that no finite and determinate idea can ever represent anything infinite and indeterminate. But the mind unreflectively joins the idea of generality which it finds in the infinite to its finite ideas. For just as the mind spreads the idea of indivisible unity over the idea of particular extension although that extension is infinitely divisible, so also the mind spreads the general idea of a perfect equality over certain particular ideas; and this is what throws it into an infinity of errors. For all the falsity of our ideas comes from our confounding them with one another and from our further mingling them with our own modifications. But we shall speak of this another time.

ARISTES. All that is very well, Theodore. But do you not think that our ideas are distinct from our perceptions? It seems to me that the idea of a circle in general is but a confused perception of several circles of diverse sizes; that is to say, a cluster of diverse modifications of my mind which are almost erased from it, each one of which is the idea or perception of a particular circle.

X. THEODORE. Yes, undoubtedly, I draw a clear distinction between our ideas and our perceptions, between ourselves who perceive and what we perceive.[*] This is because I know that the finite cannot find in itself the wherewithal to represent the infinite. This is because I know, Aristes, that I contain no intelligible reality within myself and that, far from finding the ideas of everything in my substance, I do not even find there the idea of my own being.[**] For I am entirely unintelligible to myself and will never see what I am, except when it pleases God to reveal to me the idea or archetype of minds which universal Reason contains. But that is a matter we shall discuss another time.

Surely, Aristes, if your ideas were only modifications of your mind, the confused assemblage of thousands and thousands of ideas would never be anything but a confused composite, incapable of any generality. Take twenty different colors and mix them together to excite a general color in yourself. At the same time produce several different sensations in yourself in order to form a general sensation; you will soon see this is impossible. For in blending various colors you will make green, gray, or blue, always some particular color. Dizziness is produced by an infinity of various disturbances of the fibers of the brain and animal spirits; nonetheless, it is simply a particular sensation. This is because every modification of a particular being, such as our mind, can only be particular. It can never rise to the generality found in ideas. It is true that you can think of pain in general, but you can never be modified except by a particular pain. And if you can think of pain in general this is because you can join generality to all things. However, once again,

[*] Cf. *Réponse au Livre des vrayes & fausses Idées* [*OC* VI 11–189], or my *Réponse à la III. Lettre de Monsieur Arnauld* [*OC* XI 897–989].
[**] Cf. *De la Recherche de la vérité,* Bk. 3, Pt. 2, Ch. 7, § IV [*OC* I 451ff.], and Elucidation XI, corresponding to this chapter [*OC* III 163ff.].

you can never derive this idea of generality from your own resources. It has too much reality; the infinite must furnish it for you from its own abundance.

ARISTES. I have nothing to say in reply. Everything you tell me seems evident. But I am surprised that these general ideas, which have infinitely more reality than particular ideas, strike me less than they do and appear to me to have much less solidity.

XI. THEODORE. That is because they are sensed less, or rather because they are not sensed at all. Aristes, do not judge the reality of ideas in the way children judge the reality of bodies. Children believe that all the spaces between the earth and sky are not real at all, because they are not sensed. And there are only a few people who know that there is as much matter in a cubic foot of air as there is in a cubic foot of lead, because the lead is harder, heavier, in a word more sensible than the air. Do not imitate them. Judge the reality of ideas not by the sensation you have of them which confusedly indicates their action to you, but by the intelligible light which reveals their nature to you. Otherwise you will think that the sensible ideas which strike you, such as the one you have of the floor you press with your foot, have more reality than purely intelligible ideas, although fundamentally there is no difference.

ARISTES. "No difference," Theodore! What! The idea of the extension I think of is not different from the idea of the extension which I see, press with my foot, and which resists me!

XII. THEODORE. No, Aristes, there are neither two kinds of extension nor two kinds of ideas representing them. And if that extension you think of were to touch you or modify your soul by some sensation, however intelligible it may be, it would appear sensible to you. It would seem hard, cold, colored, and perhaps painful; for perhaps you would attribute to it all the sensations you have. Once again, things must not be judged by the sensations we have of them. We must not believe that ice has more reality than water because it resists us more.

If you believed that fire has more force or efficacy than earth, your error would have some foundation. For there is some reason to judge the magnitude of forces by that of their effects. However, to believe that the idea of extension, which touches you by some sensation, is of another nature or has more reality than that of which you think without receiving any sensible impression from it, is to take the absolute for the relative; it is to judge what things are in themselves by their relation to you. This is how to give more reality to the point of a thorn than to all the rest of the universe, even to the infinite being. But when you become accustomed to distinguishing your sensations from your ideas you will recognize that the same idea of extension can be known, * imagined, or sensed, according to the way the divine substance containing it applies it diversely to our mind. Thus, do not believe that the infinite or being in general has less reality than the idea of a particular object which touches you at present in a very lively and sensible way. Judge things by the ideas representing them and do not attribute to them anything resembling the sensations by which you are affected. In due time you will understand more distinctly what I am now suggesting.

ARISTES. Everything you have said to me, Theodore, is highly abstract, and I am at great pains to keep it before me. My mind is working amazingly; a little rest, if you please. I must think leisurely on these great and sublime truths. I shall try to familiarize myself with them by strenuous efforts of a completely pure attention. At present, however, I am incapable of this. I must relax, to regain new energy.

THEODORE. I knew well, Aristes, you would not be of pure mind for long. Go; lead your body to pasture. Refresh your imagination through the variety of objects which can hearten and please it. But try, nevertheless, to preserve some taste for the truth, and when you feel yourself capable of nourishing yourself on it and meditating upon it, leave everything for it. Forget even what you are, insofar as you can. You must necessarily think of the body's needs, but it is a great disorder to occupy yourself with its pleasures.

* Cf. *Entretiens sur la Mort* II [*OC* XIII 385–415].

Dialogue III

The difference between our sensations and our ideas. We must judge things only by the ideas representing them and never by the sensations by which we are affected in their presence or on their occasion.

THEODORE. Hello, Aristes! How you dream! What are you thinking of so deeply?

ARISTES. Who is it? Ah, Theodore, you surprised me. I am returning from that other world to which you transported me these last days. I am now going there alone, without fearing the phantoms which bar entrance. However, once there I find so many obscure places that I fear being led astray and losing myself.

I. THEODORE. It is a lot, Aristes, to know how to leave one's body when one wishes and to elevate oneself mentally into the land of intellects. But that is not enough. It is necessary to know the map of that land a little, what places are inaccessible to poor mortals, and the places where they can travel freely, without fear of illusions. It seems to me that it is because they have not sufficiently heeded what I am about to draw your attention to that most travelers in these dangerous regions have been seduced by certain attractive specters which entice us to precipices from which return is morally impossible. Listen to me very seriously; today I am going to tell you something you should never forget.

Never, Aristes, take your own sensations for our ideas, the modifications which affect your soul for the ideas which enlighten all minds. This is the greatest of all the precepts for the avoidance of error. You will never contemplate ideas without discovering some truth; but whatever attention you give your own modifications, you will never be enlightened by them. You cannot quite understand what I am saying to you; I shall have to explain myself further.

II. You know, Aristes, that the divine Word, as universal Reason, contains in its substance the primordial ideas of all beings, created and possible. You know that all intellects, which are united to that sovereign Reason, discover some of these ideas in it, inasmuch as God wishes to reveal these ideas to them. This happens as a consequence of the general laws He has established to make us rational and to form a kind of society between us and Him. Someday I shall unravel this entire mystery for you. You do not doubt that intelligible extension, for instance, which is the primordial idea or the archetype of bodies, is contained in the universal Reason which enlightens all minds, even that mind with which this reason is consubstantial. But perhaps you have not sufficiently reflected on the difference between the intelligible ideas it contains and our own sensations or the modifications of our soul, and perhaps you consider it unnecessary to take careful note of this difference.

III. What a difference there is, my dear Aristes, between the light of our ideas and the obscurity of our sensations, between knowing and sensing, and how necessary it is to become accustomed to distinguishing them easily! People who fail to reflect sufficiently on this difference, continually believing themselves to know quite clearly what they sense most vividly, cannot but be misled in the darkness of their own modifications. For, after all, you must understand this important truth. Human beings are not their own light unto themselves. Their substance, far from enlightening them, is in itself unintelligible to them. They know nothing except by the light of the universal Reason which enlightens all minds, by the intelligible ideas it reveals to them in its wholly luminous substance.

IV. Created reason, our soul, the human mind, the purest and most sublime intellects, can indeed see the light, but they cannot produce it or draw it from their own resources; they cannot engender it from their substance. They can discover the eternal, immutable, necessary truths in the divine Word, in the eternal, immutable, necessary Wisdom; but in themselves they can find only sensations, often quite lively but always obscure and confused, only modalities full of darkness. In a word, they can never discover the truth by contemplating themselves. They cannot be nourished by their own substance. They can find the life of the intellect only in the universal Reason which animates all minds, which enlightens and leads all people. For it is universal Reason which provides inner consolation to those who follow it; it is universal Reason which recalls those who leave it; it is, finally, universal Reason which, by means of terrible reproaches and threats, fills those resolved to abandon it with confusion, anxiety, and despair.

ARISTES. I am indeed persuaded, Theodore, by the reflections I have made on what you have told me these last days, that it is solely the divine Word which enlightens us by the intelligible ideas it contains. For there are not two or several Wisdoms, two or several universal Reasons. Truth is immutable, necessary, eternal, the same in time and in eternity, the same among us and among foreigners, the same in heaven and in hell. The eternal Word speaks the same language to all nations, to the Chinese and the Tartars as well as to the French and the Spanish. And if they are not equally enlightened, it is because they are not equally attentive; because they mingle – some more, others less – their modalities with ideas, the particular inspirations of their self-love with the general responses of inner truth. Two times two is four among all peoples. Everyone understands the voice of truth which ordains that we not do unto others what we would not wish done unto ourselves. And those who do not obey this voice feel the internal reproaches which threaten and punish them for their disobedience, provided they return into themselves and listen to Reason. I am now indeed convinced of these principles. But I still do not understand too well this difference between knowing and sensing which you consider so necessary to avoid error. Please clarify it for me.

V. THEODORE. If indeed you had meditated on these principles of which you tell me you are convinced, you would see clearly what you are asking me. However, without involving you in too arduous a course, answer me. Do you think God feels the pain we suffer?

ARISTES. Undoubtedly not. For the feeling of pain causes unhappiness.

THEODORE. Very well. But do you believe He knows it?

ARISTES. Yes, I believe so. For He knows everything that happens to His creatures. God's knowledge has no limits, and knowing my pain makes Him neither unhappy nor imperfect. On the contrary . . .

THEODORE. Oh oh, Aristes! God knows pain, pleasure, heat, and so on, and He does not feel these things! He knows pain, because He knows what this modification of the soul is, in which pain consists. He knows it because it is He alone who causes it in us, as I shall show you in the following, and He knows well what He does. But He does not feel it, for He would be unhappy. Thus, to know pain is not to feel it.

ARISTES. True. But is it not the case that to feel pain is to know it?

VI. THEODORE. Undoubtedly not, since God does not feel it at all and knows it perfectly. However, so that we are not detained by the ambiguity of these terms, if you would have 'feeling' pain mean 'knowing' it, at least agree that it is not clearly knowing it, not knowing it by light and evidence; in a word, it is not knowing its nature and thus, strictly speaking, it is not knowing it. To feel pain, for example, is to feel unhappy, knowing neither what we are nor what that modality of our being is which makes us unhappy. But to know is to have a clear idea of the nature of the object, and by light and evidence to discover its particular relations.

I know the parts of extension clearly because I can see their relations evidently. I see clearly that the sides of similar triangles are proportional, that there is no plane triangle whose three angles do not equal two right angles. I see these truths or relations clearly in the idea or archetype of extension. For that idea is so luminous that it is by contemplating it that geometers and good physicists are made; and it is so fertile in truths that all minds together will never exhaust it.

VII. The same is not true of my being. I have no idea of it, I do not see its archetype. I cannot discover the relations of the modifications affecting my mind. In turning inward I cannot recognize any of my faculties or capacities. The inner feeling I have of myself teaches me that I am, that I think, that I will, that I feel, that I suffer, etc., but it does not let me know what I am, the nature of my thought, of my will, of my feelings, of my passions, of my pain, nor the relations all these things have to each other. For, once again, not having an idea of my soul, and not seeing its archetype in the divine Word, in contemplating it I can discover neither what it is nor what the modalities are of which it is capable, nor finally what the relations are between its modalities, relations which I sense vividly without knowing them but which God knows clearly without sensing them. All this is the case, my dear Aristes, because, as I have already said, I am not a light unto myself, because my substance and modalities are but darkness, and because for many reasons God has not found it fitting to reveal to me the idea or archetype which represents the nature of spiritual beings. For were my substance intelligible of or in itself, were it luminous, were it capable of enlightening me, as I am not separated from myself, in contemplating myself I would certainly see that I am capable of being affected by certain sensations I have never experienced and of which I shall perhaps never have any knowledge. I would not have had need of a concert to know the sweetness of harmony, and although I had never tasted a particular fruit I would be able, I do not say to sense, but to know with evidence the nature of the sensation it excites in me. But as we can know the nature of beings only in Reason which contains them in an intelligible manner, and although I can sense myself only in myself, it is only in Reason that I can discover what I am and the modalities of which my nature is capable. And *a fortiori* it is only in Reason that I discover the principles of the sciences and all the truths capable of enlightening the mind.

ARISTES. Let us move on a little, Theodore. I believe there are essential differences between knowing and sensing, between the ideas which enlighten the mind and the sensations which affect it; and I agree that although I sense myself only in myself I can know what I am only in Reason, which contains the archetype of my being and the intelligible ideas of all things.

VIII. THEODORE. Very well, Aristes. You are now ready to make thousands and thousands of discoveries in the land of truth. Distinguish ideas from sensations, but distinguish them well. Once again, distinguish them well, and all those beguiling phantoms I have told you about will not lead you into error. Always rise above yourself. Your modalities are only darkness, remember that. Ascend higher to Reason and you will see the light. Silence your senses, your imagination and your passions, and you will hear the pure voice of inner truth, the clear and evident responses of our common master. Never confound evidence, which results from the comparison of ideas, with the vivacity of the sensations which affect and disturb you. The more vivid our sensations, the more they spread darkness. The more terrible or pleasing our phantoms, the more substance and reality they appear to have, the more dangerous they are, and the better suited to mislead us. Dispense with them, do not trust them. In a word, avoid all that affects you and quickly embrace all that enlightens you. We must follow Reason despite the seductions, the threats, the insults of the body to which we are united, despite the action of the objects surrounding us. Do you conceive all this quite distinctly? Are you quite convinced of it by the reasons I have given you and by your own reflections?

ARISTES. Your exhortation, Theodore, appears quite lively to me for a discussion of metaphysics. It seems that you excite sensations in me instead of producing clear ideas. I am using your language. In all honesty, I do not understand everything you are telling me. I see it, and a moment later I no longer see it. For I still only glimpse it. It seems to me you are right, but I am not understanding you too well.

IX. THEODORE. Ah, my dear Aristes, your response is yet another proof of what we have been saying. There is no harm in your reflecting on it. I tell you what I see and you do not see it. That is a proof that one person does not teach another. This is because I am not your teacher or your professor. This is because I am simply a monitor, vehement perhaps but imprecise and poorly understood. I speak to your ears. Apparently I make only a lot of noise. But our sole master does not yet speak clearly enough to your mind; or, rather, Reason constantly speaks quite distinctly to it but, since you lack attention, you do not sufficiently hear what it tells you. I thought, however, from the things you have told me and from what I have said myself, that you sufficiently understood my principle and the conclusions that must be drawn from it. But now I see it is not enough for me to give you general views based on abstract and metaphysical ideas. I must still provide you with some particular proofs of the necessity of these views.

I have exhorted you to accustom yourself to recognizing easily the difference between knowing and sensing, between our clear ideas and our forever obscure and confused sensations. And I suggest to you that that alone is sufficient to discover an infinity of truths. I suggest this to you, I say, on the ground that it is only Reason which enlightens us, that we are not a light unto ourselves nor an intelligence to anyone else. You will see clearly whether this ground is solid when you cease listening to me and, in your study, attentively consult inner truth. However, to facilitate your understanding my principle and have you better know its necessity and consequences, please answer me. You know music well, for I see you often play instruments in a very knowledgeable and assured way.

ARISTES. I know enough to charm away my sorrow and dispel my melancholy.

X. THEODORE. Very well. Explain to me a little the nature of these various sounds which you combine in so exact and pleasing a way. What is an octave, a fifth, a fourth? How does it happen that when two strings are in unison one cannot be touched without the other being disturbed? You have a very refined, very delicate ear. Consult it, so that it tells you what I hope to learn from you.

ARISTES. I think you are mocking me. It is Reason and not the senses that we must consult.

THEODORE. True. It is necessary to consult the senses only about facts. Their power is quite limited, but Reason extends to everything. And beware of confounding its responses with the testimony of your senses. Well, then, what is its answer?

ARISTES. You are hurrying me too much. Nonetheless, it seems to me that sound is a quality spread out in the air which can affect only the sense of hearing, for each sense has its own object.

THEODORE. Is that what you call consulting Reason?

ARISTES. What would you have me say to you? Here, this is an octave: Do–Do. This is a fifth: Do–So. Here is a fourth: Do–Fa.

THEODORE. You sing well. But how badly you reason! I think it is because you want to enjoy yourself.

ARISTES. Of course, Theodore. But as for your other question, I reply that it is by sympathy that strings of the same pitch affect one another. Have I not answered well?

THEODORE. Let us speak seriously, Aristes. If now you want to please me, try to instruct me.

ARISTES. I shall do nothing of the kind, if you please. You play your part, and let me play mine. Mine is to listen.

THEODORE. How courteous and pleasing your manners are! Lend me this monochord, then, and note what I am about to do and what I am going to tell you. In plucking or drawing this string toward me, I move it out of the position in which the bridge holds it; and when I let it go you can see, without my needing to prove it to you, that for some time it moves back and forth, thereby making a large number of vibrations and consequently many other small movements which are imperceptible to our senses. For as a straight line is shorter than a curved one, a string cannot vibrate or become alternately straight and curved, unless the parts composing it lengthen and contract quite rapidly. Now, I ask you, is not one moving body capable of moving another one it encounters? This string can, therefore, disturb the air around it and even the subtle matter penetrating its pores, and this disturbs another, and so on as far as your ear and mine.

ARISTES. This is true. But it is a sound that I hear, a sound spread out in the air, a quality very different from the vibrations of a string or the movements of disturbed air.

THEODORE. Careful, Aristes. Do not consult your senses and do not judge according to their testimony. True, sound is something entirely different from disturbed air. But it is precisely for this reason that you say, without foundation, that sound is spread out in the air. For, take note, in touching this string I simply move it, and a moving string can only agitate the air surrounding it.

ARISTES. "A moving string can only agitate the air surrounding it"! What, do you not hear it produce a sound in the air?

THEODORE. Apparently I hear what you hear. But when I wish to instruct myself in a certain truth, I do not consult my ears, whereas you consult yours, notwithstanding all the firm resolutions you have made. Therefore, retreat into yourself and consult the clear ideas Reason contains. Do you really conceive of the air, the tiny bodies of whatever shape you please agitated in a particular way, being able to contain this sound you hear, and of a string being able to produce it? Once again, do not consult your ears, and for added assurance imagine you are deaf. Consider attentively the clear idea of extension. It is the archetype of bodies; it represents their nature and properties. Is it not evident that all the possible properties of extension must be simply relations of distance? Think about this seriously.

ARISTES. That is evident. All the properties of extension can consist only in its diverse ways of being. They are simply relations of distance.

THEODORE. Thus, all the possible properties or modalities of extension are simply shapes, or stable and permanent relations of distance, and motions or successive and continually changing relations of distance. Therefore, Aristes, sound, which you agree is something different from motion, is not spread out in the air and a string cannot produce it there. Thus, it can only be a sensation or modality of the soul.

ARISTES. I see now I must either surrender, or deny the principle that the idea of extension represents the nature of bodies. Perhaps it represents only one of its properties. Indeed, who told you bodies are but extension? Perhaps the essence of matter consists in something else, and this something else may be capable of containing and even producing sounds. Show me the contrary.

THEODORE. But you show me yourself that this something else in which you would have the essence of matter consist, will not be capable of thinking, of willing, of reasoning. I maintain that the strings of your lute also think just as you do, or at least that they complain about your disturbing their rest. Show me the contrary, and I shall convince you that they spread no sound.

ARISTES. It is true that if the nature of body consists in something other than extension, then as I have no idea of this thing I cannot prove to you that it does not think. But please prove to me that matter is nothing other than extension and is thus incapable of thinking. For that appears to me necessary to silence the libertines who confound the soul with the body, and who maintain that it is mortal like the body; because, according to them, all our thoughts are but modalities of this unknown thing we call body, and all modalities can cease to be.

XI. THEODORE. I have already answered the question you put to me,[*] but it is so important that, although it is removed from present concerns, I am delighted to point out that its resolution depends, like all other truths, on the great principle that universal Reason contains the ideas which enlighten us, and that as God's works have been formed on the basis of these ideas, we can do no better than contemplate them, in order to discover the nature and properties of created beings. Therefore

[*] Dialogue I, §II.

take note. We can think of extension without thinking of anything else. It is, therefore, a being or a substance, and not a way of being. For we cannot think of a way of being without thinking of the being it modifies, since ways of being are simply the being itself in a particular fashion. We cannot think of shapes and motion without thinking of extension, because shapes and motion are simply ways of being of extension. That much is clear, unless I am mistaken. And if it does not appear so to you, I suggest that you have no means of distinguishing the modalities of substances from substances themselves. If that does not appear evident to you, let us philosophize no further. For . . .

ARISTES. Please, let us philosophize.

THEODORE. Let us continue. The idea or archetype of extension is eternal and necessary. We see this idea, as I have already proved to you, and God sees it too, since there is nothing in Him that He does not discover. We see it, I say, clearly and distinctly, without thinking of anything else. We are able to perceive it alone or, rather, we are unable to perceive it as the way of being of some other thing, for it contains no necessary relation to other ideas. Now, God can do whatever He sees and whatever He makes us see clearly and distinctly in His light. He can do anything that does not involve a contradiction, for He is all-powerful. Thus, He can create extension all by itself. This extension will be, therefore, a being or a substance, and the idea we have of it will represent its nature to us. Hence, if God has created this extension there will surely be matter. For what sort of being would this extension be? Now I believe you really see that this matter is incapable of thinking, of sensing, of reasoning.

ARISTES. I grant you that, as our ideas are necessary and eternal and the same ones God consults, if He acts He will create what these ideas represent, and we are not deceived if we attribute to matter only what we see in its archetype. But perhaps we do not see this archetype in its entirety. As the modalities of extension can be only relations of distance, extension is incapable of thinking. This I admit. However, the subject of extension, that other thing which is perhaps contained in the archetype of matter and which is unknown to us, may well be able to think.

XII. THEODORE. It may well be able to do much more. For it will be able to do everything you would have it do, without anyone being able to challenge you. It will be able to have thousands and thousands of admirable faculties, virtues, properties. It will be able to act on your soul, enlighten it, make it happy and unhappy. In a word, there will be as many powers and, if you push the matter, as many divinities as there are different bodies. For, in effect, how do I know whether that other thing you take as the essence of matter does not have any quality it pleases you to attribute to it, since I have no knowledge of it? Thus, you can perhaps see that to know God's works we must consult the ideas He gives us of them, those which are clear, those on the basis of which He has created them; and that we risk very great dangers if we follow another path. For if we consult our senses, if we blindly submit ourselves to their testimony, they will persuade us that there are at least certain bodies whose power and intelligence are wonderful.

Our senses tell us that fire spreads heat and light. They persuade us that animals and plants aim at the conservation of their being and their species with considerable skill and a kind of intelligence. Now, we see in fact that these faculties are something other than shapes and motion. Thus, on the basis of the obscure and confused testimony of our senses we judge that there must be something other than extension in body, since all the modes of extension can be only motion and shapes. However, let us consult Reason attentively. Let us stop at the clear idea we have of bodies. Let us not confound them with our own being and perhaps we shall discover that we attribute qualities and properties to them which they do not have and which belong to us alone.

It may be the case, you say, that we do not entirely see the archetype or idea of matter. If that were so, we should attribute to it only what that idea represents of it to us, for we must not judge of what we do not know. Surely, if freethinkers believe they are allowed to reason on the basis of chimeras about which they have no idea, they must grant that we can reason about things of which we do have ideas. But, in order to deprive them of anything likely to lead to failure and to confidence in their strange errors, note once again that we can think of extension without thinking of anything else. For this is the principle. Thus, God can create extension without creating anything else. Hence this extension will subsist without that unknown thing they attribute to matter. This extension will therefore be a substance and not a modality of substance. And that is what for many reasons I think should be called body or matter, not only because we cannot think of the modalities of beings without thinking of the beings themselves of which they are the modalities, and because there is no other way to distinguish beings from their modalities than to see if we can think of the former without the latter; but, again, because by means of extension itself and the properties everyone attributes to it, we can sufficiently explain all natural effects. That is, we observe no material effect whose natural cause we cannot discover in the idea of extension, provided this effect is clearly known.

ARISTES. What you are now saying appears convincing to me. I understand more clearly than ever that to know God's works we must attentively consult the ideas He contains in His wisdom, and silence our senses and above all our imagination. But this way of discovering the truth is so difficult and taxing that hardly anyone can follow it. To see that the sun is dazzling with light we need only open our eyes. To judge whether sound is in the air it suffices to make a noise. Nothing is easier. But the mind labors furiously in the attention it gives those ideas which do not strike the senses. We tire soon, I know it from experience. How fortunate you are to be able to meditate on metaphysical matters!

THEODORE. I am made like others, my dear Aristes. Judge me by yourself, and you will do me honor; you deceive yourself only to my advantage. What do you want? This difficulty we all experience in uniting ourselves to Reason is a punishment and a proof of sin, and the rebellion of the body is its source. We are condemned to earn our living by the sweat of our brow. The mind must now work to be nourished by the truth. This is common to all people. But, believe me, this food of the mind is so delicious and gives the soul such ardor when we have tasted it, that although we tire of seeking it we never weary of desiring it and of renewing our search, because it is for this that we have been created. However, if I have tired you too much give me that musical instrument, so that I may relieve your attention and make sensible the truths I want to teach you, as far as that is possible.

ARISTES. What do you want to do? I understand clearly that sound is not spread out in the air and that a string cannot produce it. The reasons you have given me appear convincing to me. For neither sound nor the power to produce it are contained in the idea of matter, since all the modalities of body consist only in relations of distance. That is sufficient for me. Nonetheless, here is another proof which occurs to me and convinces me. In a fever I had some time ago I continually heard the howl of an animal which undoubtedly did not howl any more for it was dead. I also think that in sleep it happens to you as to me that we hear a concert, or at least the sound of a trumpet or drum, although at the time everything is in deep silence. At that time, while sick, I heard cries and howls. For even today I remember they caused me much unrest. Yet those disagreeable sounds were not in the air, although I heard them there as much as the one this instrument makes. Thus, although we hear sounds as if spread out in the air, it does not follow that they are there. They are really found only in the soul, for they are simply sensations which affect it, modalities which belong to it. I might push matters even further. For everything you have told me up to this point leads me to believe there is nothing in the objects of our senses which is similar to the sensations we have of them. These objects are related to their ideas, but it seems to me they have no relation to our sensations. Bodies are but extension capable of motion and various shapes. That is evident when we consult the idea representing them.

THEODORE. Bodies, you say, have no resemblance to the sensations we have, and to know their properties we must not consult the senses, but the clear idea of extension which represents their nature. Hold on firmly to this important truth.

ARISTES. That is evident, and I shall never forget it.

XIII. THEODORE. Never! Well then, pray tell me what an octave is, and a fifth, or rather teach me what must be done to hear these consonances.

ARISTES. That is quite easy. Pluck this entire string, and then put your finger there, and pluck one or the other part of the string, and you will hear the octave.

THEODORE. Why put my finger there, and not here?

ARISTES. Because here you will make a fifth, and not an octave. Look, look. The tones are all marked here ... You are laughing.

THEODORE. How knowledgeable I am, Aristes. I can make you hear any sound I wish. But if we had broken our instrument, our whole science would be in pieces.

ARISTES. Not at all, I would simply make another. It is only a string on a board. Anyone can make that.

THEODORE. Yes. But that is not enough. We must mark the consonances on this board exactly. How will you divide it, then, in order to mark where we must put our finger to hear the octave, the fifth, and the other consonances?

ARISTES. I would strike the whole string, and sliding my finger along it I would get the tone I wanted to mark. For even I know enough music to tune instruments.

THEODORE. Your method is hardly exact, since you find what you are looking for only by trial and error. However, were you to become deaf, or, rather, if the small nerve which tightens your eardrum and tunes it to your instrument were to be loosened, what would become of your science? Would you no longer be able to mark the different tones exactly? Can we not become deaf without forgetting music? If not, your science is not based on clear ideas. Reason has no part in it, for Reason is immutable and necessary.

ARISTES. Ah, Theodore! I have already forgotten what I told you I would never forget. What am I thinking of? I have given you amusing answers, you had reason to laugh at them. That is because I naturally listen more to my senses than my Reason. I am so accustomed to consulting my ears that I did not really think about what you were asking me. Here is another answer which will better satisfy you. To mark the octave on this instrument we must divide the space corresponding to the string into two equal parts. For if, having struck the whole, we then strike one or the other of its parts, we will have an octave. If we strike the whole string, and then two-thirds, we will obtain a fifth. And, finally, if we strike the whole, and then three-quarters, we will get a fourth; and these two last consonances will make up the octave.

XIV. THEODORE. That answer instructs me. I understand it distinctly. I see thereby that the octave, or rather the natural cause which produces it, is as 2 to 1, the fifth as 3 to 2, the fourth as 4 to 3. These numerical relations are clear. And since you tell me that a string, divided and struck according to the magnitude expressing these numbers, produces these consonances, if I were to become deaf I would be able to indicate them on the monochord. This is what reasoning on the basis of clear ideas is: people are instructed solidly. But why do a fifth and a fourth equal an octave?

ARISTES. Because sound is to sound as string is to string. Thus, since the octave is heard when we strike a string and then half of it, the octave is as 2 to 1 or what amounts to the same thing, as 4 to 2. Now, the relation of 4 to 2 is composed of the relations 4 to 3, which is the fourth, and 3 to 2, which is the fifth. For you actually know that the relation of one number to another is composed of all the relations between all the numbers these two numbers contain. The relation of 3 to 6, for example, which is that of 1 to 2, is composed of the relations of 3 to 4, of 4 to 5, and of 5 to 6. Thus, you see that the major third and the minor third equal a fifth. For the ratio or relation of 4 to 6, which is equal to that of 2 to 3, is composed of those of 4 to 5, which produces the major third, and of 5 to 6, which is the minor third.

THEODORE. I clearly conceive all this, on the supposition that sound is to sound as string is to string. But I do not properly understand this principle. Do you think it is based on clear ideas?

ARISTES. Yes, I believe so. For the string or its various vibrations are the cause of various sounds. Now, the whole cause is to its half as 2 to 1, and effects correspond exactly to their causes. Thus, the effect of the whole cause is double the effect of the half. Hence the sound of the whole string is to the sound of the half as 2 to 1.

THEODORE. Do you distinctly conceive what you are telling me? As for me, I find obscurity in it, and insofar as I can I submit only to the evidence accompanying clear ideas.

ARISTES. What do you find fault with in my reasoning?

XV. THEODORE. It has considerable ingenuity. For you are not lacking in that respect. However, its principle is obscure. It is not based on clear ideas. Take note. You think you know what you merely sense, and for a principle you adopt a prejudice whose falsity you have already recognized. But to make you aware of the falsity of your proof, allow me to conduct a little experiment on you. Give me your hand, I will not do you any great harm. While I rub the hollow of your hand with the cuff of my sleeve, do you not feel anything?

ARISTES. I feel a little heat, or a kind of tickling which is pleasant enough.

THEODORE. And now?

ARISTES. Oh, Theodore, you are hurting me. You are striking me too hard. I feel a pain that bothers me.

THEODORE. You are mistaken, Aristes. Let me continue. You feel a pleasure twice or three times as great as the one you felt just now. I shall prove it to you by your own reasoning. Take note. "My rubbing your hand is the cause of what you feel there. Now, the whole cause is to its half as 2 to 1, and effects correspond exactly to the action of their causes. Thus, the effect of the whole cause or the whole action of the cause is double the effect of its half." Thus, by rubbing twice as strongly or as quickly, this doubled motion should produce twice as much pleasure. Hence, I have not caused you pain, unless you would have pain be to pleasure as 2 to 1.

ARISTES. I am certainly being punished for having reasoned on an obscure principle. You have hurt me, and by way of excuse you prove to me that you have caused me a double pleasure. That is not pleasant.

THEODORE. You have been let off easily, for if we had been next to the fire perhaps I would have done worse.

ARISTES. What would you have done?

THEODORE. I might have taken a burning coal, and first I would have taken it a little closer to your hand. And if you had said that it caused you pleasure, I would have applied it to your hand in order to give you more pleasure. Then I would have proved to you, by your reasoning, that you were wrong to complain.

ARISTES. Truly I have escaped lightly. Is that how you instruct people?

THEODORE. What would you have me do? When I give you metaphysical proofs you forget them immediately. I must make them sensible so that you understand them without difficulty and always remember them. Why have you so soon forgotten that we must reason only on clear ideas, that a vibrating string can at most only agitate the air surrounding it, and cannot produce the various sounds you hear?

ARISTES. Because when I strike the string I hear the sound.

THEODORE. I see that indeed. But you do not clearly conceive that the vibrations of a string can spread or produce sound. You have agreed to that. For sound is not contained in the idea of matter, and still less is the power to act on the soul and to make it hear sound. Because the vibrations of a string or of the air are followed by a sound and by a particular sound, you conclude that that is necessary for us to hear it, things being as they are. But do not imagine that there is a necessary relation between these things. Apparently, I do not hear the same sounds as you, although perhaps I hear the same tones or consonances. For if my eardrum is thicker or thinner than yours by a certain amount,

46

which causes it to resonate more easily in receiving one tone than another – which is quite probable – then surely, all other things being equal, I will hear a sound louder than you when this string is struck. Finally, I see no relation of magnitude between consonances. It is not clear that the difference between the sounds composing them is one of more or less, like the strings that produce them. That seems evident to me.

ARISTES. So it appears to me. But since the vibrations of a string are not the cause of the sound, how do I hear the sound when the string is struck?

THEODORE. It is not the time, Aristes, to resolve this question. When we have treated the efficacy of causes, or the laws of the union of the soul and body, it will be resolved without difficulty. At present I am thinking simply of making you indicate the difference between knowing clearly and sensing confusedly. I am thinking simply of convincing you properly of that important truth, that to know God's works we must not pay attention to the sensations we have of them, but to the ideas representing them. For I cannot reiterate this to you too often: we must not consult our senses, our own modalities, which are only darkness, but Reason which enlightens us by its divine ideas, by the immutable, necessary, eternal ideas.

ARISTES. I agree with this. I am fully convinced of it. Let us move on to other matters, for I am tired of hearing you incessantly repeat the same things.

XVI. THEODORE. We will move on to whatever you please. But, believe me, it is not enough to see a principle; it must be properly seen. For between seeing and truly seeing there are infinite differences, and the principle I am teaching you is so necessary and of such great use that it must always be present to the mind and one should not forget it, as you do. But let us see if you are really convinced of it and really know how to avail yourself of it. Tell me why, given two strings in unison, we cannot strike one string without disturbing the other.

ARISTES. This question appears quite difficult to me, for in certain authors I have read many explanations of it which do not much satisfy me. I fear that my answer will again elicit some slight mocking, or that you will conduct some experiment at my expense.

THEODORE. No no, Aristes, you have nothing to fear. But do not forget the principle of 'clear ideas.' I should not warn you of it so often. But I fear that 'sympathy,' or some other chimera, prevents you from following it.

ARISTES. Let us just see. When I strike this string it disturbs the air by its vibrations. Now that agitated air can communicate some motion to other strings it encounters.

THEODORE. Very well. But the dissonant strings, as well as those which produce the same sound, will be disturbed.

ARISTES. That is what I thought. A little sympathy would do well enough here, but you want none of it.

THEODORE. I willingly take this word for what it is worth. There is sympathy between strings of the same sound. That is certain since they act upon each other, for this is what the word signifies. But whence this sympathy? That is the difficulty.

ARISTES. It is not because of their length or thickness. For there is sympathy between unequal strings, and there is no sympathy between equal strings if they do not produce the same sound. Thus everything must depend on the sound. But in this regard sound is not a modality of the string, and the string cannot produce it. Whence, therefore, this sympathy? Here I am confused.

THEODORE. You are confused over a small matter. There is sympathy between strings of the same sound. This is the fact you wish to explain. See, then, what makes two strings produce the same sound, and you will have everything necessary to discover what you are seeking.

ARISTES. If two strings are equal in length and thickness, there will be equality in their tension, which will make them produce the same sound; and if they are unequal in length alone, if one is, for example, double the other, it will have to be stretched by quadruple the force.[1]

THEODORE. What, then, does a greater or lesser tension produce in equal strings?

ARISTES. It makes them capable of a higher or lower pitched sound.

THEODORE. Yes, but that is not what we need. We have simply established the difference between sounds, and no sound can disturb this string. For sound is the effect rather than the cause of motion. Therefore tell me how tension increases sound's pitch.

[1] Malebranche's formulation of this principle underwent several changes from the first to the third editions (cf. *OC* XII 84).

ARISTES. Apparently this is because it causes the string to vibrate more quickly.

THEODORE. Good, here is everything we require. For the vibration, and not the sound of my string, will be able to cause yours to vibrate. Two strings of equal length, thickness, and tension produce the same sound, because they vibrate equally quickly; and if one rises higher than the other, this is a sign that it is more taut and makes each of its vibrations more quickly. Now one string moves another only by means of its vibrations. For one body moves another only by means of its motion. This being the case, tell me now why strings of the same sound communicate their vibration, and why dissonant strings do not, at least in any sensible way.

XVII. ARISTES. I clearly see the reason for this. Here are two strings of the same sound. There is yours and here is mine. When I release my string, it pushes the air toward you, and this displaced air disturbs your string a little. In a very short time mine again makes a number of similar vibrations, each of which disturbs the air and pushes your string, as did the first movement. This is what makes it vibrate. For several small suitably administered shocks can produce a sensible disturbance. But when these small shocks appear out of beat, they interfere with each other. Thus, when two strings are dissonant or cannot vibrate in equal or multiple time or at least in commensurable time because they are unequally stretched or are of unequal length and thickness and are incommensurable, they cannot disturb one another. For if the first moves and pushes the air and the second string toward you, while that second string returns toward me, it will then decrease its motion instead of increasing it. Thus, the vibrations of the strings must occur in equal or multiple time, in order that they mutually communicate a motion large enough to be sensible; and their motion becomes more sensible, the more the consonance they cause approaches unison. That is why they move more in an octave than in a fifth, and more in a fifth than in a fourth; because the two strings more often begin their vibrations at the same instant. Are you satisfied with this explanation?

THEODORE. Entirely, Aristes. For you have followed the principle of clear ideas. I understand quite well that strings of the same sound move each other not by the sympathy of their sound, for sound cannot be the cause of motion, but by the agreement of their vibrations which disturb or jolt the air in which they are stretched. As long as you reason about the properties of bodies on the basis of ideas of shapes and motion, I shall be happy with you. For you have such an exact mind that it is difficult for you to reason poorly while following a clear principle. In effect, if we fall into error so frequently, this arises from the falsity or obscurity of our ideas rather than from the weakness of our mind. Geometers are rarely deceived, physicists almost always. Why? Because ordinarily the latter reason on the basis of confused ideas, and the former on the basis of the clearest ideas we have.

ARISTES. I see the necessity of your principle better than ever. You have done well to repeat it to me often and to make it sensible for me. I shall try to remember it. We must not judge sensible objects on the basis of the sensations with which they strike us, but on the basis of the ideas representing them. Our sensations are confused. They are simply the modalities of our soul which are incapable of enlightening us. But the ideas Reason reveals to us are luminous; evidence accompanies them. It suffices to consider them attentively to discover their relations and to be solidly instructed in the truth. Is this not what you wanted me to keep clearly in mind, Theodore?

THEODORE. Yes, Aristes. And if you do this, you will travel fearlessly in the land of intellects. You will prudently avoid places that are inaccessible or too dangerous, and you will no longer fear those seductive phantoms that imperceptibly lead new travelers in these countries into error. But do not imagine you really know what I have told you and what you have yourself repeated. You will know it exactly only when you have meditated often upon it. For we never really understand what we hear said, unless inner truth repeats it to us in the silence of all creatures. Therefore goodbye, Aristes. I shall leave you alone with Reason. Consult it seriously, and forget everything else.

Dialogue IV

The nature and properties of the senses in general. The wisdom of the laws of the union of the soul and body. This union changed into dependence by the sin of the first man.

ARISTES. Where are you coming from, Theodore? I was getting impatient not meeting you.

I. THEODORE. What! Is Reason not sufficient for you, and are you unable to pass the time agreeably with it, if Theodore is not present? To blessed intellects Reason suffices for an eternity; and although I have left you with it for only several hours, impatience at not seeing me overtakes you. What are you thinking of? Do you expect me to allow you to have a blind and unrestrained attachment to me? Love Reason, consult it, follow it. For I declare to you that I renounce the friendship of those who neglect it and refuse to submit to its laws.

ARISTES. Gently, Theodore. Listen a moment.

II. THEODORE. There cannot be a lasting and sincere friendship unless it is based on Reason, on an immutable good, on a good everyone can possess without dividing it. For friendships founded on goods which are divisive and dissipate with use always have unfortunate consequences and last only a short while. Are these not false and dangerous friendships?

ARISTES. I agree. All that is true, nothing is more certain. Ah, Theodore!

THEODORE. What do you want to say?

III. ARISTES. What a difference there is between seeing and truly seeing, between knowing what people tell us while they say it, and knowing what Reason tells us while it answers us! What a difference between knowing and sensing, between ideas which enlighten us and confused sensations which stir and trouble us! How fertile this principle is, how it spreads light! What errors, what prejudices it dispels! I have meditated on this principle, Theodore. I have followed its consequences and was impatient to see you in order to thank you for teaching it to me. Permit me to say to you what the faithful of Samaria said to the Samaritan woman after they, as well as she, had heard our common master: "We now believe, not for thy saying," they said to that woman, "for we ourselves have heard him, and know."[*] Yes, now I am convinced not by the force of your words but by the evident responses of inner truth. I understand what you have told me, but how many other things have I understood about which you had not spoken to me! I have understood them clearly, and what remains most profoundly engraved in my memory is the fact that I have lived all my life in an illusion, always seduced by the testimony of my senses, continually corrupted by their attractions. How contemptible sensible goods are! How impotent bodies appear to me! No, this sun, however brilliant it appears to my eyes, neither possesses nor diffuses that light which enlightens me. All those colors which delight me by their variety and vivacity, and all those beauties which charm me when I turn my eyes toward everything surrounding me, belong to me. All these things neither come from nor are in bodies. For none of them is contained in the idea of matter. And I am persuaded that we must not judge God's works by the various sensations we have of them, but by the immutable, necessary, eternal ideas representing them, by the archetype on which they have all been formed.

THEODORE. What a pleasure it is to hear you! I really do see you have consulted Reason in the silence of creation, for you are still completely enlightened, animated, and imbued by it. Ah, what good friends we shall be, if Reason is always our common good and the bond of our society! We shall one and all enjoy the same pleasures, we shall possess the same riches. For the truth is given entirely to everyone, and entirely to each one of us. All minds are nourished by it without any

[*] John 4[: 42].

diminution in its abundance. What joy I have once again seeing you fully imbued by the truths you tell me!

IV. ARISTES. I am also fully aware of the debt of gratitude I owe you. That was the cause of my impatience. Yes, you have taught me about that tree of the earthly paradise which gives life and immortality to minds. You have shown me the celestial manna by which I must be nourished in the desert of the present life. You have guided me insensibly to the inner master who alone enlightens all intellects. A quarter of an hour's serious attention to the clear and luminous ideas He presents to the mind has taught me more truth, has delivered me from more prejudice than everything I have read in the books of the philosophers, than everything I have heard my teachers and even you say, Theodore. For however precise your expressions are, whenever you speak to me and I consult Reason, at the same time there is a confused noise of two different answers, the one sensible and the other intelligible. And the least drawback that thereby arises is that the answer which strikes my ear divides my mind's capacity and diminishes its vivacity and penetration. For you require time to pronounce your words, whereas all the replies of Reason are eternal and immutable. They have always been stated or, rather, they are always stated without any temporal succession; and although we require some time to hear them, none is required to make them, because actually they are not made. They are eternal, immutable, and necessary. Allow me the pleasure of revealing to you a part of what I believe I have learned from our common master, to whom you have had the kindness to introduce me.

V. As soon as you left me, Theodore, I retreated into myself to consult Reason, and I saw in a completely different manner from when you spoke to me and when I submitted to your proofs, that the ideas of creatures are eternal, that God has formed bodies on the basis of the idea of extension, that this idea must therefore represent their nature, and that thus I should consider it attentively to discover their properties. I understood clearly that to consult my senses and search for the truth in my own modalities was to prefer darkness to light and to renounce Reason. At first my senses were opposed to my conclusions, as if they were jealous of ideas and saw themselves excluded by them from a prerogative they had long possessed in my mind. But I found so much falsity and contradiction in the opposition they had formed that I condemned them as deceivers and false witnesses. Indeed, I saw no evidence in their testimony and on the contrary I noted a wonderful clarity in the ideas they attempted to obscure. Thus, although they still spoke to me with confidence, with arrogance, with the utmost importunity, I forced them into silence and recalled the ideas which had left me because they could not endure that confused noise and tumult of the rebellious senses.

I must admit, Theodore, that the sensible proofs you gave me against the authority of the senses have been wonderfully useful to me. For by means of them I silenced those importunate senses. I convicted them of falsity by their own testimony. They contradicted themselves at every moment. For besides saying nothing that was not incomprehensible and entirely unbelievable, they gave me the same reports of entirely different things, and completely opposite reports of the same things, according to the interest they took therein. I silenced them, therefore, fully resolved no longer to judge God's works by their testimony but by the ideas representing these works and on the basis of which they have been formed.

It was in following this principle that I understood that light was neither in the sun nor in the air where we see it, nor colors on the surface of bodies; that the sun could perhaps move the subtle parts of the air, and these make the same impression of motion on the optic nerve, and so on to the part of the brain where the soul resides; and that these tiny bodies, agitated upon encountering solids, could reflect differently according to the diversity of the surfaces which made them rebound. Hence their light and the variety of their supposed colors.

VI. I have likewise understood that the heat I feel was in no way in the fire, nor the cold in the ice – what am I saying! – nor the pain itself in my own body, where I have often felt it so vividly and so cruelly; nor the sweetness in sugar, nor the bitterness in aloes, nor the acidity in sour grapes, nor the sourness in vinegar, nor in wine that sweetness and strength which deceive and intoxicate so many drunkards. All this obtains for the same reason that sound is not in the air, and because there is an infinite difference between the vibrations of strings and the noise they cause, between the proportions of those vibrations and the variety of consonances.

I would take too long,[*] Theodore, were I to enter into the details of the proofs which have convinced me that bodies have no qualities other than those resulting from their shapes, nor any action other than their various motion. But I cannot conceal from you a difficulty I have been unable to overcome, whatever effort of mind I have made to deliver myself from it. I follow without difficulty the action of the sun, for example, through all the spaces between it and me. For, assuming everything is a plenum, I easily conceive that it cannot produce the impression of where it is without it being communicated to the place where I am, to my eyes, and through my eyes to my brain. But in accordance with the clear idea of motion, I have been unable to understand how the sensation of light comes to me. I saw easily that the simple motion of the optic nerve caused me to sense it. For by pressing the corner of my eye with my finger at the place to which I know this nerve extends, I saw a bright light in a dark place, on the opposite side from where my eye was pressed. But this change from motion into light appeared and still appears completely incomprehensible to me. What a strange metamorphosis, from a vibration or pressure on my eye to a flash of light! A flash, moreover, which I see neither in my soul of which it is the modality, nor in my brain where the vibration terminates, nor in my eye where the pressure occurs, nor on the side where I press my eye, but in the air; in the air, I say, which is incapable of such a modality, and on the side opposite the side of the eye that I press. How wonderful!

VII. At first I thought that my soul, being informed of the disturbance that took place in my body, was the cause of the sensation it had of the things surrounding it. But a little reflection disabused me of that thought. For it is not true, it seems to me, that the soul is informed that the sun disturbs the fibers of the brain. I saw light before I knew anything of this disturbance. For children, who do not even know they have a brain, are struck by a flash of light as well as philosophers. Moreover, what is the relation between the vibrations of a body and the various sensations following it? How can I see light in bodies, since it is a modality of my mind; and how can I see it in the bodies surrounding me, since the disturbance is only in mine? I press the corner of my eye on the right side; why do I see the light on the left side, notwithstanding the certain knowledge I have that that is not the side that is pressed?

[*] Cf. *De la Recherche de la vérité*, Bk. I, Chs. 6ff. [*OC* I 79ff.].

From all this, and from a number of other things I would be too long in telling you, I recognized that sensations were in me despite myself, that I was therefore not their cause, and that if bodies were capable of acting on me and of making themselves be sensed in the way I sense them, they would have to be of a nature more excellent than mine, be possessed of a terrific power and some even of a wonderful wisdom, always uniform in their behavior, always efficacious in their action, always incomprehensible in the surprising effects of their power. All this appeared to me monstrous and horrible to think of, although my senses supported this folly and accommodated themselves to it. But, Theodore, please explain this matter to me.

THEODORE. This is not the time, Aristes, to resolve your difficulties, unless you wish us to leave the general truths of metaphysics in order to enter into the explanation of the principles of physics and the laws of the union of the soul and the body.

ARISTES. A word or two on this, please. I very much wish to meditate on this matter. My mind is now completely prepared for it.

VIII. THEODORE. Listen, then, but remember to meditate on what I have just told you about it. When we seek the reason for certain effects, and ascending from effects to causes we come at last to a general cause or a cause which we can easily see involves no relation between itself and the effect it produces or, rather, appears to produce; then, instead of inventing chimeras, we must have recourse to the author of the laws of nature. For example, if you asked me the cause of the pain we feel when we are pricked, I would be wrong if I answered you straight away that one of the laws of the author of nature is that a prick is followed by pain. I should tell you that the prick cannot separate the fibers of my flesh without disturbing the nerves which connect to the brain, and without disturbing the brain itself. However, if you wanted to know how it happens that when a certain part of my brain is disturbed in a particular manner I feel the pain of a prick, then, since this question concerns a general effect and since by going further we can no longer find a natural or particular cause, it is necessary to have recourse to the general cause. For it is as if you were to ask who is the author of the general laws of the union of the soul and body. Because you see clearly that there can be no relation or necessary connection between the disturbances of the brain and particular sensations of the soul, it is evident that we must have recourse to a power not found in these two beings. It is not enough to say that because the prick injures the body the soul must be warned of this through pain, in order for it to undertake to conserve the body. That would be to substitute the final cause for the efficient cause, and the difficulty would remain, for it consists in knowing the cause which brings it about that when the body is injured the soul suffers, and suffers a particular pain in respect of a particular injury.

IX. To say further, as some philosophers do, that the soul is the cause of its pain because, as they say, pain is simply the sadness the soul conceives concerning what occurs in the body it loves; concerning, that is, some disorder of which it is informed by means of the difficulty it experiences in the exercise of its functions; to say this is surely not to heed the inner feeling we have of what occurs in us. For each one of us certainly senses that we are not the cause of our pain when we bleed, for example, or when we burn ourselves. We feel it despite ourselves and we cannot doubt that it comes from an external cause. Moreover, the soul does not wait to feel pain or a particular pain once it has learned there is some disturbance or particular disturbance in the brain. Nothing is more certain. Finally, pain and sadness are very different. Pain precedes knowledge of harm, sadness follows it. Pain involves nothing pleasant, and sadness pleases us so much that those who would banish it from our mind without at the same time delivering us from the harm causing it make themselves so unpleasant and inconvenient that they disrupt our joy. For sadness is effectively the state of the soul which best suits us when we actually suffer some harm or are deprived of some good, and the feeling accompanying this passion is the sweetest we can enjoy in the condition in which we find ourselves. Thus, pain is very different from sadness. But I claim further that the soul is not the cause of its sadness and that the thought we have of the loss of some good produces this passion only as a consequence of the natural and necessary movement toward the good which God alone constantly impresses upon us. However, let us return to the difficulties you have concerning the action and qualities of light.

X. 1. There is no metamorphosis. Motion of the brain can be changed neither into light nor into colour. For as the modalities of bodies are simply bodies themselves existing in a certain way, they cannot be transformed into modalities of minds. That is clear.

2. You press the corner of your eye and you get a certain feeling. This is because He who alone can act on minds has established certain laws,[*] through the efficacy of which the soul and body reciprocally act and react.

3. In pressing your eye you see light, although there is no luminous body there, because it is by means of a pressure similar to that which your finger applies to your eye and from there to your brain that the bodies we call luminous act on those surrounding them and by means of them on our eyes and our brain. All this results from natural laws. For it is one of the laws of the union of the soul and body, according to which God acts unceasingly on these two substances, that a particular pressure or movement is followed by a particular sensation.

4. You see the light which is a modality of your mind and which can consequently only be found in it, for it is a contradiction that the modality of a being exists where that being does not. You see it, I say, in the great spaces your mind does not fill, for the mind occupies no place. This is because these great spaces you see are simply intelligible spaces which fill no place.[**] For the spaces you see are very different from the material spaces you look at. We must not confound the ideas of things with things themselves. Remember that we do not see bodies in themselves and that it is only through their ideas that they are visible. Often we see them, though they are not there, which is certain proof that those we see are intelligible and very different from those we look at.

5. Finally, you see light not from the side on which you press your eye but on the other side because, as the nerve is constructed and prepared to receive the impression of luminous bodies through the pupil and not otherwise, the pressure of your finger on the left has the same effect on your eye that a luminous body on the right would have, whose rays were to pass through the pupil and the transparent parts of the eye. For in pressing the eye on the outside you press the optic nerve inside against a humor called 'vitreous,' which resists somewhat. Thus, God makes you sense light from the side on which you see it because He constantly follows the laws He has established to conserve a perfect

[*] Cf. Dialogue XII.
[**] I. *Lettre touchant la Défense de Monsieur Arnauld* [*OC* VI 193–274].

58

uniformity in His conduct. God never performs miracles, He never acts against His own laws by means of particular volitions, unless order either requires or permits it. His conduct always bears the character of His attributes. It always remains the same if what is required by His immutability is of no less consideration than what is required by another of His perfections, as I shall prove to you in the following. Here, I believe, is the resolution of your difficulties. To dispel them I have recourse to God and to His attributes. However, Aristes, God does not rest with His arms folded, as some philosophers would have it. Certainly, if God still acts now, when can we say that He is the cause of certain effects if we are not permitted to have recourse to Him for those general effects, those effects which we clearly see have no essential and necessary relation to their natural causes? Therefore, my dear Aristes, in your memory carefully preserve what I have just told you; place it with the most precious things you possess. And although you understand it well, allow me to repeat the essence of it in a few words, so that you will retrieve it easily when you are able to meditate upon it.

XI. There is no necessary relation between the two substances of which we are composed. The modalities of our body cannot, through their own efficacy, change the modalities of our mind. Nevertheless, the modalities of a certain part of the brain, which I shall not specify for you, are always followed by the modalities or sensations of our soul, and this occurs solely as a consequence of the continually efficacious laws of the union of these two substances, that is, to speak more clearly, as a consequence of the constant and continually efficacious volitions of the author of our being. There is no relation of causality between a body and a mind. What am I saying? There is no relation at all between a mind and a body. I say, further, there is no relation between a body and a body, nor between a mind and another mind. In a word, no creature can act on any other creature through its own efficacy. I shall soon prove this to you.* But is it at least evident that a body, some extension, a purely passive substance, cannot through its own efficacy act on a mind, on a being of another nature and infinitely more excellent than it? Thus, it is clear that in the union of the soul and the body there is no other connection than the efficacy of the divine decrees; decrees which are immutable, and efficacy which is never deprived of its effect. God

* Dialogue VII.

has therefore willed, and He wills unceasingly, that the various disturbances of the brain are always followed by various thoughts of the mind united to it. And it is that constant and efficacious will of the creator which, properly speaking, effects the union of these two substances. For there is no other nature, that is, there are no other natural laws, except the efficacious volitions of the almighty.

XII. Do not ask, Aristes, why God wills to unite minds to bodies. It is an established fact but the principal reasons for it have up to now been unknown to philosophy. Nevertheless, here is one reason I might well suggest to you. Apparently God desired to give to us, as He gave to His Son, a victim we could offer to Him. He desired to have us merit the possession of eternal goods, through a kind of sacrifice and annihilation of ourselves. Surely this appears just and in conformity with order. At present we are on trial in our body. It is through it, as occasional cause, that we receive from God thousands and thousands of different sensations which constitute the stuff of our merit through the grace of Jesus Christ. An occasional cause was actually required for a general cause, as I shall prove to you shortly, in order that this general cause, acting continually in a uniform and constant manner, could produce an infinity of different effects in its works, by the simplest means and by general laws which are always the same. Nevertheless, it is not that God was unable to find occasional causes other than bodies, in order to give His conduct the simplicity and uniformity which govern it. There are actually others in the angelic nature. Perhaps these blessed spirits, through the various movements of their will, are the occasional cause – both reciprocally to one another and to themselves – of the action of God who enlightens and governs them. But let us not speak of what is beyond us. This is what I am not afraid to assure you of; it is absolutely necessary to illuminate the subject of our discussion and I beg you to retain it carefully to meditate upon at leisure.

XIII. God loves order inviolably and by the necessity of His being. He loves, He esteems all things in proportion as they are estimable and lovable. He necessarily detests disorder. This is perhaps more clear and incontestable than the proof I shall some day give you,[*] which I now pass over. Now it is obviously a disorder that a mind capable of knowing

[*] In Dialogue VIII.

and loving God and consequently made for that is obliged to occupy itself with the needs of the body. Thus, as the soul is united to the body and must interest itself in its conservation, it must be informed by instinctive proofs – I mean short but convincing proofs – of the relation that the bodies surrounding us have to the one we animate.

XIV. God alone is our light and the cause of our happiness. He possesses the perfections of all beings. He has all the ideas of them. Thus, in His wisdom He contains all speculative and practical truths, for all these truths are simply the relations of magnitude and perfection which exist between ideas, as I shall soon prove to you.* He alone, then, should be the object of the attention of our mind, as He alone is capable of enlightening it and regulating all its movements, as He alone is above us. Surely a mind occupied by creatures, directed toward creatures, however excellent they might be, is neither in the order God requires nor in the state in which God has placed it. Now, if we had to examine all the relations which the bodies surrounding us have with the current dispositions of our body, in order to judge whether, how, and how much we should interact with them, this would divide – what am I saying! – this would completely fill the capacity of our mind. And surely our body would be no better off. It would soon be destroyed by some involuntary distraction, for our needs change so frequently and some-times so suddenly that for us not to be surprised by some unpleasant accident would require a vigilance of which we are incapable. For example, when would we decide to eat? What would we eat? When would we stop eating? What a fine occupation for a mind which walks and exercises its body, to know with every step it has the body take, that it is in a fluid air which cannot injure or bother it by cold or heat, wind or rain, or by some malignant and poisonous vapor; that on every place it goes to step there is not some hard and sharp body capable of injuring it; that it must suddenly lower its head to avoid a stone, and still maintain its balance for fear of falling. People who are continually occupied with what is happening in all the parts composing their body and in an infinity of objects surrounding it cannot, therefore, think of true goods, or at least they cannot think of them as much as true goods require and consequently as much as they should, because our mind is

* Dialogue VIII.

and can be created only to concern itself with those goods which can enlighten it and render it happy.

XV. Thus, it is evident that God, desiring to unite minds to bodies, had to establish as the occasional cause of the confused knowledge we have of the presence of objects and of their properties in relation to us, not our attention, which merits a clear and distinct knowledge of them, but the various disturbances of these bodies themselves. He had to give us instinctive proofs not of the nature and properties of the bodies around us but of the relation they have to ours, so that we could work successfully for the preservation of life without being incessantly attentive to our needs. He had, as it were, to see to informing us in time and place, by means of prevenient sensations, of what concerns the good of the body, in order to leave us completely occupied in the search for true goods. To convince us quickly He had to give us short proofs of whatever is related to the body, vivid proofs to determine us effectively, certain proofs we did not think to contradict, that we might preserve ourselves more surely. Note, however, these were confused but certain proofs, not of the relation between objects, in which the evidence of truth consists, but of the relation they have to our body according to its dispositions at the time. I say, "according to its dispositions at the time" because, for example, we find and should find lukewarm water hot if we touch it with a cold hand, and we find it cold if we touch it with a hot hand. We find and should find it pleasant when we are overcome by thirst, but when our thirst is quenched we find it bland and distasteful. Therefore let us admire, Aristes, the wisdom of the laws of the union of the soul and body, and although all our senses tell us that sensible qualities are spread out over objects, let us attribute to bodies only what we clearly see belongs to them after having seriously consulted the idea which represents them. For since our senses speak differently to us about the same things according to the interest they take in them, and since they inevitably contradict themselves when the good of the body requires it, let us regard them as false witnesses in respect of the truth, but as faithful instructors in respect of the preservation and conveniences of life.

XVI. ARISTES. Oh, Theodore! How imbued I am with what you are telling me, and how embarrassed at having been the dupe of these false witnesses my whole life! But they speak with so much confidence and force that they instill, as it were, conviction and certainty in minds. They command with such arrogance and assiduity that we submit without examination. How are we to enter into ourselves when they beckon us and draw us outward? And can we hear the replies of inner truth amidst the noise and commotion they raise? You have made me understand that light cannot be a modality of bodies. But as soon as I open my eyes I begin to doubt this. The sun which strikes me dazzles me and clouds all my ideas. I now understand that if I pressed the point of this pin on my hand it could make only a small hole. But if I really pressed it, it seems to me it would cause a very great pain. Surely I would not doubt it at the moment of the jab. What power and force our senses have to propel us into error! What disorder, Theodore! And yet even in this disorder the creator's wisdom shines through wonderfully. Light and colors had to appear spread out over objects so that we could distinguish them easily. Fruit had to appear full of flavor in order for us to eat it with pleasure. Pain had to be related to the pricked finger so that the vivacity of the feeling would make us draw back. There is an infinite wisdom in this order established by God. I agree, I cannot doubt it. But at the same time I find a disorder in it which is very great and seems to me unworthy of the wisdom and goodness of our God. For in the end this order is a fertile source of error for us unfortunate creatures and the unavoidable cause of the greatest evils accompanying life. I am jabbed at the end of my finger, and I suffer. I am unhappy. I am incapable of thinking of true goods. My soul can concern itself only with my injured finger and is completely filled with pain. What strange misery! A mind depends on a body and because of it loses sight of the truth. To be divided – what am I saying? – to be preoccupied with its finger and not with its true good. What a disorder, Theodore! There is surely some mystery there. I beg you to unravel it for me.

XVII. THEODORE. Yes, no doubt, there is some mystery there. My dear Aristes, how philosophers are indebted to religion, for only religion can extricate them from the predicament in which they find themselves! Everything seems contradictory in God's conduct, and nothing is more uniform. Good and evil – I speak of physical evil – do not have two different principles. It is the same God who creates everything by the same laws. But sin makes God become the just avenger of sinners for their crimes, without changing anything of His laws. At present I cannot tell you all that would be necessary to explain this matter thoroughly. But here in a few words is the resolution of your difficulty.

God is wise. He judges all things wisely. He esteems them to the extent that they are estimable. He loves them to the extent that they are lovable. In a word, God loves order invincibly. He follows it inviolably. He cannot contradict Himself. He cannot sin. Now, minds are more estimable than bodies. Thus – take note of this – although God can unite minds to bodies, He cannot subjugate them to bodies. That the jab informs and warns me is just and in conformity with order. But that it afflicts me and makes me unhappy, that it preoccupies me despite myself, that it clouds my ideas, that it prevents me from thinking of true goods – that certainly is a disorder. It is unworthy of the wisdom and goodness of the creator. Reason makes me see this clearly. However, experience convinces me that my mind depends on my body. I suffer, I am unhappy, I am incapable of thinking when I am pricked. It is impossible for me to doubt this. There is, then, a manifest contradiction between the certainty of experience and the evidence of Reason. But here is the resolution. The human mind has lost its dignity and excellence before God. We are no longer as God made us, and the union of our soul with our body has changed to a relation of dependence, for since man disobeyed God it was right that his body ceased to be subject to him. We are born sinners and corrupted, worthy of the divine anger and entirely unworthy of thinking of God, of loving Him, of worshipping Him, or of delighting in Him. He no longer wills to be our good, and if He is still the cause of our being and does not annihilate us, it is because His clemency prepares for us a redeemer through whom we shall have access to Him, company with Him, a communion of true goods with Him, according to the eternal decree by which He resolved to reunite all things in our divine leader, the Man–God, predestined from all time to be the foundation, architect, victim, and sovereign priest of the spiritual temple in which the divine majesty will dwell eternally. Thus Reason dispels this terrible contradiction which worried you so much. It makes us clearly comprehend the most sublime truths. But this is because faith leads us to understanding, and because through its authority it converts our doubts and uncertain and troubled suspicions into conviction and certainty.

XVIII. Therefore remain steadfast, Aristes, in this thought to which Reason gives birth in you, that the infinitely perfect Being always follows the immutable order as its law and that thus it can indeed unite the more to the less noble, the mind to body, but cannot subject the former to the latter; that it cannot deprive the mind of its liberty and of the exercise of its most excellent functions in order to employ it, despite itself, and by the most cruel punishment, in losing sight of its sovereign good for the vilest of creatures. And conclude from all this that prior to sin there were exceptions favoring human beings in the laws of the union of the soul and the body. Or, rather, conclude from it that there was a law which has been abolished, by which the human will was the occasional cause of that disposition of the brain by which the soul is shielded from the action of objects though the body is struck by them, and that thus despite this action it was never interrupted in its meditations and ecstasy. Do you not sense some vestige of this power in yourself when you are deeply absorbed in thought and the light of truth penetrates and delights you? Apparently noise, colors, odors, and other less striking and less lively sensations hardly interrupt you. But you are not above pain: you find it bothersome despite all your mind's efforts. I am judging you, Aristes, by myself. But to speak accurately of innocent man, created in the image of God, we must consult the divine ideas of immutable order. It is there that we find the model of a perfect man, such as our father was before his sin. Our senses cloud our ideas and tire our attention. But with Adam they informed him respectfully. They were silenced by the least sign. They even ceased informing him of the approach of certain objects when he so wished. He was able to eat without pleasure, look without seeing, sleep without dreaming of all those useless phantoms which unsettle the mind and disturb our rest. Do not regard this as a paradox. Consult Reason, and on the basis of what you sense in a disordered body do not judge of the condition of the first man, in whom all was in conformity with the immutable order which God follows inviolably. We are sinners, and I am speaking of the innocent man. Order does not allow that the mind be deprived of the liberty of its thoughts, when the body replenishes its forces during sleep. Thus, during that and every other time the just man thought about what he willed. But, having become sinners, human beings no longer deserve that there be exceptions to the laws of nature on their behalf. They deserve to be stripped of their power over an inferior nature, having been rendered the most contemptible of creatures by their rebellion; they deserve not only to be likened to nothingness, but to be reduced to a condition which for them is even worse than nothingness.

XIX. Thus, do not cease admiring the wisdom and wonderful order of the laws of the union of the soul and body, by which we have so many various sensations of the objects surrounding us. They are very wise. Considering them as they were instituted, they were actually beneficial to us in all respects, and it is quite just that they subsist after sin, although they have unfortunate consequences, for the uniformity of God's conduct ought not to depend on the irregularity of ours. But after man's rebellion it is not right that his body be perfectly subject to him. It ought to be so only insofar as this is necessary for the sinner to preserve his miserable life for a while, and to perpetuate the human species until the consummation of the work in which his posterity will enter through the merits and power of the redeemer to come. For all these successive generations, all these lands peopled by idolaters, the entire natural order of the universe which is preserved, is simply to furnish Jesus Christ abundantly with the materials necessary for the construction of the eternal temple. The day will come when the descendants of the most barbarous peoples are illumined by the light of the Gospel and will flock to the church of the elect. Our fathers died in idolatry and we recognize the true God and our adorable savior. The arm of God is not shortened. His power will extend over the most distant nations, and perhaps our descendants will lapse again into darkness when light will illumine the new world. However, Aristes, let us in a few words review the main things I have said to you, so that you can retain them easily and make them the subject of your meditations.

XX. Humans are composed of two substances, mind and body. Thus they have two very different kinds of goods to distinguish and look for, those of the mind and those of the body. God has also given them two very sure means to distinguish these different goods: reason for the good of the mind, the senses for the good of the body; evidence and light for true goods, confused instinct for false goods. I call the goods of the body false or deceiving goods because they are not such as they appear to our senses and because, although good in relation to the preservation of life, they do not of themselves possess the efficacy of their goodness; they have it only as a consequence of divine volitions or the natural laws whose occasional causes they are. At present I cannot explain myself more clearly. Now, it was fitting that the mind sense qualities, as if they were in bodies, which bodies do not have, so that it would decide, not to love or fear them but to unite itself to or separate itself from them according to the urgent needs of the machine, whose delicate springs require a vigilant and prompt guardian. The mind had to receive a kind of reward for the service it provides a body which God ordains it to conserve, in order to interest it in its conservation. That is now the cause of our errors and prejudices. That is why, not content to unite ourselves to certain bodies and separate ourselves from others, we are stupid enough to love or fear them. In a word, that is the cause of the corruption of our heart, all of whose movements should tend toward God, and the cause of the blinding of our mind, all of whose judgments should settle for light alone. But let us note this, however, and we shall see that it is because we do not employ these two means of which I have spoken for the purpose for which God has given them to us; and because instead of consulting Reason to discover the truth, instead of submitting ourselves to the evidence accompanying clear ideas, we submit ourselves to a confused and deceiving instinct which speaks reliably only for the body's goods. Now this is what the first man did not do before his sin. For undoubtedly he did not confound the modalities of which his mind was capable with those of extension. His ideas were not then confused, and his perfectly subjugated senses did not prevent him from consulting Reason.

XXI. At present the mind is as punished as it is compensated in relation to the body. If we are pricked we suffer from it, whatever effort we make not to think of it. This is true. But as I have told you, this is because it is not just that there are exceptions to the laws of nature in favor of the rebel, or rather that we have a power over our body which we do not deserve. It is sufficient for us that by the grace of Jesus Christ the miseries to which we are subject today will be the stuff of our triumph and glory tomorrow. We are unaware of the true goods. Meditation repels us. We are not naturally affected by any prevenient pleasure in things which perfect our mind. This is because the true good deserves to be loved solely by reason. It must be loved by a love of choice, an enlightened love, and not by that blind love which instinct inspires. Indeed, it deserves our industry and care. It does not need, like bodies, assumed qualities to make itself lovable to those who know it perfectly. And if now, to love it, we must be informed by spiritual delight, this is because we are weak and corrupt. It is because concupiscence derails us and because to vanquish it God must inspire in us a different, entirely holy concupiscence. It is because to acquire the equilibrium of perfect liberty, we need a counterweight raising us to heaven, since we have a weight carrying us toward the earth.

XXII. Let us then continually retreat into ourselves, my dear Aristes, and attempt to silence not only our senses, but also our imagination and passions. I have spoken to you only of the senses because it is from them that the imagination and passions derive everything they possess of malignancy and force. Generally everything that comes to the mind through the body, specifically as a consequence of natural laws, is only for the body. Therefore let us not consider it. But let us follow the light of Reason, which must guide the judgments of our mind and regulate the movements of our heart. Let us distinguish the soul and the body and the completely different modalities of which these two substances are capable, and reflect frequently on the admirable order and wisdom of the general laws of their union. By such reflections we acquire knowledge of ourselves and deliver ourselves from an infinite number of prejudices. For it is thus that we learn to know people, and we have to live among people and with ourselves. It is in this way that the whole universe appears to our mind as it is, that it appears, I say, stripped of a thousand beauties which belong uniquely to us, but with the springs and motions which make us admire the wisdom of its author. Finally, it is thus, as you have seen, that we see palpably not only the corruption of nature and the necessity of a mediator – two great principles of our faith – but also an infinity of other truths essential to religion and to morality. Therefore, Aristes, continue to meditate as you have already begun and you will see the truth of what I am telling you. You will see that the occupation of meditators must be that of all reasonable people.

ARISTES. How confusing this word 'meditator' is to me, now that I partly understand what you have told me and now that I am completely imbued by it! I believed you, Theodore, to be in a kind of illusion, because of the blind contempt I had for Reason. I must confess this to you. I treated you and some of your friends as 'meditators.' I found fun and wit in this silly joke, and I think you are well aware what is meant by it. Nevertheless, I protest I did not want this to be thought about you, and indeed I have prevented the bad effect of this term of jest by means of serious praise which I have always believed to be very true.

THEODORE. Of that I am persuaded, Aristes. You have amused yourself a little at my expense. I am glad of that. But I think that today you will not be very sorry to learn that it has cost you more than me. Indeed, understand that there was one of these 'meditators' in the company who, when you had left, thought himself obliged to defend not me but the honor of that universal Reason you had offended in dissuading minds from consulting it. At first when the meditator spoke everyone rose in your favor. But after he had weathered some jokes and contemptuous airs which the imagination inspires in revolt against Reason, he pleaded his cause so well that the imagination succumbed. You were not made fun of, Aristes. The meditator seemed distressed by your blindness. As for the others, they were affected by a certain indignation; so that, if you are still of the same mind – you are quite far from it – I would not advise you to go to Philander's to proffer jokes and commonplaces against reason in order to make the taciturn meditators contemptible.

ARISTES. Do you believe it, Theodore? I am feeling a secret joy from what you are teaching me. The wrong I fear having done was soon remedied. But to whom am I obliged for this? Is it not to Theotimus?

THEODORE. You will know this when I am fully convinced that your love for the truth is strong enough to extend to those to whom you have a slightly ambiguous obligation.

ARISTES. This obligation is not ambiguous. I protest to you that if it is Theotimus, I shall love and esteem him all the more for it. For as I meditate I am aware of my increasing inclination for those seeking the truth, for those I called 'meditators' when I was insensitive enough to treat as visionaries those who render to Reason the attention it deserves. Thus, oblige me by telling me who this virtuous man is who wished to spare me the confusion I deserved and who upheld the honor of Reason so well, without holding me up to ridicule. I wish to have him as a friend. I wish to deserve his good graces and if I cannot succeed in this I wish him to know at least that I am no longer as I was.

THEODORE. Very well, Aristes, he will know it. And if you wish to be among the number of meditators, I promise you he will also be among the number of your good friends. Meditate, and all will be well. Soon you will win him over, when he sees in you an ardor for the truth, submission to faith, and profound respect for our common master.

Dialogue V

The use of the senses in the sciences. In our sensations there is a clear idea and confused sensations. The idea does not belong to the sensation. It is the idea which enlightens the mind, and the sensation which preoccupies it and makes it attentive, for it is by means of the sensation that the intelligible idea becomes sensible.

ARISTES. I have made great headway, Theodore, since you left me. I have indeed discovered land. I have generally reviewed all the objects of my senses, having been led, it seems to me, solely by Reason. Though already somewhat accustomed to these new discoveries, never was I more surprised. Good God, what poverty I discerned in what two days ago appeared to me to be perfect magnificence! What wisdom, what greatness, what wonders in everything the world scorns! People who see only with their eyes are surely strangers in their own land. They admire everything and know nothing, too happy if what strikes them does not kill them. There are perpetual illusions on the part of sensible objects. Everything deceives us, poisons us, speaks to the soul only for the body. Only Reason disguises nothing. How pleased I am with it and with you for having taught me to consult it, for having elevated me above my senses and myself in order to contemplate the light! I have recognized very clearly, it seems to me, the truth of everything you have told me. Yes, Theodore, what pleasure I have in telling you: our mind is only darkness, its own modalities do not enlighten it, its substance, as completely spiritual as it is, contains nothing intelligible; its senses, imagination, and passions seduce it at every moment. Today I believe I can assure you I am fully convinced of this. I speak to you with the confidence that the vision of the truth gives me. Test me and see if I do not possess a little too much temerity.

I. THEODORE. I believe what you are telling me, Aristes. For I am persuaded that an hour of serious meditation can carry a mind such as yours quite far. Nevertheless, to assure myself further of your progress, answer me. You see this line **AB**. Let it be divided into two parts at any point **C**. I shall prove to you that the square of the whole is equal to the squares of each part plus the two parallelograms formed on these two parts.

ARISTES. What do you mean by this? Who does not know that it is the same thing as multiplying a whole by itself, or all the parts comprising the whole?

THEODORE. You know it. But let us suppose that you did not. I intend to demonstrate it to your eyes and thereby to prove to you that your senses clearly reveal the truth to you.

ARISTES. Let us see.

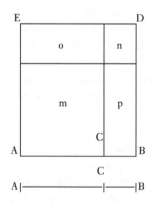

THEODORE. Look closely, that is all I ask of you. Without entering into yourself to consult Reason, you will discover an evident truth. **ABDE** is the square of **AB**. Now this square is equal to everything it contains. It is equal to itself. Therefore, it is equal to the two squares of each part **m** and **n**, and to the two parallelograms **o** and **p** formed on these parts **AC** and **CB**.

ARISTES. That is obvious to the eyes.

THEODORE. Very well. But it is also evident. There are, then, evident truths obvious to the eyes. Thus, our senses teach us of truths evidently.

ARISTES. This is a beautiful truth and quite difficult to discover. Is that all you have to say to defend the honor of the senses?

THEODORE. You are not answering, Aristes. It is not Reason which inspires this subterfuge. For, I ask you, is it not an evident truth which your senses have just taught you?

ARISTES. Nothing is easier.

THEODORE. This is because our senses are excellent teachers. They have easy ways of teaching us the truth. But Reason, with its clear ideas, leaves us in darkness. Look how people will answer you, Aristes. Prove to someone ignorant, they will tell you, that the square of 10, for example, equals the two squares of 4 and 6 plus twice the product of 4 and 6. These ideas of numbers are clear, and this truth to be proved is the same in intelligible numbers as if it were a question of a line displayed to your eyes, which was, say, ten inches long, divided into 4 and 6. And yet you will see there is some difficulty making this understood, because this principle that it is the same thing to multiply a number by itself as to multiply all its parts by themselves and separately, is not as evident as the principle that a square equals all the figures it contains. And this is what your eyes teach you, as you have just seen.

II. But if you find that the theorem your eyes taught you is too easy, here is another more difficult one. I shall prove to you that the square on the diagonal of a square is double the square on its sides. All I ask is that you open your eyes.

Look at the figure I draw on this paper. Do not your eyes tell you, Aristes, that all these triangles **A, B, C, D, E, F, G, H, I**, which I posit and each of which you see has a right angle and two equal sides, are equal to each other? Now, you see that the square formed on the diagonal **AB** has four of these triangles, and that each of the squares formed on its sides has two. Hence, the large square is double the others.

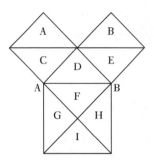

ARISTES. Yes, Theodore. But you are reasoning.

THEODORE. Reasoning! I look, and I see what you say. I am reasoning, if you wish, but it is on the faithful testimony of my senses. Simply open your eyes, and look at what I am showing you. The triangle **D** is equal to **E**, and **E** equals **B**; and on the other side **D** is equal to **F**, and **F** equals **G**. Thus, the small square equals half the large one. The same is true of the other side. That is obvious to the eyes, as you say. To discover this truth it suffices to look at this figure carefully, comparing the parts composing it by moving our eyes. Thus, our senses can teach us the truth.

ARISTES. I deny this conclusion, Theodore. It is not our senses, but Reason joined to our senses which enlightens us and reveals the truth to us. Are you not aware that, in the sensible view we have of this figure, there is simultaneously the clear idea of extension joined to the confused sensation of color which affects us. Now, it is from the clear idea of extension, and not from the white or black which make it sensible, that we discover the relations in which truth consists; I say, from the clear idea of extension which Reason contains, and not from the white or black which are simply sensations or confused modes of our senses, of which it is impossible to discover relations. There is always a clear idea and a confused sensation in the view we have of sensible objects. The idea represents their essence, and the sensation informs us of their existence. The idea makes us know their nature, their properties, the relations they have or can have between themselves – in a word, the truth; and the sensation makes us sense their difference and the relation they have to the convenience and preservation of life.

III. THEODORE. From this reply I see you have covered much ground since yesterday. I am pleased with you, Aristes. However, I ask you, is this color here on this paper not itself extended? Certainly I see it as such. Now, if it is, I shall be able clearly to discover the relations of its parts, without thinking of that extension which Reason contains. The extension of the color will be sufficient for me to learn physics and geometry.

ARISTES. I deny, Theodore, that color is extended. We see it as extended, but our eyes deceive us. For the mind will never understand that extension belongs to color. We see this whiteness as extended, but this is because we relate it to extension since it is through the sensation of the soul that we see the paper, or rather it is because intelligible extension touches the soul, modifies it in a particular way, and thereby becomes sensible to it. What, Theodore! Are you saying that pain is extended because when we have gout or some rheumatism we feel it as extended? Are you saying that sound is extended because we hear it filling the air? Are you saying that light is spread through these large spaces because we see them fully illuminated? Since we have here only the modalities or sensations of the soul, and since the soul does not draw the idea it has of extension from its own depths, all these qualities are related to extension and make the soul sense it, but they are not at all extended.

IV. THEODORE. I grant you, Aristes, that color as well as pain is not locally extended. For because experience teaches that we feel pain in an arm we no longer have, and because while asleep at night we see colors spread over imaginary objects, it is evident that we have here only sensations or modalities of the soul, which certainly do not fill all the places it sees, since the soul fills none of them and since the modalities of a substance cannot be where that substance is not. That is indisputable. Pain cannot be locally extended in my arm, nor color on the surfaces of bodies. But why do you not hold that they are sensibly extended, as it were, just as the idea of bodies, intelligible extension, is intelligibly extended? Why not hold that the light I see in pressing the corner of my eye, or otherwise, carry with it the sensible space it occupies? Why do you hold that it is related to intelligible extension? In a word, why do you hold that it is the idea or archetype of bodies that touches the soul when it sees or senses sensible qualities as spread out over bodies?

ARISTES. This is because it is only the archetype of bodies which can represent their nature to me, only universal Reason which can enlighten me through the manifestation of its ideas. The substance of the soul has nothing in common with matter. The mind does not contain the perfections of all the beings it can know. But there is nothing which does not participate in the divine Being. Thus God sees all things in Himself. But the soul cannot see them in itself. It can discover them only in divine and universal Reason. Thus, the extension I see or sense does not belong to me. Otherwise, in contemplating myself I would be able to know God's works. In attentively considering my own modalities I would be able to learn physics and many other sciences which consist simply in the knowledge of the relations of extension, as you well know. In short, I would be a light unto myself, which is something I cannot contemplate without a kind of horror. But please, Theodore, explain the difficulty you have raised for me.

V. THEODORE. It is impossible to explain directly. For this the idea or archetype of the soul would have to be revealed to us. We would then clearly see that color, pain, taste, and the other sensations of the soul have nothing in common with the extension we sense together with them. We would see intuitively that there is as much difference between the extension we see and the color that makes it visible to us, as there is between numbers, infinity, for example, or whatever other intelligible idea you please, and the perception we have of it. And at the same time we would see that our ideas are quite different from our perceptions or sensations – a truth we can discover only through serious reflection, only through long and difficult reasoning.

However, to prove to you indirectly that our sensations or modalities do not contain the idea of extension to which they are necessarily related, because this idea produces them in our soul and because the nature of the soul is to perceive what touches it, let us suppose that you look at the color of your hand and that at the same time you feel a pain there, and you will see the color of this hand as extended, and at the same time you will feel its pain as extended. Do you not agree?

ARISTES. Yes, Theodore. And even if I touched it I would still sense it as extended; and if I dipped it in hot or cold water, I would feel the heat or cold as extended.

THEODORE. Take note, then. Pain is not color, color is not heat, nor heat cold. But the extension of color, or the extension joined to color, which you see in looking at your hand, is the same as that of the pain, the heat, the cold, which you can feel there. Thus, this extension belongs neither to the color, nor the pain, nor to any other of your sensations. For you would sense as many different hands as you have different sensations if our sensations were extended of themselves as they seem to us, or if the colored extension you see were simply a sensation of the soul, such as color or pain or taste are, as some among the Cartesians imagine who well know that we do not see objects in themselves. There is, then, one and only one idea of our hand which affects us in different ways, which acts on our soul and modifies it by color, heat, pain, etc. For it is not the bodies we look at which affect us with our various sensations, since we often see bodies which do not exist. And it is also evident that bodies cannot act on the mind, modify it, enlighten it, make it happy and unhappy by means of pleasant and unpleasant sensations. Nor indeed does the soul act on itself and modify itself by means of pain, color, etc. This requires no proof after everything we have said. It is, then, the idea or archetype of bodies which affects us in different ways. I mean, it is the intelligible substance of Reason which acts in our mind through its all-powerful efficacy and which touches and modifies it with color, taste, pain, by what there is within it representing bodies.

Thus you need not be surprised, my dear Aristes, that you can learn some evident truths by the testimony of the senses. For although the substance of the soul is not intelligible to the soul itself and its modalities cannot enlighten it, because these very modalities are joined to the intelligible extension which is the archetype of bodies and because they make this extension sensible, they can show us its relations, in which the truths of geometry and physics consist. But it is always true to say that the soul is not its own light unto itself, that its modalities are but darkness, and that it discovers exact truths only in the ideas Reason contains.

VI. ARISTES. I think I understand what you are telling me. But as it is abstract I shall meditate upon it at my leisure. It is not pain or color by itself which teaches me the relations bodies have to one another. I can discover these relations only in the idea of extension which represents them, and this idea, though joined to color or pain – sensations which make it sensible – is not a modality of the soul.[*] This

---

[*] In this work I term *sentimens* what I have often termed *sensations* in other works. [In *De la*

idea becomes sensible or is sensed only because the intelligible substance of Reason acts on the soul and impresses a certain modality or sensation upon it, and thereby as it were reveals to it, albeit in a confused way, that such a body exists. For when the ideas of bodies become sensible they make us judge that there are bodies acting on us, whereas when these ideas are simply intelligible we naturally believe there is nothing outside of us acting on us. The reason for this, it seems to me, is that thinking of extension depends on us and sensing it does not. For as we sense extension despite ourselves, there must be something other than us which impresses the sensation on us. Now, we believe that this other thing is simply that which we are actually sensing. From this we judge that it is the bodies surrounding us which cause the sensation we have of them in us, and in this we always deceive ourselves. And we do not doubt that these bodies exist, and in this we often deceive ourselves. But as we think of bodies and imagine them whenever we desire, we judge that it is our volitions which are the true cause of the ideas we then have of them, or of the images we form of them. And the inner sensation we have of the effort of our attention at the time confirms us in this false thought. Although God alone can act in us and enlighten us, because His operation is not sensible we attribute to objects what He does in us independently of our volitions, and we ascribe to our power whatever He does in us depending on our volitions. What do you think, Theodore, of this reflection?

VII. THEODORE. It is quite judicious, Aristes, and worthy of a meditator. You could also add that when the idea of the body affects the soul with a very absorbing sensation like pain, this idea makes us judge not only that this body exists, but moreover that it belongs to us, as happens even to those whose arm has been amputated. However, let us return to the sensible demonstration I gave you of the equality that exists between the square on the diagonal of a square and the two squares on the sides. And let us take note that this demonstration derives its evidence and generality only from the clear and general idea of extension, from the straightness and equality of the lines and the rightness and equality of the angles and triangles, and by no means from

Recherche de la vérité, Bk. 1, Ch. 4, §1 (*OC* I 67), Malebranche appears to use the terms synonymously. In the present translation, *sentiment* is translated usually as "sensation," but frequently as "feeling" in connection with the specific faculty by which we apprehend our own existence, the *sentiment interieur*.]

78

the white and the black which make all these things sensible and particular without making them more intelligible or clear by themselves. Take note that by my demonstration it is evident that in general any square made on the diagonal of a square is equal to the squares of the two sides, but that it is by no means certain that this particular square you see with your eyes is equal to the two others. For you are not even certain that what you see is square, that this line is straight or this angle right. The relations your mind conceives between magnitudes are not the same as those of these figures. Finally, take note that although our senses do not enlighten the mind by themselves, because they make the ideas we have of bodies sensible to us, they prompt our attention and thereby indirectly lead us to an understanding of the truth. In this way we should make use of our senses in the study of all those sciences which have the relations of extension as their object; and we should not fear that they will lead us into error, provided we closely observe the precept that we judge things only on the basis of the ideas representing them and never on the basis of the sensations we have of them. This is a precept of the utmost importance, which we should never forget.

VIII. ARISTES. All that is exactly true, Theodore, and I have understood it thus since I thought about it seriously. Nothing is more certain than that our modalities are only darkness,[*] that they do not enlighten the mind by themselves, that what is most vividly sensed is not clearly known. This square here is not such as I see it. It is not the size I see it. You certainly see it as much larger or much smaller than I see it. The color I see it has does not belong to it. Perhaps you see it colored differently than I do. It is not really this square that I see. I judge that it is traced on this paper and it is not impossible that there is neither a square nor paper here, as it is certain that there is no color here. But although my eyes give me now so many false or doubtful reports concerning these figures traced on this paper, this is nothing compared to the illusions of my other senses. The testimony of my eyes often approaches the truth. This sense can help the mind discover it. It does not entirely disguise its object. In making me attentive, it leads me to understanding. But the other senses are so false that we are always under an illusion when we let ourselves be led by them. Nevertheless, it

---

[*] Cf. *De la Recherche de la vérité*, Bk. 1 [*OC* I 39–189, especially 139f., 146f.], and the *Réponse au Livre des vrayes & fausses Idées* [*OC* VI 11–189].

is not the case that our eyes are given to us to discover the exact truths of geometry and physics. They are given to us simply to clarify all the movements of our body in relation to those surrounding us, and simply for the convenience and preservation of life; and in order to preserve it, we must have some kind of knowledge of sensible objects which somewhat approaches the truth. That is why we have, for instance, some awareness of the size of a particular body at a particular distance. For if such a body were too far from us to be able to injure us, or if, being close, it were too small, we would not fail to lose sight of it. To our eyes it would be annihilated, though it would continually subsist before our mind and in that respect it could never be annihilated by division; for effectively the relation of a large but remote body, or of a body close but too small to injure us – the relation, I say, of these bodies to ours is nil or need not be perceived through the senses, which need speak only for the preservation of life. All this seems evident to me and conforms to what has passed through my mind in meditation.

THEODORE. I certainly see, Aristes, that you have been quite far in the land of truth, and that through the commerce you have had with Reason you have acquired riches much more precious and rare than those brought to us from the new world. You have discovered the source. You have drawn from it. And you are thereby rich forever, provided you do not leave it. Having found the faithful master who enlightens and enriches all those attached to Him, you no longer need me nor anyone else.

ARISTES. What, Theodore! Do you want to break off our discussion already? I know well that it is with Reason that we must philosophize. But I do not know how it must be done. Reason itself will teach me. That is not impossible. But I have no ground to hope for this, unless I have a faithful and vigilant monitor to guide and prompt me. Goodbye to philosophy, if you leave me; for by myself I fear going astray. I would soon take the answers I provide myself for those of our common master.

IX. THEODORE. I have no mind to leave you, my dear Aristes. For now that you are meditating on everything you are told, I trust you will prevent in me the misfortune you fear happening to you. We both need each other, although we receive nothing from anyone. You have taken literally a word mentioned in honor of Reason. Yes, it is from it alone that we receive the light. But Reason uses those to whom it commu-

nicates itself in order to recall its wayward children to itself and guide
them by their senses to understanding. Do you not know, Aristes, that
Reason itself became incarnate to be accessible to all people, to open the
eyes and ears of those who can see and hear only through their senses.
People have seen with their eyes the eternal Wisdom, the invisible God
who lives in them. As the dearly beloved disciple says,* they have
touched with their hands the Word that gives life. Inner truth has
appeared outside us, coarse and stupid as we are, in order to teach us in
a sensible, palpable way the eternal commands of the divine law –
commands it gives us continually from within and which we do not
hear, being extended outward as we are. Are you not aware that the
great truths faith teaches us are housed in the church, and that we can
learn them only through a visible authority emanating from incarnate
Wisdom? It is true that it is always inner truth which instructs us, but it
employs all possible means to recall us to itself and fill us with
understanding. Thus, do not fear me leaving you; for I trust it will use
you to prevent me from abandoning it and from taking my imaginings
and reveries for its divine oracles.

ARISTES. You do me much honor. But indeed I see I must accept it,
for it redounds to Reason, our common master.

THEODORE. I do you the honor of believing you to be rational.
This honor is great. For through Reason all people become superior to
all creatures when they consult and follow it. By it they judge and
condemn in a sovereign way; or, rather, Reason decides and condemns
through them. But do not think I am submitting to you. Furthermore,
do not believe that I am raising myself above you. I submit only to
Reason, which can speak to me through you as it can speak to you
through my mediation; and I elevate myself only above the brutes, only
above those who renounce the most essential of their qualities.
However, my dear Aristes, although both of us are rational let us not
forget that we are extremely prone to error, because we are both capable
of deciding without awaiting the infallible judgment of the just judge,
without waiting for the evidence to wrest our consent from us, as it
were. For if we always ceded to Reason this honor of leaving it to
pronounce its rulings in us, it would render us infallible. But instead of
awaiting its answers and of following its light step by step, we anticipate
it and go astray. As restive as we are, impatience grips us because we are

* 1 John 1[: 1].

required to stay attentive and still. Our indigence presses us and our ardor for true goods often precipitates us into the gravest misfortunes. This is because we are free to follow the light of reason or to walk in the darkness by the false and deceiving glimmer of our modalities. Nothing is more pleasant than blindly following the impressions of instinct. But nothing is more difficult than holding fast those sublime and delicate ideas of the truth, despite the weight of the body which dulls our mind. Still, let us try to support one another, my dear Aristes, without depending on each other too much. Perhaps we shall not both lose our step at the same time, provided we tread softly and be as attentive as possible not to press on weak ground.

ARISTES. Let us push on a little, Theodore. What are you afraid of? Reason is an excellent foundation. There is nothing changing in clear ideas. They do not yield to time. They are not accommodated to particular interests. They do not alter their words like our modalities, which affirm and deny according to the body's solicitations. I am fully convinced that we need to follow only the ideas which diffuse light, and that all our sensations and other modalities can never lead us to the truth. Let us proceed to another question, since I agree with you about all this.

X. THEODORE. Let us not go so fast, my dear Aristes. I am afraid that you are granting me more than I am asking of you, or that you still do not understand distinctly enough what I am saying to you. Our senses deceive us, to be sure, but this is principally because we refer our sensations of sensible objects to the objects themselves. Now, there are in us many sensations we do not refer to them. Such are the feelings of joy, sadness, hatred – in a word, all the feelings accompanying the movements of the soul. Color is not in the object, pain is not in my body, heat is neither in the fire nor in my body to where these sensations are referred. Our external senses are false witnesses. Agreed. But the feelings which accompany love and hate, joy and sadness, are not referred to the objects of these passions. We sense them in the soul and they are there. They are, therefore, good witnesses, for they speak truthfully.

ARISTES. Yes, Theodore, they speak truthfully, and the other sensations do too. For when I feel pain, it is true that I feel it; it is even true, in a sense, that I suffer it by the action of the very object which touches me. Here are great truths! What, then; are not the feelings of love, hatred and the other passions referred to the objects which are their occasion? Do they not shed their malignity on objects and represent them to us as completely other than they actually are? As for me, when I feel an aversion to people I feel myself disposed to interpret everything they do negatively. Their innocent actions seem criminal to me. I want to have good reasons to hate and despise them. For all my passions desire justification at the expense of those at whom they are directed. If my eyes spread colors over the surface of bodies, so my heart also casts, as far as possible, its inner dispositions or certain false hues over the objects of its passions. I do not know, Theodore, whether the passions in you have the same effect as they have in me, but I can assure you that I am even more afraid of listening to and following them than of subjecting myself to the frequently innocent and helpful illusions of my senses.

XI. THEODORE. I am not saying, Aristes, that we should yield to the hidden promptings of our passions, and I am pleased to see you are aware of their power and malignity. But you must agree they teach us certain truths. For it is a truth, after all, that at present I experience much joy listening to you. It is very true that the pleasure I feel now is greater than that which I had in our previous discussions. Thus, I know the difference between these two pleasures. And I do not know this other than by the feeling I have of it, other than in the modalities by which my soul is affected, modalities which are not, therefore, so dark that they do not teach me a firm truth.

ARISTES. Theodore, say that you sense this difference between your modalities and your pleasures. But please do not say you know it. God knows it and does not sense it. But as for you, you sense it without knowing it. If you had a clear idea of your soul, if you saw its archetype, then you would know what you only sense. Then you could know exactly the difference in the various feelings of joy which your goodness to me elicits in your heart. Yet assuredly you do not know it. Compare, Theodore, the feeling of joy by which you are presently affected, with that of the other day, and tell me exactly the relation between them. Then I shall believe your modalities are known to you. For we know things only when we know the relation between them. You know one pleasure is greater than another. But by how much? We know that a square inscribed in a circle is smaller than the circle. But we do not thereby know the quadrature of the circle, because we do not know the relation of the circle to the square. We can approach it to infinity and see evidently that the difference between the circle and some other figure will be smaller than any given amount. But note that this is because we have a clear idea of extension. For the difficulty there is in discovering the relation of the circle to the square arises only from the limitation of our mind, whereas it is the obscurity of our sensations and the darkness of our modalities that render the discovery of their relations impossible. Were we geniuses as great as the sublimest intellects, it seems to me evident that we could never discover the relations between our modalities, unless God manifested to us their archetype on which He formed them. For you have convinced me that we can know beings and their properties only by the eternal, immutable and necessary ideas representing them.

XII. THEODORE. Very good, Aristes. Our senses and passions cannot enlighten us. But what do you say about our imagination? It forms images of geometrical figures so clear and distinct that you cannot deny that it is by their means that we learn this science.

ARISTES. Do you think, Theodore, that I have already forgotten what you just told me or that I did not understand it? The evidence accompanying the geometers' reasonings, the clarity of the lines and figures which the imagination forms, arises solely from our ideas and in no way from our modalities, in no way from the confused traces which the course of animal spirits leaves behind. When I imagine a figure, when I construct a building in my mind, I work on a foundation which does not belong to me. For it is from the clear idea of extension, it is from the archetype of bodies that I draw all the intelligible materials which represent my design to me, all the space which provides me with my ground. It is from this idea which Reason furnishes me that I form the body of my work in my mind, and it is on the basis of the ideas of equality and of proportion that I work and order it, relating everything to an arbitrary unity which must be the common measure of all the parts composing it or at least of all the parts which can be viewed from the same point at the same time. Surely it is on the basis of intelligible ideas that we order the course of the animal spirits which trace these images or figures of our imagination. And everything of light and evidence these figures possess in no way issues from the confused sensation which belongs to us, but from the intelligible reality which belongs to Reason. It does not come from the modality specific and peculiar to us; it is a radiant burst from the luminous substance of our common master.

I cannot, Theodore, imagine a square, for instance, which I cannot at the same time conceive. And it seems evident to me that the image of this square which I form to myself is exact and regular only insofar as it corresponds exactly to the intelligible idea I have of the square, that is, of a space enclosed by four perfectly straight, completely equal lines and which, being joined at their ends, make perfectly right angles. Now, it is about such a square that I am sure that the square on the diagonal is double the square on one of the sides. It is about such a square that I am sure that there is no common measure between the diagonal and the sides. In a word, it is the properties of such a square which we can discover and demonstrate to others. But we can know nothing from this confused and irregular image which the course of animal spirits traces in the brain. The same must be said of all other figures. Thus, geometers do not derive their knowledge from the confused images of their imagination, but solely from the clear ideas of Reason. These rough images can indeed bolster their attention by lending, as it were, something bodily to their ideas; but it is these ideas which reward them, which enlighten them and convince them of the truth of their science.

XIII. Do you want me to stop here, Theodore, to represent to you the illusions and phantoms of an imagination in revolt against Reason, sustained and encouraged by the passions; those beguiling phantoms which seduce us, terrible phantoms which frighten us, monsters of all kinds which are born of our turmoil, which reproduce and multiply in a moment? They are fundamentally pure chimeras, but chimeras in which our mind revels and occupies itself with the utmost willingness. For our imagination finds much more reality in the specters to which it gives birth than in the necessary and immutable ideas of eternal truth. This is because these dangerous specters strike it, whereas ideas do not affect it. Of what use can so disordered a faculty be, a fool who likes to play the fool, someone flighty whom we have so much difficulty reining in, someone insolent who is unafraid to interrupt us in our most serious commerce with Reason? Nonetheless, I grant you that our imagination can render our mind attentive. For it exercises so much charm and influence over the mind that it makes it think willingly about what affects it. But aside from the fact that it can relate only to the ideas representing bodies, it is so subject to illusion and so quick-tempered that unless we constantly check it, unless we regulate its movements and incursions, it will transport you instantly into the land of chimeras.

THEODORE. That is enough of that, Aristes. From everything you have just told me, which fills me with astonishment and joy, I definitely see that you have understood the principle and gone quite far into the consequences it involves. I see in fact that you grasp sufficiently that it is only Reason which enlightens us through the intelligible ideas it contains in its completely luminous substance, and that you can distinguish perfectly its clear ideas from our dark and obscure modalities. However, take note: abstract principles, pure ideas elude the mind when we neglect to contemplate them and when we fix on sensible ideas. Thus, I advise you to meditate often on this matter, in order to possess it so perfectly and to make yourself so familiar with its principles and consequences, that you will never inadvertently take the vivacity of your sensations for the evidence of truth. For it is not enough to have understood well that the general principle of our prejudices is that we do not distinguish between 'knowing' and 'sensing,' and that instead of judging things by means of the 'ideas' representing them, we judge them by our 'sensations' of them. We must strengthen ourselves in this fundamental truth by following it to its conclusions. All practical principles are understood perfectly only through the use made of them. Try, therefore, through continual and serious reflection to acquire a strong and agreeable habit of readying yourself against the surprises and secret impulses of your false and deceiving modalities. There is no occupation more worthy of a philosopher. For if we properly distinguish the replies of inner truth from what we say to ourselves, if we distinguish what comes immediately from Reason from what comes to us through the body or on the occasion of the body, what is immutable, eternal, and necessary from what changes every moment, in short, the evidence of light from the vivacity of instinct, it will be almost impossible for us to fall into error.

ARISTES. I well understand everything you are telling me. And I have found so much satisfaction in the reflections I have already made on this matter that you need not fear that I will no longer think about it. Let us move on to something else if you deem it appropriate.

THEODORE. It is now rather late, Aristes, for us to start on a path that is a little long. But to which subject do you want us to turn tomorrow? Please, think about it and tell me.

ARISTES. It is up to you to guide me.

THEODORE. Not at all; it is your choice. You must not be indifferent to which way I lead you. Am I not capable of deceiving you? Might I not guide you where you should not go? Most people, my dear Aristes, imprudently enter into useless studies. These kinds of people need only hear the praises sung of chemistry, astronomy, or some other vain, barely worthwhile science, in order to throw themselves bodily into it. These people will not know whether the soul is immortal, they may well be unable to show you that there is a God, and yet they will solve the equations of algebra with surprising facility. And others will know all the finer points of language, all the rules of the grammarians, but will never have meditated on the order of their duties. What an inversion of the mind! An overpowering imagination lauds passionately the knowledge of medals, the poetry of the Italians, the language of the Arabs and Persians, in front of a young man full of zeal for the sciences. This will be enough to commit him blindly to these kinds of studies. He will neglect the knowledge of human beings, the rules of morality, and perhaps he will forget what children are taught in their catechism. For the human being is a machine that goes wherever it is impelled. Chance, much more than Reason, is what guides it. All live by opinion. All act by imitation. They even make a virtue of following those who go ahead, without knowing where. Reflect on the various activities of your friends; or, rather, go over in your mind the path you have taken in your studies, and judge whether you were right to do as the others did. Decide on this, I say, not on the basis of the praise you have received, but on the conclusive replies of inner truth. Judge this by the eternal law, the immutable order, without regard for the foolish thoughts of people. What, Aristes! Just because people pursue some trifle, each in their own way and according to their own taste, must we follow them, for fear of passing as a philosopher in the mind of fools? Indeed, must we follow above all the philosophers into their abstractions and chimeras, for fear they should consider us as ignorant or as innovators? Everything must be put in its place. Preference must be given to the knowledge which merits it. We ought to learn what we should know, and not let our heads be filled with useless furniture, however striking it appears, when we lack the necessities. Think about this, Aristes, and you will tell me tomorrow what should be the subject of our conversation. That is enough for today.

ARISTES. It would be much better, Theodore, if you told me yourself.

THEODORE. It would be infinitely better for Reason to tell us both. Consult it seriously, and I shall think on it too.

Dialogue VI

Proofs of the existence of bodies drawn from revelation. Two kinds of revelation. How it happens that the natural revelations of sensations are an occasion for error for us.

ARISTES. What a difficult question you have given me to solve, Theodore! I was quite right to tell you that it was up to you, who know the strengths and weaknesses of the sciences and the utility and fecundity of their principles, to direct my steps in that intelligible world to which you transported me. For I confess I do not know where I should turn. What you have taught me can indeed aid me in preventing me from straying in that unknown land. To this end I need simply follow the light, step by step, and yield only to the evidence attending clear ideas. But it is not enough to advance; we also have to know where we are going. It is not enough constantly to discover new truths; we must know the location of these fertile truths which bestow on the mind all the perfection of which it is now capable, these truths which should regulate the judgments we must make concerning God and His admirable works, and should regulate the movements of our heart and give us a taste, or at least a foretaste, of the sovereign good we desire.

If, in choosing from the sciences, we had to adhere to evidence alone without considering utility, arithmetic would be preferable to all the others. Numerical truths are the clearest of all, since all other relations are clearly known only insofar as they can be expressed through measures common to all the exact relations measured by unity. And this science is so fertile and profound that, were I to spend ten thousand centuries penetrating its depths, I would still discover an inexhaustible store of clear and luminous truths. However, I do not think you will find it very appropriate that, being charmed by the evidence radiating there from all sides, we go in that direction. For, after all, how would delving into the most hidden mysteries of arithmetic and algebra help us? It is not enough to race through many countries, to penetrate deeply into sterile lands, to discover places where no one ever was. We must proceed straight to those happy countries where we find fruits in abundance, solid foods capable of nourishing us.

Thus, when I compared the sciences to each other according to my lights, their various advantages either in terms of their evidence or their utility, I found myself in an odd predicament. Sometimes the fear of falling into error gave preference to the exact sciences, like arithmetic and geometry, the demonstrations of which admirably satisfy our vain curiosity. And sometimes the desire to know not the relations of ideas among themselves, but the relations of the works of God, among which we live, both among themselves and to us, involved me in physics, morality, and the other sciences which often depend on experiences and fairly uncertain phenomena. It is a strange thing, Theodore, that the most useful sciences are full of impenetrable obscurities, and that we find a sure and rather easy and single path in those which are not so necessary! Now, please tell me how to evaluate fairly the relation between the easiness of the former and utility of the latter, in order to give preference to the science that deserves it. And how can we be sure that those very sciences which seem the most useful are so in fact, and that those which seem merely evident do not have great uses which go unnoticed? I admit, Theodore, that after having thought a lot about this, I still do not know how to decide.

I. THEODORE. You have not wasted your time, my dear Aristes, in the reflections you have made. For although you do not exactly know what you should apply yourself to, I am already well assured you will not engage in a number of false studies, in which half the world is seriously involved. Indeed I am certain that were I to make a mistake in choosing the subject of our conversation, you would be able to set me aright. When people raise their head and look in all directions, they do not always follow those who go in front. They follow them only when they go where they must go or want to go themselves. And when the leader of the pack imprudently sets out on routes which are dangerous and end up nowhere, the others force him back. Thus, continue your reflections on your steps and on mine. Do not rely too much on me. Observe carefully whether I lead you where we both should go.

Thus, take note, Aristes. There are two kinds of sciences. Some consider the relations between ideas, others the relations between things by means of their ideas. The former are evident in every way, the latter can be so only by assuming that things are similar to the ideas we have of them, on the basis of which we reason about them. These latter sciences are quite useful, but they are shrouded in great obscurity, because they assume facts whose truth it is very difficult to know exactly. But if we were able to find some means of assuring ourselves of the fairness of our assumptions, we would be able to avoid error and at the same time discover those truths which closely concern us. For, once again, the truths or relations of ideas among themselves concern us when they represent the relations which obtain between the things that have some connection to us.

Hence, it seems to me evident that the best use we can make of our mind is to examine what the things are which have some connection to us, what the various kinds of connections are, what their cause is, what their effects are; and all of this in conformity with clear ideas and irrefutable experiences, the former of which assure us of the nature and properties of things, the latter of which assure us of the relation and connection they have to us. However, in order not to become trivial and useless, our entire examination must be directed only toward what renders us happy and perfect. Thus, to reduce all this to a few words, it seems evident to me that the best use we could make of our mind is to attempt to acquire an understanding of the truths we believe through faith, and of everything that leads to their confirmation. For no comparison can be made between the utility of these truths and the advantage to be derived from the knowledge of other truths. True, we believe these great truths. But faith does not exempt those who can from filling their mind with such truths and convincing themselves of them in all possible ways. For, on the contrary, faith is given to us to regulate, on its basis, all the steps of our mind as well as all the movements of our heart. It is given to us to guide us to the understanding of the very truths it teaches us. There are so many people who scandalize the faithful by means of an extravagant metaphysics and who insultingly require proofs of what they should believe on the infallible authority of the church, that although the solidity of your faith renders you impervious to their attacks, your charity should lead you to remedy the disorder and confusion they wreak everywhere. Do you approve then, Aristes, of the plan I am proposing for the course of our discussions?

ARISTES. Yes, I certainly do. But I did not think you would want to give up metaphysics. Had I thought that, it seems to me I would have indeed resolved the question of preference in the sciences. For it is clear that no discovery is comparable to an understanding of the truths of faith. I believed you simply wanted to make me something of a philosopher and a good metaphysician.

II. THEODORE. That is still all I am thinking of and I do not plan to abandon metaphysics, although in what follows I shall perhaps take the liberty of going beyond its usual limits. This general science rules over all the others. It can draw examples from them and a little detail which is necessary to render its general principles sensible. For by metaphysics I do not mean those abstract considerations of certain imaginary properties, the principal use of which is to furnish the wherewithal for endless dispute to those who want to dispute. By this science I mean the general truths which can serve as principles for the particular sciences.

I am persuaded, Aristes, that it is necessary to be a good philosopher to gain understanding of the truths of faith; and that the stronger we are in the true principles of metaphysics, the stronger we are in the truths of religion. I am assuming, you may well think, what is necessary to make this proposition admissible. But no, I shall never believe that the true philosophy is opposed to faith and that good philosophers can have different opinions from good Christians. For whether Jesus Christ in His divinity speaks to philosophers in their innermost being or instructs Christians through the visible authority of the church, it is impossible that He contradict Himself, although it is quite possible to imagine contradictions in His pronouncements or take our own decisions for His pronouncements. Truth speaks to us in various ways, but it certainly always says the same thing. Therefore, we must not oppose philosophy and religion, unless it is the false philosophy of the pagans, the philosophy founded on human authority, in short, all those non-revealed opinions which do not bear the character of truth, that invincible evidence which compels attentive minds to submit. By the metaphysical truths we have discovered in our foregoing discussions you can judge whether the true philosophy contradicts religion. On my part I am convinced it does not. For were I to present you with several propositions contrary to the truths Jesus Christ teaches us through the visible authority of His church, as these propositions are based solely in me and do not bear that character of invincible evidence, they in no way belong to the true and sound philosophy. But I do not know why I forbear telling you truths which are impossible to doubt, however little attention we have given them.

ARISTES. Allow me to tell you, Theodore, that I was delighted to see a wonderful relation between what you taught me, or rather between what reason taught me through you, and those great and necessary truths which the authority of the church makes the simple and ignorant believe, whom God desires to save as much as philosophers. For instance, you have convinced me of the corruption of my nature and of the necessity of a savior. I know that all intellects have only one single and unique master, the divine Word, and that only Reason, incarnate and rendered sensible, can deliver carnal people from the blindness into which we are all born. I grant you, with an extreme satisfaction, that these fundamental truths of our faith and many others I would be too long telling you are the necessary consequences of the principles you have demonstrated to me. Please continue. I shall try to follow you wherever you lead me.

THEODORE. Ah, my dear Aristes, take care once again that I do not go astray. I fear you are too easy on me, and that your approval prompts me into a certain negligence and causes me to fall into error. Fear for me, and mistrust everything someone subject to illusion can tell you. Moreover, you will learn nothing unless your reflections put you in possession of the truths I shall try to demonstrate to you.

III. There are only three kinds of beings about which we have any knowledge and to which we can have any connection: God, or the infinitely perfect Being who is the principle or cause of all things; minds, which we know only through the inner feeling we have of our nature; and bodies, of the existence of which we are assured by the revelation we have of them. Now what we call a human being is but a composite . . .

ARISTES. Easy, Theodore. I know there is a God or an infinitely perfect Being.* For if I think of it – and I certainly do think of it – it must exist, for nothing finite can represent the infinite. I also know that minds exist, assuming there are beings resembling me.** For I cannot doubt that I think, and I know that whatever thinks is something different from extension or matter. You have proved these truths to me. But what do you mean, that we are assured of the existence of bodies "by the revelation we have of them"? What! Do we not see them, do we not sense them? We do not need "revelation" to teach us that we have a body when we are pricked; we sense it quite clearly.

THEODORE. Yes, undoubtedly, we do sense it. But that sensation of pain we have is a kind of 'revelation.' This expression strikes you. But it is for just this reason that I use it. For you always forget that it is God Himself who produces in our soul all those various sensations by which it is affected on the occasion of the changes that happen to our body, as a result of the general laws of the union of the two substances composing humans; laws which are simply the efficacious and continual volitions of the creator, as I shall explain to you in the following. The point which pricks our hand does not cause pain by the hole it makes in the body. Nor is it the soul which produces this uncomfortable sensation in itself, since it suffers the pain despite itself. Assuredly it is a superior power. It is therefore God Himself, who through the sensations with which He affects us reveals to us what is happening outside us – I mean in our body and in those bodies surrounding us. Remember, please, what I have already told you so often.

IV. ARISTES. I was wrong, Theodore. But what you are saying evokes a very strange thought in my mind. I almost dare not suggest it to you, for I fear you will consider me a visionary. It is that I am beginning to doubt that bodies exist. The reason is that the revelation God gives us of their existence is not sure. For, after all, it is certain we sometimes see things that do not exist, as when we sleep or when fever causes some disturbance in the brain. If, as you say, God can sometimes give us deceptive sensations in consequence of His general laws, if He can reveal false things to us through our senses, why could He not do this constantly, and how could we discern truth from falsehood in the obscure and confused testimony of our senses? It seems to me that

* Dialogue II.   ** Dialogue I.

prudence obliges me to suspend my judgment concerning the existence of bodies. Please give me an exact demonstration of their existence.

THEODORE. "An exact demonstration"! That is a little too much, Aristes. I confess I do not have one. On the contrary, it seems to me that I have an "exact demonstration" of the impossibility of such a demonstration. However, be reassured. I am not lacking in proofs which are certain and capable of dispelling your doubt, and I am pleased such a doubt has occurred to you. For, after all, doubting that bodies exist for reasons which make it impossible to doubt God's existence and the incorporeality of the soul is a certain sign that we have risen above our prejudices and that, instead of subjecting reason to the senses, as most people do, we acknowledge its right to sovereign judgment in us. Unless I am deceived, here is a demonstrative proof that it is impossible to provide an exact demonstration of the existence of bodies.

V. The notion of the infinitely perfect Being does not contain a necessary relation to any creature. God is completely self-sufficient. Matter, therefore, is not a necessary emanation of the divinity. At least – and this is enough for the present – it is not evident that it is a necessary emanation of it. Now, we can give an "exact demonstration" of a truth only when we show that it has a necessary connection with its principle, only when we show that there is a necessary relation contained in the ideas we are comparing. Thus, it is not possible to demonstrate rigorously that bodies exist.

Actually, the existence of bodies is arbitrary. If there are any, it is because God willed to create them. Now, the same does not hold true of that volition to create bodies as holds true of the volitions to punish crimes and reward good deeds, to require love and fear from us, and so on. These and a thousand other similar volitions of God are necessarily contained in divine Reason, in that substantial law which is the inviolable rule of the volitions of the infinitely perfect Being, and generally of all intellects. But the volition to create bodies is not necessarily contained in the notion of the infinitely perfect Being, of the Being which is fully self-sufficient. Far from it; that notion seems to exclude such a volition from God. Thus, there is no way apart from revelation by which we can be assured that God has indeed willed to create bodies, as long as you assume what you no longer doubt, namely that bodies are not visible by themselves, that they can neither act on our mind nor be represented to it, and that our mind itself can know them only in the ideas representing them and sense them only through its modalities or sensations, and that it can be the cause of these only as a result of the arbitrary laws of the union of the soul and body.

VI. ARISTES. I quite understand, Theodore, that we cannot demonstratively deduce the existence of bodies from the notion of the infinitely perfect and self-sufficient Being, because the volitions of God relating to the world are not contained in the notion we have of Him. Now, as only these volitions can give existence to creatures it is clear that we cannot demonstrate that bodies exist. For we can demonstrate only those truths which have a necessary connection to their principle. Thus, since we cannot be assured of the existence of bodies through the evidence of a demonstration, there is no further way but through the authority of revelation. But this way does not seem sure to me. For although in the notion of the infinitely perfect Being I clearly discover that He cannot will to deceive me, experience teaches me that His revelations are deceptive. These are two truths which I cannot reconcile. For, after all, we often have sensations which reveal falsehoods to us. People feel pain in an arm they no longer have. All those whom we call mad see objects before them that do not exist. And perhaps there is no one who in sleep has not often been thoroughly unsettled and distressed by mere phantoms. God is not a deceiver. He cannot will to deceive anyone, neither the mad nor the wise. Yet nonetheless we are completely seduced by the sensations by which He affects us and through which He reveals the existence of bodies to us. Thus, it is quite certain that we are frequently deceived. But it seems less certain to me that we are not always deceived. Let us see, therefore, on what foundation you are basing the certainty you claim to possess that bodies exist.

VII. THEODORE. In general there are two kinds of revelations. Some are natural, others supernatural. I mean that some occur as a consequence of certain general laws which are known to us, according to which the author of nature acts in our mind on the occasion of what happens to our body. Others occur through general laws which are unknown to us, or through particular volitions added to the general laws to remedy the disagreeable effects they have because of the sin which has disordered everything. Now the former and the latter revelations, the natural and the supernatural, are true in themselves. But the former are now an occasion for error, not because they are false by themselves but because we do not put them to the use for which they were given to us, and because sin has corrupted nature and introduced a kind of contradiction into the relation the general laws have to us. Certainly the general laws of the union of the soul and the body, as a consequence of which God reveals to us that we have a body and that we exist in the midst of many other bodies, are very wisely established. Recall our previous discussions. They are not deceptive by themselves, in their institution, considered as they were before sin and in the design of their author. For we must realize that before his sin, before his blindness and the turmoil that the rebellion of his body caused in his mind, man clearly knew by the light of Reason:

1. That God alone can act in him, render him happy or unhappy through pleasure or pain, in short, modify or affect him.

2. He knew by experience that God always affected him in the same way in the same circumstances.

3. Thus, he recognized by experience as well as by Reason that the action of God was and had to be uniform.

4. Hence, he was determined to believe that there were beings which were the occasional causes of the general laws according to which he sensed that God acted on him. For, once again, he knew very well that God alone acted on him.

5. Whenever he wanted, he was able to prevent himself from sensing the action of sensible objects.

6. The inner feeling he had of his own volitions and of the respectful and submissive action of these objects taught him, therefore, that they were inferior to him, because they were subordinate to him, for then everything was perfectly in accordance with the divine order.

7. Thus, consulting the clear idea joined to the sensation by which he was affected on the occasion of these objects, he saw clearly that they were only bodies, since this idea represents only bodies.

8. He concluded, therefore, that the various sensations by which God affected him were simply revelations by which God taught him that he had a body and was surrounded by many other bodies.

9. But, knowing by Reason that God's action had to be uniform, and knowing by experience that the laws of the union of the soul and body were always the same; seeing indeed that these laws were established

simply to inform him of what he had to do to preserve his life, he easily discovered that he must not judge the nature of bodies by the sensations he had of them, nor let himself be persuaded of their existence by these same sensations, except when his brain was agitated by an external cause and not by a movement of animal spirits excited by an internal cause. He was able to recognize when it was that external cause which produced actual traces in his brain, because the course of animal spirits was perfectly subject to his volitions. Thus, he was not like mad or feverish people, nor like us when we are asleep, subject to taking phantoms for reality; because he could discern whether the traces in his brain were produced by the internal and involuntary course of the animal spirits, or by the action of objects, the former course being voluntary in him and dependent on his practical desires. All this seems evident to me and a necessary consequence of two incontestable truths: first, that before sin man had very clear ideas and his mind was free from prejudices; second, that his body, or at least the principal part of his brain, was perfectly subordinated to him.

If this is granted, Aristes, you can indeed see that the general laws, as a result of which God gives us these sensations or natural revelations which assure us of the existence of bodies and of the relation they have to us, are very wisely established; you see that these revelations are in no way deceptive by themselves. Nothing could have been done better, for the reasons I have already stated. How is it, then, that they now cast us into an infinity of errors? Surely it is because our mind is dimmed, because we are full of prejudices from childhood, because we do not know how to put our senses to the use for which they were given to us. And all this is so, take note, precisely because through our own fault we have lost the power we should have over the principal part of the brain, over that part in which every change is always followed by some new thought. For our union with universal Reason is extremely weakened by our dependence on our body. For, after all, our mind is so situated between God who enlightens us and the body which blinds us, that the more it is united to the one, of necessity the less it is united to the other.

As God exactly follows and must exactly follow the laws He has established of the union of the two substances of which we are composed, and because we have lost the power to prevent the traces which the rebellious animal spirits effect in the brain, we take phantoms for realities. But the cause of our error does not come precisely from the falsity of our natural revelations, but from the imprudence and temerity of our judgments, from our ignorance of the path God must take, from the disorder which, in short, sin has caused in all our faculties, and from the confusion it has introduced into our ideas, not by changing the laws of the union of the soul and body, but by elevating our body and through its rebellion depriving us of the power to put these laws to the use for which they were established. You will understand all this more clearly in our following discussions, or when you have meditated on it. However, Aristes, notwithstanding everything I have just said, I do not see that there can be any good reason to doubt that bodies exist generally. For if I am deceived in respect of the existence of a particular body, I see very well that this is because God follows exactly the laws of the union of the soul and body; I see that it is because the uniformity of God's action cannot be disturbed by the irregularity of ours, and because the loss we suffered through our own fault of the power we had over our body need not have changed anything in the laws of its union with our soul. This reason suffices to prevent me from being deceived about the existence of a particular body. I am not invincibly led to believe that it exists. But I do not have this reason, and I do not see it is possible to find any other reason to prevent me from believing generally that bodies exist despite all the various sensations I have of them, sensations so consistent, so linked together, so well ordered, that it seems to me certain that God would be deceiving us if there were nothing in everything we see.

VIII. But to deliver you completely from your speculative doubt, faith furnishes us with a demonstration which is impossible to resist. For whether bodies do or do not exist it is certain that we see them and that only God can give us sensations of them. Thus, it is God who presents to my mind the appearances of the people with whom I live, of the books I study, of the preachers I hear. Now, in the appearance of the New Testament I read of the miracles of a Man–God, His Resurrection, His Ascension into heaven, the preaching of the apostles, His joyful success, the establishment of the church. I compare all this with what I know from history, with the law of the Jews, with the prophets of the Old Testament. These are still only appearances. Yet once again I am certain that it is God alone who gives them to me, and that He is not a deceiver. I then compare anew all the appearances I just mentioned with the idea of God, the beauty of religion, the sanctity of morality, the necessity of a creed, and finally I find myself led to believe what faith teaches us. In short, I believe it without needing completely rigorous, demonstrative proof. For nothing seems more irrational to me than lack of faith, nothing more imprudent than not submitting to the greatest authority possible concerning those matters which we cannot examine with geometrical precision, either because we lack the time or for a thousand other reasons. People need an authority to teach them necessary truths, truths which should lead them to their end, and to reject the authority of the church is to overturn providence. This seems evident to me and I shall prove it in what follows.* Now, faith teaches me that God has created heaven and earth. It teaches me that Scripture is a divine book. And this book, or its appearance, teaches me clearly and positively that there are thousands and thousands of creatures. Thus, all my appearances are hereby changed into reality. Bodies exist; that is demonstrated in complete rigor, given faith. Thus, I am assured that bodies exist, not only by the natural revelation of the sensations of them which God gives me, but even more by the supernatural revelation of faith. Here, my dear Aristes, are the main arguments against a doubt which comes to mind hardly in a natural way. There are few people who are philosophers enough to propose it. And although we can, against the existence of bodies, formulate difficulties which appear insurmountable mainly to those who do not know that God must act in us by general laws, still I do not believe anyone can ever seriously doubt it. Thus, it was not really necessary to detain ourselves dispelling a doubt so minimally dangerous. For I am quite certain that you yourself did not need everything I just told you to be assured you are here with Theodore.

ARISTES. I am not very certain of this. I am certain that you are here. But this is because you are telling me things which another would not tell me and which I would never tell myself. Moreover, the friendship I have for Theodore is such that I encounter him everywhere. Do I know whether I shall always be able to distinguish properly between the true and the false Theodore, as this friendship increases even more, though that hardly seems possible?

* Dialogue XIII.

THEODORE. You are not wise, my dear Aristes. Will you never desist from these flattering ways? It is unworthy of a philosopher.

ARISTES. How severe you are! I did not expect this reply.

THEODORE. Nor did I yours. I thought you were following my reasoning. But your answer gives me some reason to fear that you have made me address your doubt well nigh in vain. Most people raise difficulties without reflection, and instead of being seriously attentive to the answers they are given, they think only of some rejoinder which would make people admire the subtlety of their imagination. Far from being mutually instructed, they think only of flattering each other. Together they are corrupted by the hidden expectations of the most criminal passions, and instead of quelling all those feelings which the passion of pride excites in them, instead of sharing the true goods which Reason imparts to them, they heap praise upon one another, which goes to their head and confuses them.

ARISTES. Ah, Theodore, how keenly aware I am of what you are saying! But what is this! Are you reading my heart?

THEODORE. No, Aristes. It is in mine that I read what I am telling you. It is in mine that I find that source of lust and vanity which makes me speak ill of humankind. I know nothing of what happens in your heart, except in relation to what I feel in my own. I fear for you what I am afraid of for myself. But I am not so rash as to judge of your actual dispositions. My manners surprise you. They are harsh and awkward – rustic, if you will. But what is this! Do you think that true friendship, based on Reason, seeks subterfuge and disguise? You do not know the privileges of the "meditators." They have the right unceremoniously to tell their friends what they find fault with in their conduct. I would like, my dear Aristes, to see a little more simplicity and much more attention in your replies. I would like Reason always to have the superior position in you and your imagination to be silenced. But if it is now too tired of its silence, let us leave metaphysics. We shall take it up another time. Do you know that the meditator of whom I spoke to you a couple of days ago wishes to come here?

ARISTES. Who? Theotimus?

THEODORE. Yes indeed, Theotimus himself.

ARISTES. Ah, that virtuous man! What a joy! What an honor!

THEODORE. He has learned somehow that I was here and that we were philosophizing together. For when Aristes is about, it is soon

known. That is because everyone wants him. See what it is to have a
fine mind and such brilliant qualities. He must be everywhere in order
not to disappoint anyone. He is no longer his own man.

ARISTES. What slavery!

THEODORE. Do you wish to be freed from it? Become meditative,
and soon the whole world will let you be. The great secret of delivering
oneself from the importunity of many people is to speak reasonably to
them. This language, which they do not understand, gets rid of them
forever, without their having reason to complain.

ARISTES. That is true. But when will Theotimus be here?

IX. THEODORE. Whenever it suits you.

ARISTES. Well, please advise him straight away that we are
expecting him, and above all assure him I am no longer what I was once.
But let this not upset the course of our discussion. I renounce my
doubt, Theodore. But I do not regret having suggested it to you. For by
the things you have told me I discern the resolution of a number of
apparent contradictions which I was unable to reconcile with the notion
we have of the divinity. When we sleep God makes us see thousands of
objects which do not exist. This is because He follows and must follow
the general laws of the union of the soul and body. It is not because He
wills to deceive us. If He acted on us by particular volitions we would
not see all these phantoms while asleep. I am no longer surprised to see
monsters and all these irregularities of nature. I see their cause in the
simplicity of God's ways. Oppressed innocence no longer surprises me;
if the stronger ordinarily prevail over it, this is because God governs the
world by general laws and defers the punishment of crimes to another
time. He is just notwithstanding the joyous success of the impious,
notwithstanding the prosperity of the forces of the most unjust
conquerors. He is wise, although the universe is full of works in which
there are a thousand defects. He is immutable, although He seems
constantly to contradict Himself, although with hail He ravages the
earth He covered with fruit through an abundance of rain. All these
contradictory effects indicate neither contradiction nor change in the
cause which produces them. On the contrary, God inviolably follows
the same laws, and His conduct bears no relation to ours. If someone
suffers pain in an arm they no longer have, it is not because God plans
to deceive them. It is solely because God does not change His plans and

because He strictly obeys His own laws. It is because He approves them and will never condemn them; it is because nothing can upset the uniformity of His conduct, nothing can oblige Him to deviate from what He has done. It seem to me, Theodore, I can discern that this principle of general laws has an infinity of consequences of very great utility.

THEODORE. That is good, my dear Aristes. You give me much joy. I did not think you had been attentive enough to grasp properly the principles on which my answers to you depend. That is quite good. But we must examine these principles thoroughly, in order for you to know more clearly their solidity and wonderful fecundity. For do not imagine that it is enough for you to catch sight of them and even to have understood them, to be able to apply them to all the difficulties which depend on them. Through practice you must make yourself master of them and acquire the ability to refer to them everything they can explain. But I am inclined to postpone the examination of these great principles until Theotimus has arrived. Nevertheless, try to discover by yourself what the things are which have some connection to us, what the causes of these connections are, and what their effects are. For it is good that your mind be prepared for the topic of our discussions, in order that you can more easily correct me if I go astray or follow me if I lead you directly to where we should proceed with all our might.

Dialogue VII

The inefficacy of natural causes, or the impotence of creatures. We are immediately and directly united only to God alone.

After many compliments between Aristes and Theotimus, Aristes, noticing that Theodore was not entirely pleased that the conversation had not finished, and wishing to cede to the newcomer the glory of this little duel of wits, withdrew. Theodore, taking up the argument, felt himself duty-bound to address Theotimus on behalf of Aristes.

THEODORE. Honestly, Theotimus, I did not realize you were such a courteous person. You have obliged Aristes to capitulate, he who never gave way to anyone. Such a victory would be a great honor if you had gained it at Philander's house. But it might have cost you more dearly. For do not deceive yourself: Aristes yields because in his own home he wishes to do the honors. He defers to you here out of kindness and a sort of duty.

THEOTIMUS. I do not doubt it, Theodore. I see very well that he wants to spare me.

ARISTES. Oh! Stop pressing me, both of you; or, Theodore, at least allow me the freedom to defend myself.

THEODORE. No, Aristes, there is simply too much useless talk. We shall say no more, Theotimus and I. Let us speak of something better. Please tell us what thoughts you have had on the subject I suggested to you in our last discussion. What are the things to which we have some relation? What are the causes of these relations, and what are their effects? For we would rather hear you philosophize than see ourselves overwhelmed by a profusion of niceties and courtesies.

ARISTES. I think you assume, Theodore, that I have sat up all night in order to treat Theotimus to some prepared speech.

THEODORE. Let us put all this aside, Aristes, and speak naturally.

I. ARISTES. It seems to me, Theodore, that there is nothing to which I am more closely united than my own body. For it cannot be touched without my being disturbed. As soon as it is wounded, I am aware of being injured and hurt. Nothing is smaller than the proboscis of those troublesome gnats that bother us on an evening walk and yet, however faintly they push the imperceptible tip of their venomous proboscis into my skin, I am aware in my soul of being pierced. The very sound they make in my ears alarms me – a sure sign that I am united to my body more closely than to anything else. Yes, Theodore, this is so true that it is only by means of our body that we are united to all these objects surrounding us. If the sun did not disturb my eyes, it would be invisible to me; and were I unfortunate enough to fall deaf, I would no longer find as much pleasure in the company I keep with my friends. It is even through my body that I hold to my religion. For through my eyes and my ears faith has entered my mind and my heart. In short, it is by means of my body that I am connected to everything. I am, therefore, united to my body more closely than to anything else.

THEODORE. Have you meditated long, my dear Aristes, in order to make this great discovery?

THEOTIMUS. All that can be very easily maintained, Theodore.

THEODORE. Yes, Theotimus, by those who consult only their senses. What do you take Aristes for, approving from his lips what any peasant might say? I no longer recognize Aristes in this reply.

ARISTES. I see clearly that I have begun very badly.

THEODORE. Very badly indeed. I did not expect this beginning. For I did not think that you would have forgotten today what you knew yesterday. But prejudices always return to the charge and drive us from our conquests, if we do not know how to hold our ground by our vigilance and sound entrenchments. Well then, I maintain that we are not in the least united to our body, let alone more closely united to it than to anything else. I exaggerate my statements a little, so that they strike you forcefully and so that you no longer forget what I am telling you. No, Aristes, to speak exactly and rigorously, your mind is not and cannot be united to your body. For it can be united only to that which can act on it. But do you think that your body can act on your mind? Do you think that it is your body that makes you rational, happy or unhappy, and so forth? Is it your body which unites you to God, to the Reason which enlightens us, or is it God who unites you to your body, and by means of your body to everything that surrounds you?

ARISTES. Most certainly, Theodore, it is God who has united my mind to my body. But could it not be said that . . .

THEODORE. What! That it is your mind that now acts on your body, and your body on your mind? I understand you. God effected this union of body and mind. But then there is your body and – through it – all the objects capable of acting on your mind. Once this union is effected, your mind is then capable of acting on your body and through it on those surrounding it. Could one not say this, perhaps?

ARISTES. There is something I do not understand very well here. How does all this come about? I am speaking to you as if I have forgotten the better part of what you have told me, for want of having thought about it.

THEODORE. I certainly doubt that. You want me to prove to you more exactly and in greater detail the principles I have so far discussed. I must try to satisfy you. But please pay attention and answer me; and you, Theotimus, please monitor us both.

II. Do you think, Aristes, that matter, which you do not perhaps deem capable of moving itself or giving itself any modality, could ever modify a mind, make it happy or sad, represent ideas to it, give it various sensations? Think about it and answer me.

ARISTES. This does not seem possible to me.

THEODORE. Once again, think about it. Consult the idea of extension and decide by this idea which represents bodies – if anything does – whether they can have any property other than the passive faculty of receiving various figures and movements. Is it not entirely obvious that all the properties of extension can consist only in relations of distance?

ARISTES. That is clear, and I have already agreed with it.

THEODORE. Thus it is impossible for bodies to act on minds.

ARISTES. Not by themselves, by their own force, it will be claimed.

But why could they not do so by a power resulting from their union with minds?

THEODORE. What do you mean, "by a power resulting from their union"? I understand nothing by these general terms. Remember, Aristes, the principle of clear ideas. If you depart from it, you will end up in darkness. With the very first step you will fall over the precipice. I can well understand how bodies, as a consequence of certain natural laws, can act on our mind in the sense that their modalities determine the efficacy of the divine volitions or general laws of the union of the soul and the body, which I shall soon explain. But that bodies should receive in themselves a certain power, by the efficacy of which they could act on the mind – this I do not understand. For what would this power be? Would it be a substance, or a modality? If a substance, then bodies will not act, but rather this substance in bodies. If this power is a modality, then there will be a modality in bodies which will be neither motion nor figure. Extension will be capable of having modalities other than relations of distance. But why do I stop here? It is up to you, Aristes, to give me some idea of this power which you conceive as the effect of the union of the soul and body.

ARISTES. We do not know, it might be said to you, what this power is. But what can you conclude from our admission of ignorance?

THEODORE. That it is better to remain silent than not to know what one is saying.

ARISTES. Agreed. But one is saying simply what one knows when one maintains that bodies act on minds. For nothing is more certain. Experience countenances no doubt on this score.

THEODORE. Nevertheless I strongly doubt it, or rather I do not believe it at all. Experience teaches me that I feel pain when a thorn pricks me. That much is certain. But let us leave it at that. For in no way does experience teach us that the thorn acts on our mind, or that it has any power. Let us believe nothing of the sort – that is my advice to you.

III. ARISTES. I do not believe, Theodore, that a thorn can act on my mind. But it will perhaps be argued that it can act on my body, and by means of my body on my mind, as a consequence of their union. For I admit that matter cannot act immediately on a mind. Take note of the word 'immediately.'

THEODORE. But is your body not material?

ARISTES. Yes, undoubtedly.

THEODORE. Your body cannot, therefore, act 'immediately' on your mind. Thus, if your finger be pricked by a thorn, although your brain is affected by its action, neither the one nor the other can act on your soul and cause it to experience pain. For neither the one nor the other can act immediately on the mind, since your brain and finger are nothing but matter.

ARISTES. Neither, however, is it my soul that produces in itself this sensation of pain which afflicts it, for it suffers the pain in spite of itself. I certainly sense that the pain comes to me from an external cause. Thus your reasoning proves too much. I see indeed that you are going to tell me that it is God who causes my pain in me, and I agree with that. However, He causes it only as a consequence of the general laws of the union of the soul and body.

THEODORE. What do you mean, Aristes? All that is true. Explain your thought more distinctly.

ARISTES. I believe, Theodore, that God has united my mind to my body, and that by this union my mind and body act mutually upon each other, as a consequence of the natural laws which God always follows very exactly. That is all I have to say to you.

THEODORE. You do not explain yourself, Aristes. That is a sure enough sign that you do not understand your own words. 'Union,' 'general laws' – what kind of reality do you understand by these terms?

THEOTIMUS. Apparently Aristes believes that these terms are clear and unequivocal, because use has made them quite common. For when one has often read something obscure or false, without having even examined it, one has difficulty believing it is not true. This word 'union' is one of the most equivocal words there is. But it is so widespread and accepted that it passes everywhere without anyone questioning it, without anyone examining whether it elicits any distinct idea in the mind. For familiar things fail to spark that attention without which it is impossible to understand anything; and everything that touches the imagination agreeably appears very clear to the mind, which mistrusts nothing when it is paid to its satisfaction.

ARISTES. What, Theotimus! Are you entirely of Theodore's mind? Can it really be doubted that the soul and body are more intimately united than anything else? I would willingly believe that you are both agreeing in order to confuse me and entertain yourselves at my expense, were I not convinced that you are too honest to have so uncharitable a design.

THEOTIMUS. You are, Aristes, a little too prejudiced. Theodore upholds the side of truth, and if he exaggerates things somewhat, it is by way of setting us aright. He sees that the weight of our prejudices is influencing us, and the force he is exercising upon us is simply to restrain us. Please, let us listen to him.

IV. THEODORE. You would have it, Aristes, that your soul is united to your body more closely than to anything else. Well, I grant that for the moment, but only on the condition that you also agree, for a day or two, not to explain certain effects by means of a principle which neither you nor I understand. Is this not quite reasonable?

ARISTES. Only too reasonable. But what do you mean?

THEODORE. This, then. There is the closest union in the world between your mind and your body. How can we doubt it! But you could not say precisely what this union is. Therefore let us not take it as the principle of explanation of those effects whose cause we are seeking.

ARISTES. But if these effects necessarily depend on it?

THEODORE. If they necessarily depend on it, we shall certainly be obliged to return to it. But let us not assume this. If I asked you, Aristes, how it is that simply in pulling the arm of the chair all the rest follows, would you believe you had sufficiently explained this effect to me by replying that it happens because the arm of this chair is united to the other parts which comprise it? Assuredly Theotimus would not be satisfied with such a reply. Children may answer thus, but not philosophers, except when they are not claiming to philosophize. To put Theotimus' mind to rest on this question, it would be necessary to return to the physical cause of this union of parts which compose hard bodies, * and prove to him that the hardness of bodies arises simply from the compression of an invisible matter surrounding them. This word 'union,' then, explains nothing. It requires explanation itself. Thus, Aristes, you may take vague and general words for reasons. But do not expect to pay us with such coin. For although many accept and make do with it, we are more exacting, in virtue of our fear of being deceived.

ARISTES. What would you have me do? I am paying you with

* Cf. *De la Recherche de la vérité*, Bk. 6, Ch. 9 [*OC* II 420–49].

money I have received in good faith. I have none better. And since it has currency in the world, you could make do with it. But let us see just how you pay people yourself. Show me with sound arguments that the body and mind act upon each another, without having recourse to their union.

THEODORE. Do not assume, Aristes, that they act upon each other, but only that their modalities are reciprocal. Assume only just what experience teaches you, and try to pay attention to what I am going to tell you. Do you think that one body can act upon another and move it?

ARISTES. Who could deny it?

V. THEODORE. Theotimus and I, and soon perhaps Aristes. For there is a contradiction – a contradiction, I say – in the claim that bodies can act on bodies. I will demonstrate for you this paradox which appears so contrary to experience, so opposed to the tradition of philosophers, so incredible to the wise and the ignorant. Answer me: can a body move itself by itself? Please consult the idea you have of body; for always remember that it is necessary to judge things by the ideas which represent them, and not at all by the sensations we have of them.[*]

ARISTES. No, I do not see that bodies can move themselves by themselves. But no more do I see that they cannot do this. I am doubtful about the matter.

THEODORE. You do well to doubt, and to hold back when you do not see clearly. But try to see clearly and to dispel your doubt. Courage, let us advance!

ARISTES. I fear taking a false step for want of light. Enlighten me a little.

THEODORE. Carefully consult your clear ideas, my dear Aristes. It is they that shed, upon attentive minds, that light which you lack. Contemplate intelligible extension, the archetype of bodies. This represents them, as it is on its basis that they have all been formed. This idea is completely luminous; therefore be guided by it. Do you not clearly see that bodies can be moved, but that they cannot move themselves? You hesitate. Well, suppose then that this chair can move itself. In which direction will it go, with what speed, and when will it decide to move itself? Give it then an intelligence as well, and a will capable of determining itself. In other words, create a human being out

[*] Dialogues III, IV, V.

of your armchair. Otherwise this power of self-motion will be useless to it.

ARISTES. A human being out of my armchair! What a strange thought!

THEOTIMUS. Only too common and real, as Theodore knows. For all those who judge things by reference to themselves or by their sensations of them, and not by means of the ideas which represent them, make something resembling themselves out of all those objects. They have God act like a human. They ascribe to animals what they sense in themselves. To fire and the other elements they attribute inclinations, of which they have no other idea than their own sensations of them. Thus they humanize everything. But do not stop here; follow Theodore and answer him.

ARISTES. I certainly think that this chair cannot move itself. But how do I know that there is not some other body to which God has given the power of self-motion? Remember, Theodore, you have to prove there is a contradiction in bodies acting upon one another.

VI. THEODORE. Well then, Aristes, I shall show you. It is a contradiction for a body to be neither at rest nor in motion. For even God – though omnipotent – cannot create a body which is nowhere or which does not have certain relations of distance to other bodies. Every body is at rest when it has the same relation of distance to other bodies; and it is in motion when this relation constantly changes. Yet it is obvious that every body either changes or does not change its relation of distance. There is no middle ground. For these two propositions, 'It changes' and 'It does not change,' are contradictory. Thus it is a contradiction that a body be neither at rest nor in motion.

ARISTES. That did not require proof.

THEODORE. But it is the will of God that gives existence to bodies and to all creatures, whose existence is certainly not necessary. Since this same volition that has created them always subsists, they always exist; and when this volition ceases – I am speaking of God according to our mode of conception – it is necessary that bodies cease to exist. Thus it is this same volition that puts bodies at rest or in motion, because it is that volition which gives them being, and because they cannot exist without being at rest or in motion. For, take note, God cannot do the impossible, or that which contains a manifest contradiction. He cannot will what cannot be conceived. Thus He cannot will that this chair exist, without at the same time willing that it exist either here or there and without His will placing it somewhere, since you cannot conceive of a chair existing unless it exists somewhere, either here or elsewhere.

ARISTES. It seems to me, however, that I can think of a body, without conceiving of it either at rest or in motion.

THEODORE. That is not what I am saying to you. You can think of a body in general, and make abstractions as you please. I recognize that. It is often that which deceives you. But once again I am telling you that you cannot conceive of a body that exists, which does not at the same time exist somewhere, and whose relation to other bodies neither changes nor does not change, and that consequently is neither at rest nor in motion. Thus it would be a contradiction were God to make a body which He creates neither at rest nor in motion.

ARISTES. Very well, Theodore, I grant you that. When God creates a body initially He must place it either at rest or in motion. But once the moment of creation has passed, this is no longer the case. Bodies dispose themselves haphazardly, or according to the law of the strongest.

VII. THEODORE. "The moment of creation has passed!" But if this moment does not pass, then you are in a spot, and will have to yield. Therefore take note. God wills that a certain kind of world exist. His will is omnipotent, and this world is thus created. Let God no longer will there to be a world, and it is thereby annihilated. For the world assuredly depends on the will of the creator. If the world subsists, it is because God continues to will its existence. Thus, the conservation of creatures is, on the part of God, nothing but their continued creation. I say on the part of God who acts. For on the part of creatures there appears to be a difference, since by the act of creation they pass from nothingness to being, whereas by the act of conservation they continue to be. But in essence the act of creation does not cease, because in God creation and conservation are but a single volition which, consequently, is necessarily followed by the same effects.

ARISTES. I understand your reasons, Theodore, but I am unconvinced by them. For the proposition, 'Let God no longer will there to be a world, and it is thereby annihilated,' appears false to me. It seems to me that to annihilate the world it is not enough that God no longer will that it exist: it is necessary that He positively will that it no longer exist. No will is required to do nothing. Thus, now that the world has been made, let God leave it alone, and it will always be.

VIII. THEODORE. You are not thinking, Aristes. You are making creatures independent. You are judging God and His works by the works of people, who presuppose nature and do not create it. Your house subsists although your architect is dead. This is because its foundations are sound and it has no connection with the life of the person who built it. It does not depend on that person in the least. But the foundation of your being depends essentially on the creator. And although the arrangement of stones in a sense depends on the will of people as a consequence of the action of natural causes, their product does not depend on it. But because the universe has been created from nothing, it is so dependent on the universal cause that it would necessarily relapse into nothingness, were God to cease conserving it. For God neither does nor indeed can produce a creature independent of His volitions.

ARISTES. I admit, Theodore, that there is a relation, a connection, an essential dependence between creatures and the creator. But could it not be claimed that to preserve the dependence of created beings it suffices that God can annihilate them as He pleases?

THEODORE. Undoubtedly not, my dear Aristes. What greater mark of independence than to subsist by oneself and without support? To put the matter precisely, your house does not depend on you. Why not? Because it subsists without you. You can set it ablaze as you wish; but you do not sustain it. This is why there is no essential dependence between it and you. Thus, let God be able to destroy creatures as He pleases, if they can subsist without the continual influence of the creator, they are not essentially dependent on Him.

That you should be entirely convinced of what I am saying, conceive for a moment that God does not exist. According to you the universe will not cease to subsist. For a cause which exercises no influence is no more necessary for the production of an effect than a cause which does not exist. That is obvious. Now, on this supposition, you cannot conceive that the world is essentially dependent on the creator, since the creator is assumed not to exist any longer. True, this supposition is impossible; but the mind can join or separate things as it pleases, in order to ascertain their relations. Thus, if bodies are essentially dependent on the creator, to subsist they need to be sustained by His continual influence, by the efficacy of the same volition which created them. If God simply stops willing their existence, it will follow necessarily and from this very fact alone that they will no longer exist. For were they to continue existing though God no longer continued willing them to be, they would be independent; and indeed, it should be noted, they would be so independent that God could no longer destroy them. This I shall now prove to you.

IX. An infinitely wise God can will nothing that is not, as it were, worthy of being willed; He can love nothing that is not lovable. Now, nothingness contains nothing lovable. Hence it cannot be the object of divine volition. Nothingness assuredly lacks sufficient reality – as it has none at all – to have any relation to the action of a God, to an action of infinite worth. Therefore God cannot positively will the annihilation of the universe. It is only creatures who, through lack of power or through error, can take nothingness for the object of their volitions. This is because such an object can be an obstacle to the realization of their desires, or so they imagine. But if you think about it you will clearly see that nothing is more evident than that an infinitely wise and omnipotent God cannot – without contradicting Himself – exercise His power in order to effect nothing! What am I saying? "to effect nothing!" It is to destroy His own work; not to remedy its disorders which He did not put there, but to annihilate those natures He has created. Thus, Aristes, assuming that to annihilate the world it is not enough that God cease willing it to be; assuming it to be further required that God positively will that it no longer exist, I hold the world to be necessary and independent, because God cannot destroy it without renouncing His attributes, and because it is a contradiction for Him to renounce them.

Do not, then, diminish the dependence of creatures, lest you commit the impiety of destroying it completely. As you say, God can annihilate them as He pleases. But this is because He ceases willing what He was free to will. Because He is entirely self-sufficient in Himself, He loves invincibly only His own substance. The will to create the world along with its immanent operations, though eternal and immutable, involves nothing necessary. Just as God was able to form the decree to create the world in time, so He was and will always be able to cease willing the world to exist; not that the act of His decree is capable of either being or not being, but because this immutable and eternal act is perfectly free, and involves the eternal duration of created beings only conditionally. From all eternity God willed, He will continue to will eternally; or, to put it more precisely, God wills continuously – but without variation, without succession, without necessity – everything He will do in the course of time. The act of His eternal decree, though simple and immutable, is necessary only because it is. It cannot not be, only because it is. But it is, only because God wills it. For just as people, at the same time they move their arm, are free not to move it, though on the supposition that it moves there is a contradiction that it does not move; so, as God wills what He wills always and without succession, although His decrees are immutable, they are still perfectly free, because they are necessary only conditionally, take note, only because God is immutable in His designs. But I fear I digress; let us return to our subject. Are you now really convinced that creatures are essentially dependent on the creator; so completely dependent, that they cannot subsist without His influence, that they can continue existing only if God continues to will that they exist?

ARISTES. I have done all I can to combat your reasons. But I surrender. I have nothing to reply to you. The dependence of creatures is entirely different from what I thought.

X. THEODORE. Let us return to what we said, then, and draw some conclusions from it. But be careful that I do not conclude anything that is not clearly contained in the principle.

Creation does not pass, because the conservation of creatures is – on God's part – simply a continuous creation, a single volition subsisting and operating continuously. Now, God can neither conceive nor consequently will that a body exist nowhere, nor that it does not stand in certain relations of distance to other bodies. Thus, God cannot will that this armchair exist, and by this volition create or conserve it, without situating it here, there, or elsewhere. It is a contradiction, therefore, for one body to be able to move another. Further, I claim, it is a contradiction for you to be able to move your armchair. Nor is this enough; it is a contradiction for all the angels and demons together to be able to move a wisp of straw. The proof of this is clear. For no power, however great it be imagined, can surpass or even equal the power of

God. Now, it is a contradiction that God wills this armchair to exist, unless He wills it to exist somewhere and unless, by the efficacy of His will, He puts it there, conserves it there, creates it there. Hence, no power can convey it to where God does not convey it, nor fix nor stop it where God does not stop it, unless God accommodates the efficacy of His action to the inefficacious action of His creatures. This is what must be explained to you, in order to have reason agree with experience and provide you with the understanding of the greatest, the most fruitful and most necessary of all principles, namely: God communicates His power to creatures and unites them with one another, only because He establishes their modalities, occasional causes of the effects which He produces Himself – occasional causes, I say, which determine the efficacy of His volitions as a consequence of the general laws He has prescribed for Himself, in order to make His conduct bear the character of His attributes and to spread throughout His work the uniformity of action necessary both to unite together all the parts that comprise it, and to rescue it from the confusion and irregularity of a kind of chaos in which minds could never understand anything. I am saying this, my dear Aristes, in order to imbue you with ardor and rouse your attention. For since what I have just said concerning the motion and rest of matter may well appear unimportant to you, you may perhaps believe that principles so unimportant and simple cannot lead you to these great and important truths which you have already glimpsed and upon which rests almost all of what I have said to you up to now.

ARISTES. Do not be afraid, Theodore, that I shall lose sight of you. I am following you quite closely, it seems, and you are charming me in a way that seems to send me into raptures. Courage, then. I can stop you if you step too lightly over places too difficult and perilous for me.

XI. THEODORE. Let us suppose, then, Aristes, that God wills that there be a certain body on this floor, a ball for example. His will is realized instantly. Nothing is more mobile than a sphere on a plane; but all the powers imaginable could not move it, unless God intervenes. For once again, insofar as God wills to create or conserve this ball at point A or at some other point you choose – and it is necessary that He put it somewhere – no force can displace it from there. Do not forget this; it is our principle.

ARISTES. I hold to this principle. It is only the creator who can be the mover, only He who gives being to bodies, who can put them in the places they occupy.

THEODORE. Very well. Thus, the motive force of a body is but the efficacy of the will of God, who conserves it successively in different places. On this supposition, let us conceive that this ball is moved and that in the line of its motion it strikes another ball at rest. Experience teaches us that this other ball will be moved inevitably and according to certain proportions which are always exactly observed. Yet it is not the first ball that moves the second. This is clear from our principle. For one body cannot move another without communicating its motive force to it. But the motive force of a moving body is simply the will of the creator who conserves it successively in different places. It is not a quality that belongs to this body. Nothing belongs to it except its modalities, and modalities are inseparable from substances. Therefore bodies cannot move each other, and their encounter or impact is only an occasional cause of the distribution of their motion. For as they are impenetrable, it is a kind of necessity that God, whom I suppose to act always with the same efficacy or quantity of motive force,[1] as it were imparts to the body so struck the motive force of the body which strikes it, in proportion to the magnitude of the impact but according to the law that, when two bodies collide with each other, the stronger one or the one transported with the greater force must overcome the weaker one, and make it rebound without receiving anything from it. I say, 'without receiving anything from the weaker body,' because a perfectly hard body like the one I am assuming cannot simultaneously receive two contradictory impressions or motions in the parts that comprise it. This can happen only to bodies which are either soft or elastic. But it is unnecessary at the moment to go into the specifics of the laws of motion.[*] It suffices that you understand that bodies can move neither themselves nor those with which they collide, as Reason has revealed to us, and that there are certain laws, which we learn from experience, according to which God inevitably moves bodies.

---

[1] In the course of his career Malebranche revised his laws of motion, and in the *Dialogues* there is considerable difference between the first two editions and the third and fourth editions. Cf. *OC* XII 162.

[*] Cf. *Loix des communications des movemens*, in *De la Recherche de la vérité* (end of volume 3 of the 1700 edition). [For the laws of motion as they appeared in the 1700 edition of *De la Recherche de la vérité*, cf. *OC* XVII–1 51–143.]

ARISTES. This seems indisputable to me. But what do you think, Theotimus? You never contradict Theodore.

XII. THEOTIMUS. I have been convinced of these truths for a long time. However, as you want me to challenge Theodore's views, please resolve a small difficulty for me. Here it is. I can certainly understand that a body cannot move itself. But, supposing it to be moved, I maintain it can move another as its true cause, as a cause between which and its effect there is a necessary connection. For supposing that God has not yet established the laws of the communication of motion, certainly there will not yet be any occasional causes. This being so, let body **A** be moved and, in following its line of motion, let it move into body **B**, which I suppose to be concave, like the mold of body **A**. What will happen? Choose.

ARISTES. What will happen? Nothing. For where there is no cause, there can be no effect.

THEOTIMUS. Why nothing? Something new must happen. For either body **B** will be moved after impact, or it will not.

ARISTES. It will not.

THEOTIMUS. So far, so good. But, Aristes, what will become of body **A** upon meeting body **B**? Either it will rebound, or it will not. If it rebounds, there will be a new effect of which **B** will be the cause. If it does not rebound things will be even worse, for there will be a force that is destroyed or at least lacking in action. Hence, the impact of bodies is not an occasional cause, but a very real and true cause, as there is a necessary connection between the impact and whatever effect you choose. Thus ...

ARISTES. Wait a minute, Theotimus. What are you proving? Given that bodies are impenetrable, it is necessary that at the moment of impact God determines His choice in the matter you have confronted me with. That is all; I failed to note this. You do not prove at all that a moving body can, by means of something belonging to it, move another body which it encounters. If God had not yet established the laws of the communication of motion, the nature of bodies – their impenetrability – would oblige Him to make such laws as He judged appropriate; and He would choose those which are the simplest, provided they are sufficient to make the things He willed to form from matter. But it is clear that impenetrability has no efficacy of its own, and that it can merely provide

God, who treats things according to their nature, with an occasion to diversify His action without altering anything in His conduct.

Nevertheless, I am willing to say that a moving body is the true cause of the motion of those bodies it encounters; for we need not quibble over a word. But what is a moving body? It is a body transported by a divine action. The action which transports it can also transport that body which it meets, if it is extended to it. Who doubts this? However, this action – this motive force – does not in any way belong to body. It is the efficacy of the will of Him who creates them or who conserves them successively in different places. Matter is essentially mobile. By nature it has a passive capacity for motion. But it does not have an active capacity, it is actually moved only by the continuous action of the creator. Thus one body cannot move another by an efficacy belonging to its nature. If bodies had in themselves the force to move themselves, the stronger would – as efficient causes – overcome those bodies they encountered. But, as a body is moved only by another body, their encounter is only an occasional cause which, in virtue of their impenetrability, obliges the mover or creator to distribute His action. And because God must act in a simple and uniform manner, He had to formulate laws which were general and as simple as possible, in order that when change was necessary He changed as little as possible and, at the same time, produced an infinity of different effects. This, Theotimus, is how I understand these matters.

THEOTIMUS. You understand them very well.

XIII. THEODORE. Perfectly well. Then we are all agreed on this principle. Let us follow it a while. Thus, Aristes, you cannot yourself move your arm, change place, situation, posture, do good or wrong to others, or effect the least change in the universe. Here you are in the world without a single power, immobile as a rock, as stupid, as it were, as a stump. Let your soul be united to your body as closely as you please, let it thereby connect you to all those that surround you; what benefit will you derive from this imaginary union? What will you do simply to move your fingertip, simply to utter a single syllable? Alas! Without God's assistance you will make only futile efforts, you will form only impotent desires. For, upon reflection, do you really know what must be done in order to pronounce the name of your best friend, in order to flex or straighten those of your fingers of which you make the most use? But let us suppose that you know what the whole world does not know, upon which even some of the learned themselves cannot agree, namely, that one can move one's arm only by means of animal spirits, which, in flowing into the muscles through the nerves, contract them and draw to them the bones to which they are attached. Let us suppose you know anatomy and the workings of your machine as precisely as a watchmaker knows his own work. But recall in any case the principle that only the creator of bodies can be their mover. This principle is sufficient to foil – what am I saying, 'to foil'! – to annihilate all your alleged faculties. For, after all, animal spirits are bodies, however small they might be: they are simply the most subtle part of the blood and humors. Thus, God alone can move these small bodies. He alone is able, and knows how, to make them flow from the brain to the nerves, from the nerves to the muscles, from a muscle to its antagonist; all of which is necessary for the movement of our limbs. Thus, notwithstanding the union of the soul and body such as it pleases you to imagine, you would be dead and motionless were it not that God wills to attune His volitions to yours; to attune His volitions which are always efficacious, to your desires which are always impotent. Here, my dear Aristes, is the solution of the mystery. All creatures are united only to God in an immediate union. They depend essentially and directly only on Him. As they are all equally impotent, they do not depend on each other. It can be said that they are united among themselves, and even that they depend on each other. I grant this, provided it is not understood according to common ideas, provided we agree that it exists only as a consequence of the immutable and continually efficacious volitions of the creator, only as a consequence of the general laws which God has established and by which He governs the ordinary course of His providence. God willed that my arm move at the moment I will it myself. (I am supposing the necessary conditions.) His will is efficacious, it is immutable. From it I derive my power and my faculties. God willed that I have certain sensations, certain emotions, whenever there are certain traces, certain disturbances of the spirits in my brain. In a word, He willed and He wills ceaselessly that the modalities of the mind and body be reciprocal. Therein lies the union and the natural dependence of the two parts of which we are composed. It is simply the mutual reciprocity of our modalities based on the unshakable foundation of divine decrees, decrees which by their efficacy communicate to me the power I have over my body and – through my body – over others; decrees which by their immutability unite me to my body and, through it, to my friends, to my goods, to everything that surrounds me. I derive nothing from my nature, nothing from the imaginary nature of the philosophers. Everything comes from God and His decrees. God has integrated together all His works, without producing any connecting entities. He has subordinated them to one another, without conferring upon them any efficacious qualities. These are vain pretensions of human pride, chimerical productions of the ignorance of philosophers! Having been sensibly influenced in the presence of bodies, and having been internally affected by the feeling of their own efforts, they have failed to discern the invisible operation of the creator, the uniformity of His conduct, the fecundity of His laws, the continuously present efficacy of His volitions, the infinite wisdom of His ordinary providence. Therefore please, my dear Aristes, do not claim any longer that your soul is united to your body more closely than to anything else, since it is immediately united to God alone, since the divine decrees are the indissoluble connections between all the parts of the universe, and the wondrous chain of the subordination of all causes.

XIV. ARISTES. Ah, Theodore! How clear and solid your principles are, and how Christian! Yet how appealing and moving! I am fully imbued with them. What! It is God Himself who is now in our midst, not as a mere onlooker or observer of our good and bad actions, but as the principle of our society, the bond of our friendship, the soul, as it were, of the exchanges and discussions we have with one another. I can speak to you only by means of the efficacy of His power, and can touch and move you only by the motion He communicates to me. I do not even know what the necessary arrangement is of those organs which serve the voice in enunciating what I unhesitatingly say to you. The interplay of these organs is beyond me. The variety of words, tones, measures, generates seemingly infinite detail. God knows this detail; He alone determines its movement at the very moment of my desires. Yes, it is He who exhales the air He himself made me breathe. It is He who produces its vibrations or disturbances by means of my organs. It is He who disperses it externally, and who from it forms these words by which I reach your mind and pour into your heart what mine cannot contain. In effect, it is not me who breathes; I breathe despite myself. It is not I who speak to you; I simply will to speak to you. However, let my breathing depend on me, let me know exactly what is required to explain myself, let me form and enunciate my words. How could they reach you, how could they strike your ears, affect your brain and touch your heart, without the efficacy of that divine power which joins together all the parts of the universe? Yes, Theodore, all this is a necessary consequence of the laws of the union of the soul and body and of the communication of motion. All this depends on these two principles of which I am convinced: it is only the creator of bodies who can be their mover; and God communicates His power to us only through the establishment of certain general laws, whose efficacy we determine by our various modalities. Oh, Theodore! Oh, Theotimus! God alone is the bond of our society. As He is its principle, let Him be its end. Let us not subvert His power. Woe to those who have it serve their criminal passions. Nothing is more sacred than this power. Nothing is more divine. It is a kind of sacrilege to use it profanely. I understand now that this makes the just avenger of crimes serve iniquity. We can do nothing by ourselves. Therefore we should will nothing. We can act only by means of the efficacy of the divine power. Thus, we should will nothing but what accords with the divine law. Nothing is more certain than these truths.

THEODORE. These are excellent conclusions.

XV. THEOTIMUS. These are wonderful principles for morality. But let us return to metaphysics. Our soul is not united to our bodies, the way this is commonly understood. It is united immediately and directly simply to God alone. It is only by the efficacy of His action that we three are here in one another's presence. What am I saying, "in one another's presence"! Rather, we three are united here in conviction, infused by the same truth, animated it seems to me by a single spirit fired, as it were, by the same passion. God joins us together through the body as a consequence of the laws of the communication of motion. He affects us with the same sensations as a result of the laws of the union of the soul and body. But, Aristes, how are we so strongly connected in spirit? Theodore utters some words into your ear. They are simply air, struck by the vocal organs. God transforms, as it were, this air into words, into various sounds. He makes you hear these diverse sounds by the modalities by which He affects you. But the sense of these words –

where do you get this from? Who reveals to you and me the same truths which Theodore contemplates? If the air he displaces while speaking does not contain the sounds you hear, surely it will not contain the truths you understand.

ARISTES. I understand you, Theotimus. It is because we are each united to the universal Reason which enlightens all intellects. I know more than you think. Theodore has already transported me to where you want to guide me. He has persuaded me that there is nothing visible, nothing that can act upon and reveal itself to the mind, except that substance – Reason – which is not only efficacious, but also intelligible. Yes, no created thing can be the immediate object of our knowledge. We see things in this material world which our bodies inhabit, only because our mind, by means of its attention, moves in another world, only because it contemplates the beauties of the archetypal and intelligible world which Reason contains. Just as our bodies live on the earth and partake of the various fruits it yields, so are our minds nourished by the very truths contained in the intelligible and immutable substance of the divine Word. Thus, the words Theodore speaks into my ears advise me, as a consequence of the laws of the union of the soul and the body, to be attentive to the truths he discovers in sovereign Reason. This turns my mind in the same direction as his. I see what he sees because I look where he looks. And through the words I offer in reply to his, although both are devoid of sense, I converse with him and enjoy with him a good common to all. For we are all essentially united to Reason, so united that without it we could not have society with anyone.

THEOTIMUS. Your reply, Aristes, surprises me extremely. Knowing all you have said to me now, how were you able to answer Theodore that we are united to our body more closely than to anything else?

ARISTES. The reason is that we say only what is present in the memory, and because abstract truths do not present themselves to the mind as naturally as what we hear said throughout our life. When I have meditated as much as Theotimus I shall no longer speak mechanically, but I shall measure my words in accordance with the deliverances of inner truth. Thus, I understand now – and as long as I live I shall not forget – that we are united immediately and directly only to God. It is in the light of His wisdom that He reveals to us the magnificence of His works, the model on which He forms them, the immutable art regulating their springs and movements, and it is by the efficacy of His volitions that He unites us to our bodies, and through our bodies to all those bodies surrounding us.

XVI. THEODORE. You could add that it is by the love He has for Himself that He communicates to us this invincible passion we have for the good. But we shall speak of this another time. For now it is enough for you to be quite convinced – quite convinced – that the mind can be immediately and directly united only to God alone; that we can interact with creatures solely by the power of the creator which is communicated to us only as a consequence of His laws; and that we cannot establish a society among ourselves and with Him, except through the Reason which is consubstantial with Him. Once this is supposed, you can certainly see that it is of the utmost importance for us to attempt to gain some knowledge of the attributes of this sovereign Being, as we are so dependent on Him. For in the end He must act in us according to His nature. His way of acting must bear the character of His attributes. Not only must our obligations be related to His perfections, but further still our conduct must be ordered to His, in order for us to adopt the right methods for the execution of our designs and find a combination of causes that promotes them. On this matter faith and experience teach us many truths by the short cut of authority and the most pleasant and easy proofs of sensation. However, none of this yields understanding for us; that must be the fruit and reward of our work and application. Moreover, as we are made to know and love God, it is clear that there is no endeavor preferable to meditation on the divine perfections, which meditation should both infuse us with love and order all the duties of a rational creature.

ARISTES. I can well understand, Theodore, that the worship which God requires of minds is a spiritual worship. It consists in His being known and loved by them, so that we might form judgments about Him which are worthy of His attributes, and might regulate all the movements of our heart in accordance with His volitions. For God is spirit, and He wills to be worshipped in spirit and in truth. However, I must confess that, with respect to the divine perfections, I have the greatest fear of forming judgments which dishonor them. Would it not be better to honor them through silence and admiration, and to occupy ourselves exclusively with the search for truths less sublime and more proportioned to the capacity of our mind?

THEODORE. What do you mean by this, Aristes? You are not thinking. We are created to know and love God, and yet you would have us neither think nor speak of Him, nor I might add, worship Him! It is necessary, you say, to honor Him through silence and admiration. Yes: through a respectful silence which the contemplation of His greatness imposes upon us; through a religious silence to which the brilliance of His majesty reduces us; through, as it were, an enforced silence which derives from our impotence and does not have as its principle a criminal negligence, a misplaced curiosity to know objects far less worthy of our application, rather than Him. What will you admire in the divinity if you know nothing of Him? How will you love Him without contemplating Him? How shall we educate one another in love if we banish from our discourse Him whom you have just recognized as the soul of our relations to each other and the bond of our small company. Surely, Aristes, the more you come to know the sovereign Being, the more you will admire His infinite perfections. Thus, do not fear either to think too much or to speak unworthily about Him, so long as faith guides you. Do not be afraid of passing false judgments concerning Him, provided they always conform to the notion of the infinitely perfect Being. You do not dishonor the divine perfections through judgments unworthy of them, provided you never judge them according to yourself and do not attribute the imperfections and limitations of creatures to the creator. Therefore think on them, Aristes. For my part I shall think on them, and I hope Theotimus will do likewise. This is necessary for the development of the principles which I think we should discuss. Until tomorrow, then, at the usual hour; for it is time I retire.

ARISTES. Goodbye, Theodore. If you please, Theotimus, let the three of us meet again at the agreed time.

THEOTIMUS. I am going with Theodore. But I shall return with him, as you wish ... Oh, Theodore! How changed Aristes is! He is attentive, he no longer jokes, he no longer stands so much on ceremony; in a word, he listens to reason and submits to it in good faith.

THEODORE. This is true. But his prejudices still return to impede him and confound his ideas somewhat. Reason and prejudice issue in turn from his mouth. Sometimes truth makes him speak, sometimes memory plays its part. But his imagination no longer dares to rebel. This bespeaks a solid foundation, and gives me everything to hope for.

THEOTIMUS. What do you want, Theodore! Prejudices do not go away like an old suit one no longer thinks of. It seems to me that we were like Aristes. For we are not born philosophers, we become philosophers. It is necessary to impress these great principles upon him unceasingly, so that he thinks of them so frequently that his mind takes them into possession and, whenever necessary, they come to him perfectly naturally.

THEODORE. Thus far this is what I have been trying to do. But it causes him difficulty, for he loves the detail and variety of thoughts. I ask you always to emphasize the necessity of a good understanding of principles, in order to check the vivacity of his mind; and please do not forget to meditate on the subject of our discussion.

Dialogue VIII
God and His Attributes

THEODORE. Very well, Aristes, how are you? We must know what condition you are in, so that we can accommodate to it what we have to say to you.

ARISTES. I have gone over in my mind what you have told me up until now, and I confess I was unable to resist the evidence of the proofs on which your principles are based. But wanting to meditate on the subject of the divine attributes, which you suggested to us, I encountered so many difficulties there that I became disheartened. I was going to tell you that this material was too sublime or abstract for me; I could not reach it or find any place to grab hold there.

THEODORE. What! You want to say nothing to us?

ARISTES. Because I have nothing good to say, nothing which satisfies me. I shall listen to both of you, if you please.

THEODORE. That does not please us at all. But since you do not want to tell us what you thought, at least follow and tell me your view on what has occurred to me.

ARISTES. Willingly. But Theotimus?

THEODORE. Theotimus will be the judge on the little differences which may well arise from the diversity of our ideas.

THEOTIMUS. The judge! What do you mean by that? It is up to Reason to preside among us and to decide absolutely.

THEODORE. I mean, Theotimus, that you will be the earthly judge through dependence on Reason, and that you can pronounce only according to the laws it prescribes for you as for us. Please, let us not lose time. Simply compare what each of us says with the deliverances of inner truth, to warn and correct whoever goes astray. Let us begin.

Aristes, follow me and stop me only when I pass over difficult matters too lightly.

I. By the divinity we all understand the infinite, Being without restriction, infinitely perfect Being. Now, nothing finite can represent the infinite. Thus it is sufficient to think of God to know He exists. Do not be surprised, Theotimus, if Aristes grants me this. For he already agreed to this before you were here.*

ARISTES. Yes, Theotimus, I am convinced that nothing finite can have enough reality to represent the infinite, that in seeing the finite we cannot discover the infinite which it does not contain. Now I am certain that I see the infinite. Thus the infinite exists, since I see it and I can see it only in itself. As my mind is finite, the knowledge I have of the infinite is finite. I do not comprehend it, I do not get its measure; in fact I am quite certain I shall never be able to get its measure. Not only do I find no end in it, I see moreover that it has none. In short, the perception I have of the infinite is limited, but the objective reality in which my mind gets lost, as it were, has no limits. This is now impossible for me to doubt.

THEOTIMUS. I do not doubt it either.

THEODORE. Granting this, it is clear that as this word 'God' is simply the abbreviated expression for the infinitely perfect Being, there is a contradiction in supposing that we might be mistaken if we attributed to God only what we see clearly belongs to the infinitely perfect Being. For if, after all, we are never deceived when we judge God's works only according to what we clearly and distinctly see in the ideas of them, as God has formed them on the basis of these ideas which are their archetype, it cannot be that they do not naturally represent their nature. For all the more reason we shall never be deceived provided we attribute to God only what we clearly and distinctly see belongs to the infinitely perfect Being, only what we discover not in an idea distinguished from God, but in His very substance. Thus, let us attribute to God or to infinitely perfect Being all perfections, however incomprehensible they appear to us, provided we are certain that they are realities or true perfections; realities and perfections, I say, which do not take after nothingness, which are not limited by imperfections or limitations similar to those of creatures. Therefore take note.

* Dialogue II.

II. God is infinitely perfect Being. Therefore God is independent. Think about this, Aristes, and stop me only when I say something you do not see clearly to be a perfection and to belong to infinitely perfect Being. God is independent. Therefore He is immutable.

ARISTES. "God is independent. Therefore He is immutable!" Why immutable?

THEODORE. Because there can be no effect or change without a cause. Now, God is independent of the efficacy of causes. Thus, if some change were to happen in God, He would be the cause of it Himself. Now, although God is the cause or principle of His volitions or decrees, He has never produced any change in Himself. For His decrees, although perfectly free, are themselves eternal and immutable, as I have already told you.* God made these decrees, or rather He formulates them unceasingly in His eternal wisdom which is the inviolable rule of His volitions. And although the effects of these decrees are infinite and produce thousands and thousands of changes in the universe, these decrees are always the same. This is because the efficacy of these decrees is determined to action only by the circumstances of those causes we call natural and which I believe should be called 'occasional,' for fear of encouraging the dangerous prejudice of a 'nature' and efficacy distinguished from God's will and omnipotence.

ARISTES. I do not understand all this well. God is free and indifferent in respect of, for example, the motion of a particular body, or of any effect you please. If He is indifferent, He can produce that effect or not produce it. That effect is a consequence of those decrees, I grant it. But it is certain that God can not produce it. Thus He can not will to produce it. Hence God is not immutable, since He can change His will and can not will tomorrow what He wills today.

THEODORE. You do not remember, Aristes, what I told you in our last discussion.** God is free and even indifferent with respect to thousands and thousands of effects. He can change His will in the sense that He is indifferent to willing or not willing a particular effect. Note, however, now that you are seated, can you be standing? Absolutely speaking you can, but on our assumption you cannot. For you cannot be standing and seated at the same time. Understand, therefore, that in God there is no succession of thoughts and volitions, that by an eternal and immutable act He knows everything and wills everything He wills.

* Preceding [VIIth] Dialogue, §ix. ** [Dialogue VII,] §ix.

God wills to create the world with a perfect freedom and complete indifference. He wills to formulate His decrees and to establish simple and general laws to govern it in a manner which bears the character of His attributes. But given these decrees, they cannot be changed, not because they are absolutely necessary, but only conditionally. Take note: this is simply because they are given, and because God, in formulating them, knew so well what He was doing that they cannot be revoked. For although He willed some for a time, He did not change His mind and will when that time was up; rather, a single act of His will is referred to the differences of time contained in His eternity. Thus, God does not change, and He cannot change His thoughts, His plans, His volitions. He is immutable; this is one of the perfections of His nature. And nevertheless He is perfectly free in everything He does outside Himself. He cannot change, because whatever He wills He wills without succession by a simple and invariable act. But He is capable of not willing it, because He freely wills whatever He actually wills.

ARISTES. I shall think about what you have told me, Theodore. Let us move on. I believe God is immutable. It seems evident to me that it is a perfection not to be subject to change. That is enough for me. Even when I cannot reconcile God's immutability with His freedom, I believe He possess these two attributes because He is infinitely perfect.

III. THEOTIMUS. Allow me, Theodore, to propose a small difficulty for you. You have just said that the efficacy of God's immutable decrees is determined to action only by the circumstances of the causes called 'natural' and which we term 'occasional.' These are your terms. But what, I ask you, is to become of miracles? The impact of bodies, for example, is the occasional cause of the communication of motion from the striking body to the struck one. What! Cannot God in such a case suspend the effect of the general law of the communication of motion, and has He not often suspended it?

THEODORE. Once for all, my dear Aristes – for I clearly see that you are responsible for Theotimus wanting me to explain myself further, since he fears you did not quite grasp my thought – once for all, Aristes, when I say God always follows the general laws He has prescribed for Himself, I am talking only of His general and ordinary providence. I do not exclude miracles or effects which do not follow from His general laws. But further, Theotimus – it is to you that I now speak – when God performs a miracle and does not act as a consequence of the general laws which are known to us, I maintain either that God acts as a consequence of other laws unknown to us, or that what He does then is determined by certain circumstances He had in view from all eternity in undertaking that simple, eternal, and invariable act which contains both the general laws of His ordinary providence and also the exceptions to these very laws. But these circumstances must not be called occasional causes in the same sense that the impact of bodies, for example, is the occasional cause of the communication of motion, because God did not make general laws in order to regulate uniformly the efficacy of His volitions on the coincidence of these circumstances. For in the exceptions to the general laws God acts sometimes in one way, sometimes in another, though always according to what is required of Him by whichever one of His attributes is, as it were, most valuable to Him at that moment. I mean that if what He owes to His justice is then more important than what He owes to His wisdom or to all His other attributes, in this exception He will follow the path of His justice. For God never acts except according to what He is, except to honor His divine attributes, and to satisfy what He owes Himself. For He is to Himself the source and end of all His volitions, whether He is punishing us, granting us mercy, or rewarding in us His own gifts, the merits we have acquired by His grace. But I fear, Theotimus, that Aristes is not content with our digression. Let us return. In the course of our discussions we must also explain those principles on which depends the explanation of the difficulties you might raise.

God, or the infinitely perfect Being, is thus independent and immutable. He is also all-powerful, eternal, necessary, immense . . .

ARISTES. Slowly. He is all-powerful, eternal, necessary. Yes, these attributes belong to the infinitely perfect Being. But why immense? What do you mean?

IV. THEODORE. I mean that the divine substance is everywhere, not only in the universe, but infinitely beyond. For God is not contained in His work; rather, His work is in Him and subsists in His substance, which conserves it by His all-powerful efficacy. It is in Him that we exist. It is in Him that we have movement and life, as the apostle says: "In him we live, and move, and are."[*]

[*] Acts 17: 28.

ARISTES. But God is not corporeal. Thus, He cannot be spread out everywhere.

THEODORE. It is because He is not corporeal that He can be everywhere. Were He corporeal He would not be able to pervade bodies in the way He pervades them. For it is a contradiction that two feet of extension make only one. As the divine substance is not corporeal, it is not locally extended like bodies, large in an elephant, small in a gnat. All of it is, as it were, everywhere it is, and it is present everywhere; or, rather, everything is in it. For the substance of the creator is the inner place of creatures.

Created extension is to the divine immensity what time is to eternity. All bodies are extended in the immensity of God, as all times succeed one another in His eternity. God is always everything He is without succession in time. He fills everything with His substance without local extension. In His existence there is neither past nor future; everything is present, immutable, and eternal. In His substance there is neither large nor small; everything is simple, equal, and infinite. God created the world, but the volition to create it is not past. God will change the world, but the volition to change it is not in the future. The will of God which was and will be is an eternal and immutable act whose effects change without there being any change in God. In a word, God was not, He will not be, but He is. We could say that God was in past time; but He was then everything He will be in future time. For His existence and duration, if it is permitted to use that term, is completely in eternity, and completely in every passing moment in His eternity. Likewise, God is not partly in heaven and partly on earth. He is completely whole in His immensity, and completely in all the bodies which are locally extended in His immensity; completely in all the parts of matter, though they are infinitely divisible. Or, to speak more precisely, God is not so much in the world as the world is in Him or in His immensity, just as eternity is not so much in time as time is in eternity.

ARISTES. It seems to me, Theodore, that you are explaining an obscure thing by means of another which is not very clear. I do not feel struck by the same evidence as in these past days.

V. THEODORE. I do not claim, Aristes, to make you clearly comprehend the immensity of God and the way in which He exists everywhere. This appears incomprehensible to me as well as to you. But

I do claim to give you some knowledge of God's immensity by comparing it with His eternity. As you granted me that God is eternal, I thought I could convince you that He is immense by comparing the eternity you accept with the immensity you refuse to recognize.

THEOTIMUS. What do you want Theodore to do? He is comparing divine things with divine things. That is the way to explain them, insofar as it is possible. But you compare them with finite things. That is just the way to deceive yourself. The human mind fills no space. Thus the divine substance is not immense. False conclusion. Created extension is larger in a large space than in a small one. Therefore, if God were everywhere He would be larger in a giant than in a pygmy. Another conclusion drawn from the comparison of the infinite with the finite. If you want to judge the divine attributes consult the infinite, the notion of infinitely perfect Being, and do not stop at the ideas of particular and finite beings. Those are the notions which Theodore uses. He does not judge the divine immensity by the idea of creatures either corporeal or spiritual. He knows well that the divine substance is not subject to the imperfections and limitations which are inseparable from created beings. That is why he judges that God is everywhere, and exists nowhere in the way bodies exist.

ARISTES. What! God is there, as it were, in His entirety, and there too, and there, there, there, and everywhere else, and in the spaces we conceive beyond the world; this is incomprehensible.

THEODORE. Yes, God is everywhere, or rather everything is in God, and the world, however large we imagine it, can neither equal nor be compared to Him. This is incomprehensible, I agree, but that is because the infinite surpasses us. What then, Aristes! Is God not here, in your garden, in the sky, and is He not in His entirety everywhere He is? Would you dare deny that God is everywhere?

ARISTES. He is present by His operation. But . . .

THEODORE. How "by His operation"? What kind of reality is God's operation as distinguished and separated from His substance? By "God's operation" you do not mean the effect He produces, for the effect is not the action, but the end of the action. Apparently by "God's operation" you mean the act by which He operates. Now, if the act by which God produces or conserves this chair is here, surely God is here Himself; and if He is here, He must be here completely and thus in all the other respects in which He operates.

ARISTES. I believe, Theodore, that God is in the world in the way you believe your soul is in your body. For in fact I know you do not think that the soul is spread through all the parts of the body. It is in the head, because it reasons there. It is in the arms and feet, because it moves them. Likewise God is in the world because He conserves and governs it.

VI. THEODORE. What prejudices, what obscurities in your comparison! The soul is not in the body nor the body in the soul, although their modalities are reciprocal as a consequence of the general laws of their union. But both are in God, who is the true cause of the reciprocity of their modalities. Minds, Aristes, are in the divine Reason, and bodies are in His immensity; but they cannot be in each other. For mind and body have no essential relation to each other. It is only to God that they have a necessary relation. The mind can think without the body but it cannot know anything except in divine Reason. Body can be extended without the mind but it can be extended only in God's immensity. This is because the qualities of body have nothing in common with those of mind. For body cannot think nor can the mind be extended. But each participates in the divine Being. God, who gives them their reality, possesses it, for He possesses all the perfections of creatures without their limitations. He knows like minds, He is extended like bodies, but all this in a way completely different from his creatures. Thus, God is everywhere in the world and beyond. But the soul is nowhere in bodies. It does not know in the brain, as you imagine. It knows only in the intelligible substance of the divine Word, although it knows in God only because of what happens in a certain portion of matter called the brain. It moves them only because He who by His immensity is everywhere executes the impotent desires of His creatures by His power. Therefore, Aristes, do not say that God is in the world, that He governs, as the soul is in the body it animates. For there is nothing true in your comparison, not only because the soul cannot be in the body nor the body in the soul, but also because minds cannot operate in the bodies they animate and consequently cannot be spread out in them by their operation, as you claim of the divine operation, by which alone, according to you, God is everywhere.

ARISTES. What you are saying now seems very difficult to me. I shall think about it. But, still, please tell me: before the world existed and God operated in it, where was He?

VII. THEODORE. I put this question to you, Aristes, you who would have God in the world only by His operation ... You do not answer. Well, I tell you that before the creation of the world God was where He is at present or where He would be were the world to return to nothingness. He was in Himself. When I tell you that God is in the world and infinitely beyond, you do not enter into my thinking if you believe that the world and those imaginary spaces are, as it were, the place occupied by the infinite substance of the divinity. God is in the world only because the world is in God. For God is only in Himself, only in His immensity. If He creates new spaces, He does not thereby acquire a new presence because of these spaces. He does not increase His immensity, He does not make Himself a place. He is eternally and necessarily where these spaces are created, but He does not exist there locally, like these spaces.

Extension, Aristes, is a reality, and all realities are found in the infinite. Thus, God is extended as well as bodies, since God possesses all absolute realities or all perfections. But God is not extended like bodies. For, as I just told you, He does not have the limitations and imperfections of His creatures. God knows, as well as minds, but He does not think like them. To Himself He is the immediate object of His knowledge. In Him there is neither succession nor variety of thoughts. One of His thoughts does not contain, as it does in you, the negation of all the others. They do not mutually exclude one another. Likewise, God is extended as well as bodies, but there are no parts in His substance. One part does not contain, as in bodies, the negation of any other, and the place of His substance is but His substance itself. He is always one and always infinite, perfectly simple and composed, as it were, of all realities or all perfections. This is because the true God is Being and not a particular being, just as He said Himself to His servant Moses, through the mouth of the angel invested with His powers.[1] He is Being without restriction, not finite being, a being composed, as it were, of being and nothingness. Thus, attribute to God, whom we adore, only what you conceive in infinitely perfect Being. Divest Him only of the finite, only of what derives from nothingness. And although you do not clearly understand everything I am telling you, as I do not understand it myself, at least you understand that God is such as I

---

[1] Allusion to Exodus 3: 14.

represent Him to you. For you should know that, in order to judge worthily of God, we must attribute to Him only incomprehensible attributes. That is evident since God is the infinite in every sense, since nothing finite pertains to Him, and since anything that is infinite in every sense is incomprehensible in every respect to the human mind.

ARISTES. Ah, Theodore, I begin to recognize that I was making very unworthy judgments about God, because I judged Him confusedly, in relation to my own self or on the basis of ideas which can represent only creatures. It seems evident to me that any judgment not based on the notion of the infinitely perfect Being, the incomprehensible Being, is not worthy of the divinity. Surely, if the pagans had not abandoned this notion they would not have made false divinities from their chimeras, and if Christians always followed this notion of Being or the infinite, which is naturally imprinted on our mind, they would not speak of God as some do.

VIII. THEOTIMUS. You appear, Aristes, quite content with what Theodore has just told you, viz. that the attributes of God are incomprehensible in all ways. But I fear there is an equivocation there. For it seems to me that we clearly conceive an extension which is immense and has no limits. The mind cannot comprehend or measure this extension, I grant. But it clearly knows its nature and properties. Now, what is the immensity of God if not an infinite intelligible extension not simply by which God is everywhere, but in which we see spaces which have no limits. Thus, it is not true that the immensity of God is in every sense incomprehensible to the human mind, since we know intelligible extension quite clearly, so clearly that it is in and by it that geometers discover all their proofs.

ARISTES. It seems to me, Theotimus, that you have not properly grasped Theodore's thought. But I have not meditated enough on this matter; I cannot properly explain to you what I only glimpse. Please, Theodore, answer for me.

THEODORE. What, Theotimus! Are you confounding the divine immensity with intelligible extension? Do you not see that there is an infinite difference between these two things? God's immensity is His very substance spread out everywhere and in its entirety everywhere, filling all places without local extension. That is what I maintain is completely incomprehensible. But intelligible extension is simply the substance of God insofar as it is representative of bodies and participable by them, with the limitations or imperfections which pertain to them and are represented by this same intelligible extension, which is their idea or archetype. No finite mind can comprehend the immensity of God, nor all those other attributes or ways of being of the divinity, if I may be permitted to speak so. Those ways of being are forever infinite in every sense, forever divine, and consequently forever incomprehensible. But nothing is clearer than intelligible extension. Nothing is more intelligible than the ideas of bodies since it is by them that we know quite distinctly not the nature of God, but the nature of matter. Surely, Theotimus, if you judge God's immensity by the idea of extension, you will be giving God a corporeal extension. Make that extension as infinite, as immense as you will; still you will not exclude from it the imperfections which this idea represents. The substance of God will not be completely whole everywhere it is. Judging God by the idea of creatures and by the vilest of creatures, you corrupt the notion of the infinitely perfect Being. Thus, both of you be careful of the judgments you make about what I am telling you about the divinity. For once and for all I warn you that when I speak of God and His attributes, if you understand what I am telling you, if you have an idea of it which is clear and proportioned to the finite capacity of your mind, either it is because I am then mistaken, or it is because you do not understand what I mean. For all the absolute attributes of the divinity are incomprehensible to the human mind, though it can clearly comprehend what there is in God relative to creatures, namely, the intelligible ideas of all possible works.

THEOTIMUS. I can well see, Theodore, that I was mistaken in confounding intelligible extension with God's immensity. This extension is not the divine substance spread out everywhere, but it is that substance insofar as it is representative of bodies and participable by them in the way corporeal creatures can participate imperfectly in being. Nevertheless I knew well that an infinite corporeal extension, as some conceive the universe, which they compose of an infinite number of vortices, would still involve nothing divine. For God is the infinite in extension, He is the infinite without qualification; He is Being without restriction. Now, it is a property of the infinite, which is incomprehensible to the human mind, as I have often heard you affirm, simultaneously to be one and all things; to be composed, as it were, of an infinity of perfections, and so simple that each perfection it possesses contains all the others without any real distinction. Certainly, this property pertains less to the material universe and to the parts of which it is composed, than to the substance of the soul which, without any composition of parts, can receive various modalities at the same time – which is a faint outline of the divine simplicity and universality.

THEODORE. You are right, Theotimus. There is no substance more imperfect, more remote from the divinity, than matter, even if it is infinite. It corresponds perfectly to the intelligible extension which is its archetype, but it corresponds only very imperfectly to the divine immensity; and it does not correspond at all to the other attributes of the infinitely perfect Being.

IX. ARISTES. What you are saying here makes me really understand that that unholy man of our time, who made his God from the universe, did not have a God.[2] He was a true atheist. But I cannot but think of a number of good people who, for want of a little philosophy, have very unworthy views about the divinity. Their God is not the universe, He is the creator of the universe. And that is almost everything they know about Him. That would be a lot, if they left it at that, without corrupting the notion of the infinite. But, in truth, I pity them when I think of the idea they form of the incomprehensible Being. Theotimus was quite right to tell me that people naturally 'humanize' everything. Still, were they simply to incarnate the divinity, as it were, by endowing it with the qualities belonging to them, that would be excusable. But there are some who divest it of all its incomprehensible attributes and of all those characteristics essential to infinitely perfect Being, except power; and they share this with what they call 'nature,' in such a way that although they leave the best part of it for God, they deprive Him of any exercise of it.

THEODORE. That happens, Aristes, for fear of tiring, or at least of debasing the divine majesty by petty concerns, by actions unworthy of His consideration and greatness. For we naturally believe that God must be content with the judgments we make about Him, when we make Him such as we would like to be ourselves. Human beings are

---

[2]   The allusion is almost certainly to Benedict Spinoza (1632–77). Malebranche's views on Spinoza and his attempts to distinguish his own position from Spinoza's are best seen in his correspondence with J. J. Dortous de Mairan (1678–1771), who claimed that Malebranche's doctrine of intelligible extension effectively leads to Spinozism, cf. *OC* XIX 852ff.

always imbued with the inner feeling they have of what is transpiring in their minds and hearts. They can only sense confusedly what they are and hope to be. Thus, they quite naturally project themselves onto the objects of their knowledge, and by their humanity measure not only everything surrounding them, but even the infinite substance of the divinity. It is true that the notion of the infinitely perfect Being is deeply engraved in our mind. We never exist without thinking of Being. But far from employing this vast and immense notion of Being without restriction to measure thereby the divinity which is continually represented to us, we consider this immense notion as a pure fiction of our mind. This is because, Aristes, Being in general does not strike our senses and we judge the reality and solidity of objects by the force by which they affect us.

ARISTES. I understand all this well, Theotimus. It is exactly what Theodore told me seven or eight days ago. My mind finds no hold on the abstract ideas you are putting forward to me. They do not strike me sensibly. But I do not thereby judge that they are only pure phantoms. I believe they are sublime truths to which we can attain only by silencing our imagination and senses, only by going beyond ourselves. And I am firmly resolved in what follows no longer to judge God by myself nor by the ideas which represent creatures, but solely by the notion of the infinitely perfect Being. Please continue, Theodore, to question and instruct me.

X. THEODORE. Very well, let us continue. You believe that God is good, wise, just, merciful, patient, and stern.

ARISTES. Careful. These terms are quite common, and I mistrust them. I believe that God is wise, good, just, and clement, and that He has all the other qualities Scripture attributes to Him. But I do not know whether all those who utter these words conceive the same things. The infinitely perfect Being is good, just, merciful! To me, that seems obscure. Define these terms for me.

THEODORE. Oh, Aristes! You fear a surprise. You do well. When philosophizing about subtle and sublime matters we must be afraid of equivocations, and the most common terms are not the most exempt from equivocation. These words must therefore be defined. However, that is not so easy. First give me an answer that can serve to explain them. Do you think that God knows and wills?

ARISTES. As for that, yes. I have no doubt whatsoever that God knows and wills.

THEODORE. How is it that you do not doubt this? Is it because you know and will yourself?

ARISTES. No, Theodore. It is because I know that knowing and willing are perfections. For although I sense, suffer, and doubt, I am certain that God does not sense or doubt. And when I say that God knows and wills, I do not claim that He does so as people do. I claim only generally that God wills and knows, and leave it to you and Theotimus to explain how He does this.

THEODORE. What do you mean by "how He does this"? All the divine ways are incomprehensible. We do not know how we ourselves know nor how we will, for having no clear idea of our soul, we cannot comprehend anything clearly in our own modalities. All the more reason why we shall not explain to you exactly how God knows and wills. Nevertheless, consult the notion of the infinitely perfect Being. See if I am following it. For I tell you outright that God is His own light unto Himself, that in His substance He finds the essences of all beings and all their possible modalities, and in His decrees He finds their existence and all their actual modalities.

ARISTES. It seems to me you are not venturing much.

XI. THEODORE. Nor do I claim to. But as you accept this principle, let us draw out its consequences. In Himself God knows everything He knows. Therefore, all truths are in God, because since He is infinitely perfect there are none which escape His knowledge. Thus, His substance contains all intelligible relations, for truths are but real relations and falsehoods are imaginary relations. Therefore, God is not only wise, but wisdom; not only knowing, but knowledge; not only enlightened, but the light which illumines His own self and indeed all intellects. For it is in His very light that you see what I see and that He Himself sees what we both see. I see that all the diameters of a circle are equal. I am certain that God Himself sees it, and that all minds either actually see it or can see it. Yes, I am certain that God sees exactly the same thing I see, the same truth, the same relation I now perceive between two and two, and four. Now, God sees nothing except in His substance. Thus, this very truth which I see, I see in Him. All this you know, Aristes, and have already agreed to it. But these principles escape so easily, and are moreover of such great importance, that we do not lose time by recalling them to the mind and making them familiar to us.

ARISTES. Here, then, is one of the great differences between the way God knows and the way we know. God knows all things in Himself, and we know nothing in ourselves. We know nothing except in a substance which is not ours. God is wise by His own wisdom; but we become wise only through the union we have with the eternal, immutable, necessary Wisdom common to all intellects. For it is quite clear that a mind as limited as ours cannot find in its own substance the ideas or archetypes of all possible beings and of their infinite relations. But, further, I am so certain that people, angels and even God see the same truths I see, that I see it is impossible for me to doubt that it is the same light which illumines all minds.

XII. THEOTIMUS. Surely, Aristes, if God sees exactly what we see when we think that two times two are four, it is in God alone that we see this truth, for God sees it only in His wisdom. He even sees that we are now thinking of it, but only in His decrees and in His eternity, for He does not derive His knowledge from what presently takes place in His creatures. But could we not say that minds do not see the same, but similar truths? God sees that two times two are four. You see it, I see it. Here are three similar truths, not a single and unique truth.

ARISTES. There are three similar perceptions of one and the same truth, but how are there three similar truths? And who told you they are similar? Have you compared your ideas with mine and with those of God, so as to recognize the resemblance clearly? Who told you that tomorrow, that through all the centuries, you will see as you do today that two times two are four? Who told you that even God cannot make minds capable of seeing clearly that two times two are not four? Surely it is because you see the same truth I see, but by a perception which is not mine, though perhaps similar to mine. You see a truth common to all minds, but by a perception which belongs to you alone; for our perceptions, our sensations, all our modalities, are particular. You see an immutable, necessary, eternal truth. For you are so certain of the immutability of your ideas that you are not afraid of seeing them all changed tomorrow. As you know that they exist before you do, so you are quite assured they will never disappear. Now, if your ideas are eternal and immutable, it is evident that they can be found only in the eternal and immutable substance of the divinity. This cannot be disputed. It is in God alone that we see the truth. It is in Him alone that is found the light which illumines Him and all intellects. He is wise by His own wisdom, and we can be so only through the union we have with Him. Let us not dispute these principles. They are evident, it seems to me, and the foundation of the certainty we find in the sciences.

THEOTIMUS. I am quite pleased, Aristes, to see you are convinced not only that God's power is the efficacious cause of our knowledge – for I think you do not doubt this – but also that His wisdom is its formal cause which enlightens us immediately and without the intervention of any creature. I certainly see that Theodore has discussed this matter with you. I am also indebted to him for that which you owe him and which he claims to draw from St. Augustine.[*]

THEODORE. Thus, we all agree that God is infinitely wise and that He is so essentially and through Himself, by the necessity of His being; that people can be wise only through the light of the divine Wisdom; that this light is communicated to them as a consequence of their attention, which is the occasional cause that determines the efficacy of the general laws of the union of their mind with universal Reason, as we shall explain in the following. Let us now prove that God is just.

XIII. God contains in the simplicity of His being the ideas of all things and their infinite relations: in general, all truths. Now, in God we can distinguish two kinds of truths or relations: relations of magnitude and relations of perfection, speculative truths and practical truths, relations which by their evidence require only judgment, and other relations which also excite movement. It is not the case, however, that relations of perfection can be clearly known unless they are expressed through relations of magnitude. But we need not stop at this. Two times two are four: this is a relation of equality in magnitude, it is a speculative truth which excites no movement in the soul, neither love nor hate, neither esteem nor contempt, etc. Human beings are more valuable than beasts: this is a relation of inequality in perfection, which requires not simply that the mind yield to it, but that love and esteem be regulated by the knowledge of this relation or truth. Thus, pay attention.

God contains in Himself all relations of perfection. Now, He knows and loves everything He contains in the simplicity of His being. Thus,

[*] Cf. *Réponse au Livre des vrayes & fausses Idées*, Chs. 7 & 21 [*OC* VI 63–9; 143–50].

He esteems and loves all things to the extent they are lovable and estimable. He invincibly loves the immutable order, which consists and can only consist in the relations of perfection obtaining between His attributes and between the ideas He contains in His substance. Therefore He is just essentially and through Himself. He cannot sin because, loving Himself invincibly, He cannot but render justice to His divine perfections, to everything He is, and to everything He contains. He cannot even will positively and directly to produce some disorder in His work, because He esteems all creatures according to the degree of perfection in their archetypes. For example, He cannot without reason will that the mind be subject to the body, and if this occurs it is because at present human beings are not as God made them. He cannot favor injustice, and if this is so it is because the uniformity of His conduct must not depend on the irregularity of ours. The time for His vengeance will come. He cannot will what corrupts His work, and if there are monsters which disfigure it this is because He renders greater honor to His attributes through the simplicity and generality of His ways than through the exclusion of the defects which He permits in the universe, or those which He produces there as a consequence of the general laws He has established for effects better than the generation of monsters, as we shall explain in the following. Thus, God is just in Himself, just in His ways, just essentially; because all His volitions are necessarily in conformity with the immutable order of the justice He owes to Himself and to His divine perfections.

However, human beings, on their own, are not just. For the immutable order of justice, which encompasses all the relations of perfection of all possible beings and all their qualities, is found only in God, and in no way in our own modalities. If people loved themselves by a movement of which they themselves were the cause, far from their self-love being able to make them just, it would corrupt them infinitely more than the self-love of the most villainous people. For there has never been a soul so black and possessed of a self-love so disordered, that the beauty of the immutable order could not move it on certain occasions. Thus, we are perfectly just only when, seeing in God what God sees in Himself, we judge things as He does, and we esteem and love what He loves and esteems. Far from being just by ourselves, then, we are perfectly just only when, delivered from this body which confuses all our ideas, we see without obscurity the eternal law on the basis of which we shall precisely regulate all the judgments and movements of our heart. It is not that we cannot say that those who possess charity are truly just, although they often form quite unjust judgments. They are just in the disposition of their heart. But they are not just strictly speaking, because they do not know precisely all the relations of perfection which must regulate their esteem and love.

XIV. ARISTES. I understand, Theodore, because you are telling me here that justice as well as truth live, as it were, eternally in an immutable nature. The just and the unjust, as well as the true and the false, are not inventions of the human mind, as certain corrupt minds maintain.[3] People, they say, have made laws for their mutual conservation. It is on the basis of self-love that they have founded them. They agree among themselves and are thereby obligated. For people who break the agreement, discovering themselves weaker than the other contracting parties, find themselves among enemies who satisfy their self-love by punishing them. Thus, they should observe the laws of the country in which they live from self-love, not because they are just in themselves, for they say that overseas entirely contrary ones are observed, but because in submitting to them they have nothing to fear from those who are stronger. According to them, everything is permitted to everyone by nature. Each individual has the right to everything, and if I cede my right it is because the force of competitors obliges me to do so. Thus, self-love is the rule of my actions. My law is an external power, and were I the stronger I would by nature recover all my rights. Can anything more brutal and insane be said? Force has given the lion control over the other animals; and I grant that it is often by force that people usurp it over one another. But to believe that this is permitted and that the stronger has the right to everything without ever being able to commit an injustice, is surely to place oneself among the animals and to make an assembly of brute beasts out of human society. Yes, Theodore, I agree that the immutable order of justice is a law from which even God can never be exempted, and on the basis of which all minds must regulate their conduct. God is just essentially and by the necessity of His being. But let us consider just whether He is good,

---

[3]   The likely target of Malebranche's attack here is Thomas Hobbes (1588–1679).

merciful, forbearing; for it seems to me that all that can scarcely be reconciled with the severity of His justice.

XV. THEODORE. You are right, Aristes. God is neither good, nor merciful, nor forbearing, according to common ideas. These attributes, as they are ordinarily conceived, are unworthy of the infinitely perfect Being. But God does possess these qualities in the sense that Reason teaches us this and Scripture, which cannot contradict itself, has us believe it. To explain all this more distinctly, let us first see whether God is essentially just in the sense that He necessarily rewards good actions and unfailingly punishes everyone who offends Him or who injures, as it were, His attributes.

ARISTES. I do indeed see, Theodore, that if creatures are capable of offending God He will not fail to avenge Himself, He who loves Himself by the necessity of His being. But that God should be offended by this does not seem conceivable to me. And if that were possible, as He loves Himself necessarily, He would never have given being, or at least this freedom or power, to creatures capable of resisting Him. Is this not evident?

THEODORE. You are raising for me, Aristes, a difficulty which will soon be explained. Follow me, please, without forestalling me. Is it not clear from what I have just told you that the immutable order is the law of God, the inviolable rule of His volitions, and that He cannot prevent Himself from loving things in proportion as they are lovable?

ARISTES. That is what you have just proved.

THEODORE. Thus, God cannot will that His creatures do not love according to this same immutable order. He cannot exempt them from following this law. He cannot will that we love more what deserves to be loved less. What, you hesitate! Does this not appear certain to you?

ARISTES. I find some difficulty in it. I am convinced by a kind of inner feeling that God cannot will that we love and esteem more what deserves to be loved and esteemed less; but I do not see it very clearly. For what is our love and esteem to God? Nothing at all. Perhaps we wish to be esteemed and loved because we all need one another. But God is so above His creatures that apparently He takes no interest in the judgments we pass on Him and His works. This has at least some plausibility.

THEODORE. It has only too much plausibility for corrupted minds.

It is true, Aristes, that God does not fear and hopes for nothing from our judgments. He is independent, He is abundantly self-sufficient. However, He necessarily takes an interest in our judgments and in the movements of our heart. Here is the proof of this. Minds have a will or are capable of willing or loving only because of the natural and invincible movement toward the good which God constantly impresses on them. Now, God acts in us only because He wills to act, and He can will to act only through His will, only through the love He bears for Himself and His divine perfections. And it is the order of these divine perfections which is, properly speaking, His law, since He is just essentially and by the necessity of His being, as I have just proved to you. He cannot, therefore, will that our love, which is simply the effect of His own, be contrary to His, or tend where His does not tend. He cannot will that we love more what is less lovable. He wills necessarily that the immutable order, which is His natural law, is ours as well. He can exempt neither Himself nor us from it. And since He made us such that we can either follow or not follow this natural and indispensable law, we must be such that we can be punished or rewarded. Yes, Aristes, if we are free, it follows that we can be either happy or unhappy, and if we are capable of happiness or of unhappiness, this is a certain proof that we are free. People whose hearts are disordered by the poor use of their freedom share in the order of the justice which God owes His divine perfections, if these sinners are unhappy in proportion to their disorders. Now, God invincibly loves order. Thus, He unfailingly punishes whoever violates it. This is not because sinners offend God, in the sense in which humans offend one another, nor because God punishes them out of the pleasure He finds in vengeance. But it is because God can act only according to what He is, according to the demands of the immutable order of the necessary relations of everything He contains, the character of which the disposition of the parts of the universe must bear. Thus, God is not indifferent with respect to the punishment of our disorders. He is neither clement, nor merciful, nor good, according to common ideas, since He is just essentially and through the natural and necessary love He has for His divine perfections. He can defer reward and penalty as the order of His providence requires or permits; this requires Him ordinarily to follow the general laws He has established to govern the world in a manner which bears the character of His attributes. But He cannot exempt Himself from rendering to people, sooner or later, according to their actions. God is good to the good and wicked, as it were, to the wicked, as Scripture says: "And with the elect thou wilt be elect: and with the perverse thou wilt be perverted."* He is clement and merciful, but in and through His Son: "For God so loved the world, as to give his only begotten Son; that whosoever believeth in him, may not perish, but may have life everlasting."** He is good to the sinners in this sense, that through Jesus Christ He gives them the graces necessary to change the wicked disposition of their heart, in order that they cease being sinners, that they do good works and that, having become good and just, He can be good to them, pardon them their sins in view of the atonement of Jesus Christ, and crown His own gifts or the rewards they have acquired through the good use of His grace. But God is always severe, always an exact observer of the eternal laws, always acting according to what He is, according to the requirements of His own attributes or of that immutable order of the necessary relations of the divine attributes which His substance contains and which He loves invincibly and through the necessity of His being. All this, Aristes, conforms to Scripture as well as to the notion everyone has of the infinitely perfect Being, though it does not at all accord with the crude ideas of those stupid and hardened sinners who desire a humanely affable and indulgent God, or a God who does not meddle in our affairs and who is indifferent to the life we lead.

ARISTES. I do not believe we can doubt these truths

THEODORE. Consider them well, Aristes, in order to remain convinced of them, not simply by a kind of inner feeling by which God inwardly persuades all those whose heart is not hardened and entirely corrupted, but also by an evidence such that you can demonstrate it to those rare geniuses who believe that in self-love they have found the true principles of natural morality.

* Psalm 17: 27.   ** John 3: 16.

Dialogue IX

God always acts according to His nature. He has done everything for His glory in Jesus Christ, and He has not formed His plans without regard for the ways of executing them.

I. THEODORE. What do you think today, Aristes, of what we were talking about yesterday? Have you properly contemplated the notion of the infinite, of Being without restriction, of the infinitely perfect Being? And can you now envisage it in a completely pure way, without endowing it with the ideas of creatures, without as it were embodying it, without limiting it, without corrupting it to accommodate it to the weakness of the human mind?

ARISTES. Ah, Theodore, how difficult it is to separate the ideas of particular beings from the notion of Being! How difficult it is not to attribute to God what we sense in ourselves! We continually humanize the divinity, we naturally limit the infinite. This is because the mind wishes to comprehend what is incomprehensible, it wishes to see the invisible God. It seeks Him in the ideas of creatures, it fixes on its own sensations which touch and penetrate it. But how far all this is from representing the divinity! And what strange judgments are made about the attributes of God and His adorable providence by those people who judge the divine perfections by the inner feeling of what happens in themselves! I glimpse what I am telling you, but I still do not see it well enough to explain it.

THEODORE. You have meditated, Aristes. I can tell it by your answer. You understand that in order to judge soundly concerning the divine attributes and the rules of providence we must continually remove the ideas of particular beings from the notion of Being, and never consult our own inner feeling. That is enough. Let us stay our course, and let us all three guard against striking that dangerous reef of judging the infinite by something finite.

ARISTES. We shall surely strike it, Theodore, for all currents are carrying us there. I have felt it since yesterday.

THEODORE. I believe so, Aristes. But perhaps we shall not be wrecked by it. At least let us not strike it thoughtlessly, like most people. I hope that by our mutual vigilance we shall avoid a good number of the dangerous errors into which people rush blindly. Let us not pander to our natural laziness, Aristes. Be brave! Our common master, who is the author of our faith, will give us some understanding of the infinite, if we know how to question Him with a serious attention and with the respect and submission due to His word and to the infallible authority of His church. Therefore let us begin.

II. Yesterday, Aristes, you agreed that God knows and wills, not because we know and will, but because knowing and willing are true perfections. What do you think of that now? Today I plan to consider the divinity in terms of His ways, and as going outside of Himself, as it were, as assuming the plan of diffusing Himself in the production of His creatures. Thus, we must be sure that God knows and wills, since without that it is impossible to understand Him producing anything outside of Himself. For how would He act wisely without knowledge? How would He form the universe without willing it? Do you believe, Aristes, that He who is self-sufficient is capable of forming any desire?

ARISTES. You question me in such a way that you always give rise to new doubts in me. I see that this is because you want neither to surprise me nor to leave behind any refuge for our prejudices. Very well then, Theodore, I have no doubt at all that God knows, but I doubt that He can ever will anything. For what could He will, He who is fully sufficient unto Himself? We wish for other things, but that is a sign of our poverty. Not having what we need, we desire it. But the infinitely perfect Being can will nothing, can desire nothing, since He sees perfectly that He lacks nothing.

THEODORE. Oh, oh, Aristes! You surprise me. "God can will nothing." What! Can the infinitely perfect Being have created us despite

Himself or without having even willed it? We exist, Aristes, this is an established fact.

ARISTES. Yes, we exist, but we are not made. Our nature is eternal. We are a necessary emanation of the divinity. We constitute part of Him. The infinitely perfect Being is the universe; it is the aggregate of all that is.

THEODORE. Again!

ARISTES. Do not think, Theodore, that I am impious and demented enough to yield to these daydreams. But I am very glad that you teach me to refute them. For I have heard there are minds corrupted enough to let themselves be captivated by them.

THEODORE. I do not know, Aristes, whether all that is now said of certain people is altogether true, nor even whether those ancient philosophers, who dreamed up the opinion you are putting forward, ever believed it to be true. For although there are few extravagances of which people are incapable, I would readily believe that those who produce such chimeras are not persuaded of them. For even the author who has revived this impiety agrees that God is the infinitely perfect Being.[1] And that being so, how could he believe that all created beings are but parts or modifications of the divinity? Is it a perfection to be unjust in one's parts, unhappy in one's modifications, ignorant, demented, impious? There are more sinners than good people, more idolaters than believers. What disorder, what discord between the divinity and its parts! What a monster, Aristes, what an appalling and ridiculous chimera! A God necessarily hated, blasphemed, scorned, or at least unknown by the better part of what He is. For how few people would think of recognizing such a divinity? A God who is necessarily either unhappy or unfeeling in most of His parts or modifications, a God who punishes or exacts vengeance on Himself. In a word, an infinitely perfect being nonetheless comprising all the disorders of the universe. What notion is more full of visible contradictions! Surely if there are people capable of constructing a God on the basis of so monstrous an idea, it is either because they do not want to have one or they are minds born to seek all the properties of a triangle in the idea of a circle. Believe me, Aristes, never has someone of good sense been truly persuaded of this madness, although several people have professed

---

[1]   Malebranche is likely referring to Spinoza.

it as if they were truly convinced by it. For self-love is so bizarre that it can indeed provide us with a motive to confide that view to our companions in debauchery, and to want to appear sincerely convinced of it. But it is impossible to believe it to be true, however little we are capable of reasoning and of fearing that we err. Those who maintain it cannot be inwardly persuaded of it, unless the corruption of their heart has so blinded them that it would be a waste of time to attempt to enlighten them. Let us therefore return to our subject, Aristes.

III. We exist: this is an established fact. God is infinitely perfect. Thus, we depend on Him. We do not exist despite Him. We exist only because He wills that we exist. But how can God will that we exist, He who has no need of us? How can a Being who lacks nothing, who is entirely self-sufficient, will anything? This is what creates the difficulty.

ARISTES. It seems to me that it is easy to resolve it. For we need simply say that God did not create the world for Himself, but for us.

THEODORE. But us? For whom did He create us?

ARISTES. For Himself.

THEODORE. The difficulty returns. For God has no need of us.

ARISTES. Therefore let us say, Theodore, that God made us simply out of pure goodness, pure love for us.

THEODORE. Let us not say that, Aristes, at least not without explanation. For it seems evident to me that the infinitely perfect Being loves Himself infinitely, loves Himself necessarily; that His will is but the love He has for Himself and for His divine perfections; that the movement of His love cannot, as with us, come to Him from without, nor consequently lead Him outside Himself; that being uniquely the principle of His action, He must be its end; in short, that in God all love other than self-love would be disordered or contrary to the immutable order which He contains and which is the inviolable law of the divine volitions. We can say that God has made us out of pure goodness in the sense that He has made us without needing us. But He made us for Himself. For God cannot will except through His will, and His will is simply the love He bears for Himself. The reason, the motive, the end of His decrees can be found only in Him.

ARISTES. I find accepting your arguments difficult, although they appear evident to me.

THEOTIMUS. Do you not see, Aristes, that it humanizes the

divinity to seek the motive and end of His action outside of Him? But if this thought of having God act for people solely out of pure goodness appeals to you so much, how is it that there are twenty times, a hundred times more damned than elect?

ARISTES. That is because of the sin of the first man.

THEOTIMUS. Yes. But would God not prevent this sin which is so disastrous for the creatures He made,* and made out of pure goodness?

ARISTES. He had His reasons.

THEOTIMUS. Thus, in Himself God has good reasons for everything He does, reasons which do not always accord with a certain idea of goodness and love which is quite pleasant to our self-love but which is contrary to the divine law, to that immutable order which contains all the good reasons God can have.

ARISTES. But, Theotimus, since God is self-sufficient, why adopt the plan to create the world?

THEOTIMUS. God has His reasons, His end, His motive, all in Himself. For prior to His decrees what could there be to determine Him to formulate them? As God is self-sufficient, it is with a complete freedom that He is determined to create the world. For if God had need of His creatures, then because He loves Himself invincibly He would produce them necessarily. Yes, Aristes, all that we can legitimately conclude from the fact that God is self-sufficient is that the world is not a necessary emanation of the divinity, which faith teaches us. But to imagine that the divine abundance can render God impotent is to go against an established fact and to deprive the creator of the glory He will derive eternally from His creatures.

IV. ARISTES. How so, Theotimus? Is it because God created the world because of the glory He might derive from it? If this glory were the motive which determined the creator, then we have something external to God which determines Him to act. How does it come about that God is deprived of this glory for an eternity? "Glory"! What do you mean by that word? Surely, Theotimus, you are entering on a path from which you will have difficulty extricating yourself.

THEOTIMUS. This path is difficult. But, Theodore, whoever negotiates it successfully will not leave me stranded there.

ARISTES. What, Theodore! God made the universe for His glory.

* Cf. *Conversations chrétiennes*, 1702 edition, pp. 64ff. [*OC* IV 45ff.].

You approve this thought so human and so unworthy of the infinitely perfect Being! Please answer instead of Theotimus; explain yourself.

THEODORE. It is here, Aristes, that much attention and vigilance is required, not to strike that reef you discern. Be careful that I am not wrecked on it.

When architects have constructed a comfortable and architecturally excellent building, they derive a secret satisfaction from it, because their work bears witness to their skill in their art. Thus, we can say that the beauty of their work does them honor, because it bears the character of the qualities in which they take pride, qualities they esteem and love and are pleased to possess. When, moreover, it happens that someone stops to contemplate their building and to admire its arrangement and proportions, the architects are proud of it a second time, and this pride is still founded principally on the love and esteem they have for the qualities they possess and would be happy to possess to a more eminent degree. For if they believed that the profession of architect were unworthy of them, if they scorned this art or science, their work would cease to do them honor, and those who praised them for having built it would shame them.

ARISTES. Be careful, Theodore; you are going straight for the reef.

THEODORE. All this, Aristes, is but a comparison. Follow me. It is certain that God necessarily loves Himself and all His qualities. Now it is evident that He can act only according to what He is. Thus, His work bears the character of the attributes by which He glorifies Himself and does Himself honor. As God esteems and loves Himself invincibly He finds His glory and takes gratification in a work which in some way expresses His excellent qualities. Here, then, is a sense in which God acts for His glory. And, as you see, this glory is not external to Him, for it is based simply on the esteem and love He has for His own qualities. Assume there are no intellects who admire His work; assume there are only demented or stupid people who do not discern its wonders, people who on the contrary scorn this admirable work, who blaspheme it, who regard it as the necessary effect of a blind nature because of the monsters found in it, who are scandalized to see innocence oppressed and injustice on the throne; God does not derive from it less of this glory for which He acts, this glory which for its principle has the love and esteem He has for His qualities, this glory which always determines Him to act according to what He is or in a manner which bears the character of His attributes. Thus, supposing God wills to act, He can act only for His glory in this first sense, since He can only act according to what He is and through the love He has for Himself and His divine perfections. But as He is self-sufficient, this glory cannot invincibly determine Him to will to act, and I even believe that this glory alone cannot be a sufficient motive to make Him act, unless He finds the secret of rendering His work divine and proportioning it to His action, which is divine. For, after all, however large and however perfect the universe might be, insofar as it is finite it will be unworthy of the action of God, whose worth is infinite. Thus, God will not adopt the plan of producing it. That is, in my view, what causes the greatest difficulty.

V. ARISTES. Why is that, Theodore? It is easy to resolve this difficulty. Let us make the world infinite. Let us construct it out of an infinite number of vortices. For why suppose a large heaven which surrounds all others and beyond which there is nothing more?

THEODORE. No, Aristes, let us leave to creation the character that suits it; let us give it nothing approaching the divine attributes. However, let us nevertheless try to deliver the universe from its profane condition and to render it worthy of divine gratification by means of something divine, worthy of the action of a God whose worth is infinite.

ARISTES. How?

THEODORE. Through the union with a divine person.

ARISTES. Ah, Theodore, you always have recourse to the truths of faith, in order to avoid an issue. That is not philosophizing.

THEODORE. What do you want, Aristes? The reason is because I find that it suits me, and because without it I am unable to find the solution to thousands upon thousands of difficulties. What! Is not the universe, sanctified by Jesus Christ and subsisting in Him, so to speak, more divine and more worthy of the action of God than all your infinite vortices?

ARISTES. Yes, undoubtedly. But if we had not sinned the Word would not have been incarnated.

THEODORE. I do not know, Aristes. But even if we had not sinned, a divine person would not have failed to unite Himself with the universe, in order to sanctify it, to deliver it from its profane condition, to render it divine, to bestow on it an infinite dignity, in order that God, who can act only for His glory, should receive from it glory corresponding perfectly to His action. Was the Word incapable of being united to the work of God without being incarnated? He became man; but could He not have become an angel? It is true that in becoming man He simultaneously became united to the two substances, mind and body, of which the universe is composed, and that through this union He sanctified the whole of nature. That is why I do not believe that sin was the sole cause of the incarnation of the Son of God. But God could have conferred upon angels the grace that He conferred upon people. Moreover, God foresaw and permitted sin. That was enough. For that is a certain proof that the universe, restored through Jesus Christ, is worth more than the same universe in its initial construction; otherwise God would never have let His work be corrupted. That is a sure sign that the principal design of God is the incarnation of His Son. Thus, let us see, Aristes, how God acts for His glory. Let us justify this proposition, which has seemed to you so commonplace and perhaps so devoid of sense and so untenable.

VI. First, God thinks of a work which through its excellence and beauty expresses the qualities He loves invincibly and is pleased to possess. But nonetheless that is not enough for Him to adopt the plan of producing it, because since a finite world, a profane world, still contains nothing divine, it cannot have any real relation to the divinity; it cannot express the attribute essential to God, His infinity. Thus God can neither derive His gratification from it, nor consequently create it, without denying Himself. What, then, does He do? Religion teaches us this. He renders His work divine through the union of a divine person to the two substances, mind and body, from which He composes it. And He thereby elevates it infinitely and, principally because of the divinity He communicates to it, He receives from it that first glory which is related to that of the architects who constructed a house which does them honor because it expresses the qualities they are proud to possess. God receives, I say, this first glory embellished, as it were, with an infinite brilliance. Nonetheless, God derives from Himself alone the glory He receives from the sanctification of His church or of that spiritual house of which we are the living stones, sanctified by Jesus Christ, since the subject of His glory is simply the relation of His work to the perfections of which He is proud.

These architects also receive a second glory from the observers and admirers of their building, and it is also in view of this kind of glory that they do their best to make the most magnificent and most superb building they can. It is also principally in view of the worship, which our sovereign priest had to establish in honor of the divinity, that God resolved to make Himself a temple in which He was eternally glorified. Yes, Aristes, vile and contemptible creatures that we are, through our divine leader we render and shall eternally render divine honors to God, honors worthy of the divine majesty, honors which God receives and will always receive with pleasure. Our adorations and praises are in Jesus Christ sacrifices of pleasing fragrance. God takes pleasure in these spiritual and divine sacrifices, and if He repented of having established an earthly worship and even of having created man,* He has vowed by Himself never to repent having sanctified it, having made us His priests under our sovereign pontiff, the true Melchizedek.** God regards us in Jesus Christ as Gods, as His children, as His heirs, and as co-heirs of His dearly beloved Son.† In this dear Son He adopted us. It is through Him that He gives us access to His supreme majesty. It is through Him that He takes pleasure in His work. It is by this secret He has found in His wisdom that He goes beyond Himself, if it is permitted to speak so, beyond His holiness, which separates Him infinitely from all creatures; that He goes, I say, with a magnificence from which He derives a glory capable of satisfying Him. The Man–God precedes Him on all His paths, He justifies all His plans, through His creatures He makes Him render honors with which He must be content. Jesus Christ appears only in the fullness of time, but He exists prior to all the centuries in the plans of the creator; and when He is born in Bethlehem, it is then that God is glorified, it is then that He is satisfied with His work. All blessed spirits recognize this truth, when the angel announces the birth of the savior to the shepherds. "Glory to God," they all say together, "peace on earth, God is pleased with men."‡ Yes, surely the incarnation of the Word is the first and principal design of God. That is what justifies His action. Unless I am mistaken, that is the sole solution of thousands upon thousands of difficulties, thousands upon thousands of seeming contradictions.§

Human beings, Aristes, are sinners; they are not such as God made them. Thus, God has let His work be corrupted. Reconcile this with

---

* Hebrews 7: 20–21; 6: 17.   ** 1 Peter 2: 9.   † 1 John 3: 1–22; Romans 8: 16–17.
‡ Luke 2[: 14].
§ *Traité de la nature et de la grâce* I [*OC* V 11–64], & *Eclaircissements I, II* [*OC* V 172–96].

His wisdom and with His power. Extricate yourself from this problem without the aid of the Man–God, without admitting a mediator, without conceiving that God had principally the incarnation of His Son in view. I defy you to do it with all the principles of the best philosophy. For my part I admit I find myself at a loss every time I try to philosophize without the aid of faith. It is faith which guides me and supports me in the search for the truths which have some relation to God, such as those of metaphysics. For, in the case of the truths of mathematics, which measure the magnitudes, numbers, times, movements, and everything which is distinguished simply by more or less, I agree that faith is of no help in discovering them, and that experience suffices, along with reason, to become knowledgeable in all the branches of physics.

VII. ARISTES. I well understand what you are saying, Theodore, and I find it quite consistent with reason. I even feel an inner joy in seeing that by following faith we elevate ourselves to the understanding of the truths which St. Paul teaches us in several places in his admirable Epistles. However, two small difficulties come to my mind. The first is that it seems that God was not perfectly free in the production of His work, since He derives from it a glory which is infinite and satisfies Him so greatly. The second is that in any case He should not be eternally deprived of the satisfaction He has of seeing Himself so divinely honored by His creatures.

THEODORE. I answer you, Aristes, that the infinitely perfect Being is fully self-sufficient, and that thus He invincibly and necessarily loves only His own substance, only His divine perfections. That is evident, and is sufficient for your first difficulty. But as for the second, note that God must never do anything that belies His qualities, and He should leave all the marks of dependence on creatures which are essentially dependent. Now, the essential character of dependence is not to have existed. An eternal world appears to be a necessary emanation of the divinity. God must show that He is self-sufficient in such a way that for an eternity He was able to do without His work. Through Jesus Christ He derives from it a glory that satisfies Him. But He would not receive this glory if the incarnation were eternal, because that incarnation would violate His attributes, which He must honor insofar as that is possible.

ARISTES. I grant you that, Theodore. Only the necessary and

independent Being must be eternal. Anything that is not God must bear the essential mark of its dependence. That appears evident to me. But without making the world eternal God could have created it sooner than He did by a thousand million centuries. Why such delay with a work from which He derives so much glory?

THEODORE. He did not delay it, Aristes. Sooner and later are properties of time which have no relation at all to eternity. If the world had been created a thousand million centuries earlier than it had been, the same problem could be raised against you and repeated constantly to infinity. Thus, God did not create His work too late, since an eternity had to precede it and since, in relation to eternity, creation a thousand million years earlier or a thousand million years later marks neither an advance or a regress.

ARISTES. I do not know how to answer you, Theodore. I shall think about what you have just told me, that God acts only for His glory, only for the love He bears for Himself, for I think this principle contains many consequences. However, Theotimus, what do you think of it?

VIII. THEOTIMUS. This principle appears incontestable to me. For it is evident that the infinitely perfect Being can find the motive of His volitions and the reasons for His action solely in Himself. But I do not know; I might indeed wish, it seems to me, that God loved us a little more, or that He did something uniquely for love of us. For, after all, Scripture teaches us that God so loved us that He gave us His only Son. That is a great gift, Aristes, and it seems the mark of a love a little more disinterested than that which Theodore attributes to Him.

ARISTES. Very well, Theodore, what do you say to that?

THEODORE. That Theotimus is striking the reef, or rather that he senses he is in the current leading him there, unless perhaps he wishes to see how you are disposed on the matter.

ARISTES. You are not answering.

THEODORE. That is because I would actually like you to do that yourself. But since you wish to remain silent, at least try properly to follow my thinking. I believe, Aristes, that God so loved us that He gave us His Son, as Scripture says.[*] But I also believe what that same Scripture teaches me, that He so loved His Son that He gave us and all the nations of the earth to Him.[**] Finally, I also believe, because of

[*] John 3: 16.   [**] Psalm 2: 8; Matthew 28: 18.

Scripture, that if He predestined us in His Son,[*] and if He chose His Son as the first among the predestined, this is because He wanted to make Him His pontiff, in order to receive from Him and from us through Him, the adoration He is due. For here, in a few words, is the order of things. All is for us, we are for Jesus Christ, and Jesus Christ is for God. "All things are yours," says St. Paul, "things present, or things to come; and you are Christ's; and Christ is God's."[**] That is because God is necessarily the end of all His works.

Conceive distinctly, Aristes, that God loves all things in proportion as they are lovable, that the law He inviolably follows is but the immutable order which I have said many times consists only in the necessary relations of the divine perfections. In a word, conceive that God acts according to what He is, and you shall understand without difficulty that He loves us so strongly that He does everything He can for us, acting as He must act. You will understand that God loves the natures He made insofar as they are the way He made them; that He loves them, I say, to the degree of perfection their archetypes contain; and that He will render them happier inasmuch as they deserve that, by conforming to His law. You will understand that in the beginning God created human beings just and without any defect; and that if He made them free that is because He wished to make them happy, without forgoing what He owes Himself. You will easily believe that, though human beings became sinners, worthy of the divine anger, still God can love them with so much kindness and goodness as to send His Son to deliver them from their sins. You will not doubt that God so cherishes humans as sanctified through Jesus Christ that He gives them a share of His heritage and of an eternal bliss. But you will never understand that God acts solely for His creatures, or through a movement of pure good whose motive does not find its reason in the divine attributes. Once again, Aristes, God is able not to act; but if He acts, He can do so only if He regulates Himself on the basis of Himself, on the basis of the law He finds in His substance. He can love people; but He can do so only because of the relation they have to Him. In the beauty which the archetype of His work contains He finds a reason for implementing it, but that is because this beauty does Him honor, because it expresses the qualities in which He glorifies Himself and which He is pleased to possess. Thus, the love God bears us is not interested in the sense that

[*] Ephesians 1[: 4].   [**] 1 Corinthians 3: 22.

He has some need of us; but it is interested in the sense that He loves us only through the love He bears Himself and His divine perfections, which we express through our nature (which is the first glory that all beings necessarily render their author), and which we adore through the judgments and actions owed to Him. That is the second glory, which we give to God through our sovereign priest, our savior, Jesus Christ.

THEOTIMUS. All that, Theodore, appears sufficiently explained to me. The infinitely perfect Being is fully self-sufficient; that is one of the names God gives Himself in Scripture. And yet He made everything for Himself: "The Lord hath made all things for himself."* He made everything in Jesus Christ, and through Jesus Christ: "All things were created by him and in him."** Everything for the glory He derives from His church in Jesus Christ: "To him be glory in the church, and in Christ Jesus unto all generations, world without end."† The Epistles of St. Paul are all full of these truths. That is the foundation of our religion, and you have made us see that there is nothing more in conformity with Reason and with the most exact notion of the infinitely perfect Being. Let us move on to something else. When Aristes has properly thought about all this, I hope he will be convinced by it.

ARISTES. I am indeed already persuaded of it, Theotimus, and it is not my fault that Theodore does not go a little more into detail than he does.

IX. THEODORE. Let us attempt to understand properly the most general principles, Aristes. For afterwards all the rest follows of itself, everything is unfolded to the mind with order and a wonderful clarity. Thus, let us again consider, in the notion of the infinitely perfect Being, what the plans of God can be. I am not claiming that we shall be able to discover their details, but perhaps we shall recognize what is most general in them, and in what follows you will see that the little we have discovered about them will be of great use to us. Thus, do you think that God wills to create the most beautiful and the most perfect work He can?

ARISTES. Yes, undoubtedly, for the more perfect His work, the more it will express the qualities and perfections in which God glories. That is evident by everything you have just told us.

THEODORE. Therefore, the universe is the most perfect God can

* Proverbs 16: 4.   ** Colossians 1: 16.   † Ephesians 3: 21.

create? What! So many monsters, so many disorders, the great number of impious people; does all this contribute to the perfection of the universe?

ARISTES. You confuse me, Theodore. God wills to make the most perfect possible work. For the more perfect it is, the more it will honor Him. That appears evident to me. But I clearly conceive that it would be more accomplished if it were free of the thousands and thousands of defects which disfigure it. That is a contradiction which stops me short. It seems that God has not executed His plan or has not adopted the plan most worthy of His attributes.

THEODORE. That is because you have still not properly understood the principles. You have not sufficiently meditated on the notion of the infinitely perfect Being which contains them. You still do not know how to make God act according to what He is.

THEOTIMUS. But, Aristes, might it not be that the irregularities of nature, monsters, and even the impious are like the shadows of a painting, which lend force to the work and relief to the figures?

ARISTES. That thought has an 'I know not what' which pleases the imagination, but the mind is not satisfied by it. For I understand quite well that the universe would be more perfect if there were nothing irregular in any of the parts comprising it, and on the contrary there is almost no place where there is not some defect.

THEOTIMUS. Thus, it is because God did not will His work to be perfect.

ARISTES. That is not the reason either. For God cannot positively and directly will the irregularities which disfigure His work and which express none of the perfections He possesses and in which He is glorified. That appears evident to me. God permits disorder, but He does not create it, He does not will it.

THEOTIMUS. "God permits": I do not really understand this expression. Whom does God permit to freeze the vines and ruin the harvest He made grow? Why does He permit monsters in His work which He does not make and does not will? What then! Is the universe not such as God willed it?

ARISTES. No, for the universe is not such as God made it.

THEOTIMUS. That may be true in respect of the disorders which have crept into it through the poor use of freedom. For God did not make the impious. He permitted people to become that way. I do indeed understand that, although I do not know the reasons for it. But certainly it is only God who makes monsters.

ARISTES. What strange creatures these monsters are, if they do not do honor to Him who gives them being. Do you know, Theotimus, why God, who today covers the entire countryside with flowers and fruit, will tomorrow ravage it with frost or hail?

THEOTIMUS. That is because the countryside will be more beautiful in its sterility than in its fecundity, although that does not suit us. Often we judge the beauty of God's works by the utility we derive from them, and we deceive ourselves.

ARISTES. Still, it is better to judge them by their utility than by their inutility. What a beautiful thing, a country desolated by a tempest!

THEOTIMUS. Quite beautiful. A country inhabited by sinners should be in desolation.

ARISTES. If the tempest spared the lands of good people, perhaps you would be right. It would be even more appropriate to refuse rain to the field of a brute, than to make his wheat germinate and grow in order to cut it down by hail. That would surely be the shortest route. But it is often, however, the less culpable who are the more ill-treated. What seeming contradictions in the action of God! Theodore has already given me the principles which dispel these contradictions. But I understood them so poorly that I no longer remember them. If you do not wish, Theotimus, to set me on the correct path, let Theodore speak, for I see that you are entertained by the difficulty in which I find myself.

THEOTIMUS. That is fair.

X. THEODORE. You see, Aristes, that it is not enough to have glimpsed the principles; it is necessary to have understood them properly, in order that they be present to the mind when necessary. Listen, therefore, since Theotimus does not wish to tell you what he knows perfectly well.

You are not deceived in believing that the more perfect a work is, the more it expresses the perfections of the workman, and that it does him greater honor the more the perfections it expresses please him who possesses them, and that thus God wills to make His work the most perfect possible. But you grasp only half of the principle, and that is what leaves you perplexed. God wills that His work honors Him; you understand that well. Note, however, that God does not will that His ways dishonor Him. That is the other half of the principle. God wills that His action as well as His work bear the character of His attributes. Not content that the universe honors Him through its excellence and beauty, He wills that His ways glorify Him through their simplicity, their fecundity, their universality, through the characteristics which express the qualities He is glorified in possessing.

Thus, do not imagine that God willed absolutely to make the most perfect work possible, but only the most perfect in relation to the ways most worthy of Him. For what God wills uniquely, directly, absolutely in His plans is always to act as divinely as possible. It is to make His action as well as His work bear the character of His attributes; it is to act exactly according to what He is and according to all that He is. From all eternity God saw all possible works and all the possible ways of producing each of them, and as He acts only for His glory, only according to what He is, He determined to will that work which could be produced and conserved in those ways which, combined with that work, would honor Him more than any other work produced in any other way. He formed the plan which would better convey the character of His attributes, which would express more exactly the qualities He possesses and glories in possessing. Fully embrace this principle, Aristes, lest it escape you, for of all principles it is perhaps the most fertile.

Once again, do not imagine that God ever forms His plan blindly, I mean, without having compared it with the ways necessary for its implementation. That is how people act who often regret their decisions because of the difficulties in which they find themselves. Nothing is difficult to God. Note, however, that not everything is equally worthy of Him. His ways as well as His work must bear the character of His attributes. Thus, God must have regard for the ways as well as the work. It is not enough that His work honors Him through its excellence; His ways must further glorify Him through their divinity. And if a world more perfect than ours could be created and conserved only in ways which are correspondingly less perfect, in such a manner that the expression, as it were, which this new world and its new ways gave the divine qualities was less than their expression in our world, I am not afraid to say this to you: God is too wise, He loves His glory too much, He acts too exactly according to what He is, to prefer this new world to the universe He has created. For in His plans God is indifferent only when they are equally wise, equally divine, equally glorious for Him, equally worthy of His attributes, and only when the relation, composed of the beauty of the work and the simplicity of His ways, is exactly equal. When this relation is unequal, although God is able to do nothing since He is self-sufficient, He cannot choose and adopt the worse one. He is able not to act, but He cannot act in vain, nor can He multiply His ways without proportionally augmenting the beauty of His work. His wisdom protects Him against adopting, from all possible plans, that which is not the wisest. The love He bears Himself does not allow Him to choose the plan which does not honor Him the most.

XI. ARISTES. I grasp your principle well, Theodore. God acts only according to what He is, only in a manner which bears the character of His attributes, only for the glory He finds exclusively in the relation which His work and His ways together jointly have to the perfections He possesses and is glorified in possessing. It is the greatness of this relation which God considers in the formation of His plans. For here is the principle. God can act only according to what He is, and He can absolutely and directly will only His glory. If the defects of the universe in which we live diminish this relation, then the simplicity, the fecundity, the wisdom of the ways or laws God follows, augment it even more. A world more perfect but produced in ways less fertile and simple would not bear the character of the divine attributes as much as ours. Here is why the world is filled with impious people, monsters, disorders of all kinds. God could convert all people and prevent all disorders. But He must not thereby upset the simplicity and uniformity of His action. For He must be honored through the wisdom of His ways as well as through the perfection of His creatures. He does not allow monsters; it is He who makes them. But He makes them only in order to alter nothing in His action, only out of respect for the generality of His ways, only to follow exactly the laws of nature He has established and has nonetheless established not for the monstrous effects they must produce, but for those effects more worthy of His wisdom and goodness. For He wills them only indirectly, only because they are the natural consequence of His laws.

THEODORE. How quickly you draw your conclusions!

ARISTES. That is because the principle is clear, because it is fertile.

THEODORE. At first, Aristes, it seems that this principle has no solidity because of its generality. But when we follow it closely it strikes us so forcefully and so quickly, by the number of amazing truths it reveals, that we are charmed by it. Learn from this that the most general principles are the most fertile. At first they seem like pure chimeras. Their generality is the cause of that, for the mind regards as nothing whatever does not touch it. However, grasp these principles well, if you can, and follow them; in short order they will allow you to see the land properly.

ARISTES. I feel that, Theodore, when I meditate a little on what you are telling me. And even now, without any effort of mind, it seems to me that in your principle I see at a glance the resolution of a number of difficulties I have always had concerning God's action. I conceive that all those effects which contradict one another, those works which conflict with one another, those disorders which disfigure the universe, all indicate no contradiction whatsoever in the cause which governs them, no defect in intellect, no impotence. Rather, they indicate a prodigious fertility and a perfect uniformity in the laws of nature.

THEODORE. Slowly, Aristes. For we shall explain all this more exactly in what follows.

XII. ARISTES. I even understand that the reason for the predestination of people must necessarily be found in your principle. I believed that from all eternity God chose particular people precisely because He desired to do so, without reason for His choice either on His part or on ours, and that subsequently He consulted His wisdom about the ways to sanctify them and lead them safely to heaven. But now I see I was mistaken. God does not form His plans blindly, without comparing them with His means. He is wise in the formation of His decrees as well as in their execution. There are reasons in Him for the predestination of the elect. For the future church, formed by the ways God employs in respect of it, does Him more honor than any other church formed by any other way. For God can act only for His glory, only in the manner which best attests to the character of His attributes. God predestined neither us, nor even our divine leader, in virtue of our natural merits, but in virtue of the reasons furnished Him by His inviolable law, the immutable order, the necessary relation among the perfections He contains in His substance. He willed to unite His Word to a particular nature and to predestine particular people in His Son, because His wisdom indicated to Him that He ought to use them in this way for His own glory. Am I following your great principle properly, Theodore?

THEODORE. Quite properly. But are you not worried about going too far into theology? Here you are in the midst of the greatest mysteries.

ARISTES. Let us return. For I am unsuited to penetrate into them.

THEOTIMUS. You do well, Aristes, to return promptly. For St. Augustine, the great doctor of grace, does not want us to seek reasons for the choice God made about people. Predestination is purely gratuitous, and the reason why God takes one and leaves another is that He is merciful to whomever it pleases Him to be merciful.

ARISTES. What, Theodore! Does St. Augustine claim that God does not consult His wisdom in the formation of His plans, but only for their execution?

THEODORE. No, Aristes. But apparently Theotimus explains St. Augustine after the thought of certain people. This holy doctor, writing against the heretics of his day, rejects the poor reason they gave for God's choice and for the distribution of His grace. But he was always prepared to accept those reasons which are in the analogy of faith and which do not destroy the gratuitous nature of grace. Here, in a couple of words, is the reasoning of these heretics; it is good that you know it and are able to respond to it. God wills that all people are saved and arrive at knowledge of the truth. Therefore, they can all be saved through their natural powers. But, said the more moderate of them, if that is not possible without the aid of inner grace, let us then see to whom God will give it. God chooses some rather than others. Very well, agreed; but at least His choice should be rational. Now, it is a common notion that whoever chooses worse chooses badly. Thus, if God does not bestow His grace equally upon all, if He chooses He must then prefer the best or at least prefer the less to the more wicked. For we cannot doubt that the choice He makes of some rather than others is wise and rational. There is no favoring people in Him. Thus, the reason for His choice in the distribution of His grace must necessarily be found in the good use we can still make of our natural powers. It is up to us to will, to desire our redemption, to believe in the mediator, to beg His mercy; in a word, to begin, and God will come to our aid. Through the good use of our free will we shall merit God's giving us His grace.

ARISTES. These people reason well.

THEODORE. Perfectly well, but on the basis of false ideas. They do not consult the notion of the infinitely perfect Being. They make God act like people. For, take note, why do you think that God disperses the rains?

ARISTES. In order to render the ground we cultivate fertile.

THEODORE. Then we need simply sow or plant a field for it to rain there. For as God does not make it rain equally on all lands, as He makes a choice, He must choose rationally and make it rain on cultivated lands rather than on others, rather than on sand and sea. In this comparison find the defect in reasoning of the enemies of grace; but, please, do not quibble.

ARISTES. I understand you, Theodore. Whether we cultivate the lands or let them lie fallow, it does not rain either more or less. This is because ordinarily it rains only as a consequence of the general laws of nature, according to which God conserves the universe. Likewise, the reason for the distribution of grace is not derived from our natural merits. God bestows His initial graces only as a consequence of certain general laws. For God does not act in the manner of particular causes and limited intellects. The reason for His choice derives from the wisdom of His laws, and the wisdom of His laws from the relation they have to His attributes, from their simplicity, from their fecundity, in short, from their divinity. God's choice of people in the distribution of His graces is therefore rational and perfectly worthy of the wisdom of God, although it is founded neither on the difference between natures nor on the inequality among merits.

THEODORE. You have it, Aristes. In short order you have undermined the firmest support of Pelagianism. Someone who watered the sand or who carried to the sea the water necessary for the field, would not be wise. Nonetheless, that is what God does as a consequence of His laws, and in this respect He acts very wisely, or divinely. That is enough to silence those heretical, proud people who would teach God to make a wise and rational choice among people.

Very well, Theotimus, are you still afraid of Aristes falling into the precipice with which St. Augustine frightens, and rightly frightens, those who seek the cause of their election in their natural merits? Aristes

---

* Cf. Dialogue XII, §§xvi ff.; *Traité de la nature et de la grace* II [*OC* V 65–116]; *Réponse à la Dissertation de M. Arnauld*, Chs. 7–11, etc. [*OC* VII 512–57ff.].

would have the distribution of grace be purely gratuitous. Let us cease worrying about him. Let us rather pity certain people, whom you know, who claim that God chooses His elect out of pure goodness toward them, without wisdom and reason on His part. For it is a horrible impiety to believe that God is not wise in the formation of His plans as well as in their execution. The predestination to grace is gratuitous in respect of us. Grace is not distributed according to our merits, as St. Augustine maintains, after St. Paul and with the entire church, but it is regulated according to a law with which God never dispenses. For God formed the plan which contains the predestination of particular people rather than a number of others, because there was no plan more wise, more worthy of His attributes, than that one. That is what your friends could not understand.

XIII. THEOTIMUS. What else, Theodore! For we naturally strike that reef of judging God by ourselves. We all love independence. For us, to submit to Reason is a kind of slavery; to be unable to do what it forbids is a kind of impotence. Thus, we fear rendering God impotent by making Him wise. But God is His own wisdom. Sovereign Reason is coeternal and consubstantial with Him. He loves it necessarily, and although He is obliged to follow it, He remains independent. Everything God wills is wise and rational, not because God is above Reason, not because what He wills is just, simply and solely because He wills it; but because He cannot belie Himself, cannot will anything which does not conform to His law, to the immutable and necessary order of the divine perfections.

THEODORE. Surely, Theotimus, everything is inverted if we claim that God is above Reason and has no rule in His plans other than His mere will. This false principle spreads such blanket darkness that it confounds the good with the evil, the true with the false, and creates out of everything a chaos in which the mind no longer knows anything. St. Augustine proved original sin invincibly by the disorders we experience in ourselves. Human beings suffer, therefore they are not innocent. The mind depends on the body, therefore people are corrupt, they are not such as God made them. God cannot submit the more noble to the less, for order does not permit it. What conclusions these are for those not afraid to say that God's will is the sole rule of His actions! They have only to reply that God willed it so; that it is our self-love which causes us to find the pain we suffer unjust; that it is our pride which is offended that the mind is subordinated to the body; that as God has willed these supposed disorders, it is an impiety to appeal to Reason against them, since God's will does not recognize it as the rule of His conduct. According to this principle, the universe is perfect because God willed it. Monsters are works as perfect as others according to the plans of God. It is good to have eyes high in our head, but they would have been as wisely placed anywhere else, had God so placed them. However we invert the world, whatever chaos we make out of it, it will always be equally admirable, since its entire beauty consists in its conformity with the divine will, which is not obliged to conform to order. But this will is unknown to us! All the beauty of the universe must therefore disappear in view of that great principle that God is above the Reason which enlightens all minds, and that His wholly arbitrary will is the sole rule of His actions.

ARISTES. Ah, Theodore, how well all your principles are connected! By what you have just told me I understand further that it is in God and in an immutable nature that we see beauty, truth, justice, since we are not afraid to criticize His work, to note the defects in it, and even to conclude thereby that it is corrupt. Indeed, the immutable order, which we see partly, must be the law of God Himself, written in His substance in eternal and divine characters, since we are unafraid of judging His conduct by the knowledge we have of that law. We affirm outright that people are not such as God made them, that their nature is corrupted, that in creating them God could not subject the mind to the body. Are we impious or rash in so judging of what God should or should not do? Not at all. Rather, we would be either impious or blind if we suspended our judgment about this. This is because, Theodore, we do not judge God by our authority but by the sovereign authority of the divine law.

THEODORE. There, my dear Aristes, is a reflection worthy of you. Do not forget to study this law, then, since it is in that sacred code of the immutable order that we find such important decisions.

Dialogue X

The magnificence of God in the magnitude and infinite number of His different works. The simplicity and fecundity of the ways in which He conserves and develops them. The providence of God in the first impression of motion He communicates to matter. This first step in His conduct, which is not determined by general laws, is governed by an infinite wisdom.

THEOTIMUS. What do you think, Aristes, of those general principles which Theodore proposed yesterday? Did you follow them all the time? Has their generality, their sublimity neither discouraged nor tired you? As for me, I confess to my confusion; I wanted to attend to them but they escaped me like phantoms, so that I expended a lot of effort quite uselessly.

ARISTES. When a principle has nothing which affects the senses, it is rather difficult to follow and grasp it; when what we embrace has no body, by what means do we hold it?

THEOTIMUS. We take it quite naturally to be a phantom. For as the mind is distracted the principle is eclipsed, and we are completely surprised to be holding nothing. We recapture this principle but it escapes us anew. And although it escapes us only when we close our eyes, because we close them frequently without being aware of it we think that it is the principle which vanishes. This is why we consider it like a phantom beguiling us.

ARISTES. True, Theotimus. For this reason I believe that general principles bear some resemblance to chimeras, and that the average person, who is not made for attentive work, treats them as chimerical.

THEOTIMUS. Nonetheless there is an extremely great difference between these two things. For general principles please the mind, which they enlighten by their evidence, and phantoms please the imagination, which gives them being. And although it seems that it is the mind which forms these principles and all truths generally, because they are presented to it as a consequence of its attention, I think you well know that they are prior to us and do not derive their reality from the efficacy of our action; for all these immutable truths are but the relations which are found between ideas whose existence is necessary and eternal. But the phantoms which the imagination produces, or which are produced in the imagination by a natural result of the general laws of the union of the soul and the body, exist only for a time.

ARISTES. I agree, Theotimus, that nothing is more solid than the truth, and that the more general the truths are, the more reality and light they have. Theodore has convinced me of that. But I am so sensual and unsophisticated that I often find nothing to savor there, and I am sometimes tempted to leave them altogether.

THEOTIMUS. There it is, Theodore.

THEODORE. You will do nothing of the kind, Aristes. Truth is more valuable than onions and cabbage; it is an excellent manna.[1]

ARISTES. Quite excellent, I agree. But sometimes it appears rather empty and not very solid. I do not find much taste in it, and every day you want us to gather it afresh. That is none too pleasant.

THEODORE. Very well, Aristes, let us spend this day as the Jews do their Sabbath. Perhaps yesterday you worked enough for two days.

ARISTES. Assuredly, Theodore, I worked a lot, but I gathered nothing.

THEODORE. I left you, however, well on the way to drawing conclusions. The way you took up the matter, you should have two nice full measures of them.

ARISTES. What measures, two omers?[2] Then give your principles more body, Theodore, if you want me to fill these measures. Make them more sensible and palpable. They slip through my fingers; the least heat dissolves them and after much work I find I have nothing.

THEODORE. You are being nourished, Aristes, without noticing it.

---

[1] Allusion to Exodus 16: 15.　　[2] Allusion to Exodus 16: 16ff.

These principles which pass through the mind and escape it, always leave some light there.

ARISTES. True, I can feel it. But to begin again every day and change my usual diet! Can you not render the principles of your philosophy more sensible for us?

THEODORE. I am afraid, Aristes, that they would thereby become less intelligible. Believe me, I always make them as sensible as I can. But I am afraid of corrupting them. It is permitted to embody the truth in order to accommodate it to our natural weakness and to maintain the mind's attention, which gets no hold on what has no body. But it is always necessary that the sensible should carry us to the intelligible and the flesh lead us to Reason, and that the truth appear as it is, without any disguise. The sensible is not what is solid. It is only the intelligible which, through its evidence and light, can nourish intellects. You know this. Try to remember it and follow me.

ARISTES. What do you wish to talk about?

I. THEODORE. About general providence or the ordinary conduct of God in His governance of the world.

You have grasped, Aristes, and perhaps even forgotten, that the infinitely perfect Being, though sufficient unto Himself, was able to adopt the plan of forming this universe; that He created it for His own glory; that He placed Jesus Christ at the head of His work, at the beginning of His designs and ways, so that all would be divine; that He was not required to undertake the most perfect work possible, but only the most perfect work that could be produced through the wisest or most divine ways, so that any other work produced in any other way could not express more exactly the perfections God possesses and glories in possessing. This, then, is how the creator is ready, as it were, to go outside Himself, outside His eternal sanctuary; ready to begin the production of creatures. Let us see something of His magnificence in His work; but let us follow Him closely in the majestic process of His ordinary action.

As for the magnificence of His work, it shines through from all sides. Wherever we cast our gaze in the universe, we see there a profusion of wonders. And if we cease admiring them this is surely because we cease considering them with the attention they deserve. For astronomers, who measure the size of astral bodies and would indeed like to know the number of the stars, are more struck with admiration the more knowledgeable they become. At one time the sun appeared large, like the Peloponnesus,[*] but today the more skilled of them find it to be a million times larger than the earth. The ancients counted only one thousand and twenty-two stars,[3] but today no one would dare count them. Indeed, God once told us that no one will ever know their number,[4] but the invention of telescopes forces us now to recognize that the catalogues we have of them are quite imperfect. They contain only those we can discover without telescopes, and that is surely the smallest number. I believe even that there are many more than we shall ever discover, more than are visible through the best telescopes; and yet it really does appear that quite a large number of those stars do not exceed, either in size or in majesty, this vast body which to us here below appears the most luminous and beautiful. How great, then, God is in the heavens! How elevated He is in their depths! How magnificent He is in their brilliance! How wise He is, how powerful in their regulated movements!

II. However, Aristes, let us leave the great. Our imagination gets lost in these immense spaces which we dare not limit and are afraid to leave without limits. How many admirable works there are on the earth we inhabit, on this point which is imperceptible to those who measure only celestial bodies! However, this earth which the good gentlemen astronomers count for nothing, is still too vast for me. I confine myself to your gardens. What animals, birds, insects, plants, flowers, and fruits!

The other day as I lay in the shade, it occurred to me to note the variety of herbs and small animals I found under my eyes. Without changing place I counted more than twenty kinds of insects in a quite small space, and at least as many various plants. I took one of those insects whose name I do not know, and perhaps it has none; for people who give various and often very magnificent names to whatever comes from their hands, simply do not believe they need to name those works of the creator which they do not know how to admire. I took, as I said, one of those insects. I considered it attentively, and I am not afraid to say of it to you what Jesus Christ says of the lilies of the field, that

---

[3] Ptolemy's catalogue of fixed stars, the first of its kind published in the ancient world, lists 1,022 stars.

[4] Genesis 15: 5.

[*] Today, this is called Morea.

Solomon in all his glory did not have such magnificent ornaments.[5] After having for some time admired this tiny creature so unjustly scorned, and indeed so unworthily and cruelly treated by other animals to whom it apparently serves as food, I began reading a book I had with me, and I found something quite amazing there: in the world there are an infinite number of insects at least a million times smaller than the one I had just considered, and ten thousand times smaller than a grain of sand.[*]

Do you know, Aristes, what the fathom or measure is, used by those who wish to express the smallness of these living atoms or, if you will, their magnitude, for although they are small in relation to us they are still quite large in relation to others? That measure is the diameter of the eye of those tiny domestic animals that have bitten people so much that they have forced them to honor them with a name. It is by this fathom, but reduced to feet and inches as it is too large as a whole; I say, it is by the parts of this new standard that these observers of the curiosities of nature measure the insects which are found in liquids and about which they prove, through the principles of geometry, that we can discover an infinity of them at least a thousand times smaller than the eye of an ordinary louse. Do not be shocked by this measure; it is one of the most exact and most common. This small animal has made itself sufficiently known, and it can be found in every season. These philosophers are pleased that the facts they advance can at any time be verified and that the multiplicity and delicacy of the admirable works of the author of the universe can be safely judged.

ARISTES. That surprises me a little. But please, Theodore, are these animals, which are imperceptible to our eyes and which with good microscopes appear almost like atoms, the smallest? Might there not be many others which forever escape the ingenuity of people? Perhaps the smallest ever seen are to others, which will never be seen, as the elephant is to the gnat. What do you think of that?

THEODORE. We are losing ourselves, Aristes, in the small as well as in the large. No one can claim that they have at last discovered the smallest animal. Once it was the mite, but today this little mite has become monstrous in size. The more we perfect microscopes, the more

---

[5] Matthew 6: 28–9.
[*] Letter from Mr. Leeuwenhoek to Mr. Wren. [From Anton van Leeuwenhoek (1632–1723) to Sir Christopher Wren (1632–1723), dated 25 July 1684 (*OC* XII 459, n. 45).]

we are persuaded that the smallness of matter does not limit the wisdom of the creator; and that even from nothing, as it were, from an atom, which is undetected by our senses, He forms works which surpass the imagination and even extend well beyond the greatest intellects. I shall explain this to you.

III. When we are truly convinced, Aristes, that this variety and succession of beauties which adorn the universe is simply a consequence of the general laws of the communication of motion, which all depend on the law, so simple and so natural, that moving or impelled bodies always move in the direction and proportion in which they are least impelled. When, I say, we are truly persuaded that all the figures or modalities of matter have no other cause than motion, and that motion is communicated according to several laws which are so natural and so simple that it seems that nature acts only by a blind impetuosity, we understand clearly that it is not the earth which produces plants and that it is not possible that the union of the two sexes forms a work as wonderful as the body of an animal. We can indeed believe that the general laws of the communication of motion are sufficient to develop and grow the parts of organic bodies. But we cannot be persuaded that they could ever form so complex a machine. We see, rather, that unless we wish to have recourse to an extraordinary providence, we must believe that the seed of a plant contains in miniature the plant which it engenders, and that in its womb an animal contains the animal which should come from it.[6] We even understand it to be necessary that each seed contains the entire species it can conserve; that every grain of wheat, for instance, contains in miniature the ear it germinates, each grain of which contains in turn its own ear, all the grains of which can always be as fertile as those of the first ear. Surely it is impossible that the laws of motion alone can, in respect of certain ends, adjust together an almost infinite number of organic parts which comprise what we call an animal or a plant. It is much more the case that these simple and

---

[6] Malebranche is building on the preformation theory of Jan Swammerdam (1637–80), who wrote the *General History of Insects* (Utrecht, 1669). In Malebranche's version of this theory, the body and organs of any member of a species are contained preformed in the embryo of the first, originating member of that species. Along with Marcello Malpighi (1628–94) and Swammerdam, Malebranche represents the 'ovist' branch of seventeenth-century preformation theory, as opposed to its "spermist" or "animalculist" branch, as represented by van Leeuwenhoeck.

general laws are sufficient to cause all those wonderful works, all of which God formed in the first days of the creation of the world, to grow insensibly and appear in due time. Nonetheless, it is not the case that the tiny animal or the germ of the plant has precisely the same proportion of size, solidity, and figure among all its parts, as the animals and plants. But it is the case that all the parts essential to the machine of the animals and plants are so wisely disposed in their germs, that they will, in time and as a consequence of the general laws of motion, assume the shape and form which we observe in them. That is assumed.

IV. Think, Aristes, that a fly has as many organic parts as a horse or an ox, and perhaps more. A horse has only four feet, and a fly has six; but it also has wings of a wonderful structure. You know how the head of an ox is formed. Observe sometime, then, the head of a fly under a microscope, and compare the one with the other. You will see indeed that I am not imposing on you. We find only a single crystalline lens in the eye of an ox; but these days we can discern several thousand in the eye of a fly. Consider, further, that a cow produces only one or two calves every year, whereas a fly produces a swarm containing more than a thousand flies; for the smaller the animal, the more fertile it is. And perhaps you know that now bees no longer have a king whom they honor, but solely a queen whom they tend and who alone produces an entire population.* Thus, try now to imagine the terrifying smallness, the wonderful delicacy of all the bees, the thousand organic bodies which the queen bee carries in its womb. And although your imagination is frightened by this, do not think the fly is formed from a maggot without being contained in it, nor the maggot from the egg, for that is inconceivable.

ARISTES. As matter is infinitely divisible, I understand quite well that God was able to produce in miniature everything we see on a larger scale. I have heard that a Dutch scientist discovered the secret of showing, in the cocoons of caterpillars, the butterflies which issue from them.** I have often seen, even in the middle of winter, in the bulbs of tulips, complete tulips with all the parts they have in spring. Thus, I may indeed suppose that all seeds contain plants, and all eggs animals similar to the ones from which they came.

* According to Swammerdam a bee produces approximately 4000 of them.
** Swammerdam, *History of Insects.*

V. THEODORE. You are still not there. It is roughly six thousand years since the world was made and bees produced swarms.[7] Supposing, then, that each of these swarms contains a thousand insects, the first bee had to be at least a thousand times larger than the second, and the second a thousand times larger than the third, the third a thousand times larger than the fourth, decreasing continually down to the six thousandth, at a ratio of a thousand to one. That is clear on the hypothesis, since whatever contains is larger than what is contained. Conceive, then, if you can, the wonderful delicacy that the bees of the year 1696 had while in the first bee.[8]

ARISTES. That is very easy. We need simply look for the correct value of the last term of a series of thousandths having six thousand and one terms, whose first term expressed the natural size of the honeybee ... At the beginning of the world the bees of this year were smaller than they are today, a thousand thousand thousand times, etc., Theodore: five thousand nine hundred and ninety-seven times a thousand times. That was their correct size, on your hypothesis.

THEODORE. I understand you, Aristes. To express the relation between the natural size of a bee and the size that the bees of this year 1696 had at the beginning of the world, given that six thousand years or, rather, six thousand generations have passed since they were created, we need simply write a fraction having one for its numerator and one accompanied by a mere eighteen thousand zeros for its denominator. Now that is a fine fraction! However, are you not worried that such a divided and ruptured unit will be dissipated, and that your bee and nothing will amount to the same thing?

ARISTES. Certainly not, Theodore. For I know that matter is infinitely divisible, and that the small is such only in relation to the larger. Although my imagination resists it, I easily conceive that since what we call an atom can be continually divided, every part of extension is in one sense infinitely large, and that from it God can make in miniature everything we see on a large scale in the world at which we wonder. Yes, the smallness of bodies can never impede the power of God, this I conceive clearly. For geometry demonstrates that there is no atom in extension, and that matter can be eternally divided.

[7] This figure is deduced from biblical chronology.
[8] The reference to the year 1696 is retained in the fourth edition.

THEODORE. That is quite good, Aristes. You conceive, therefore, that if the world endured several thousand centuries, within a single bee God could form all the bees to come from it and could so wisely adjust the simple laws of the communication of motion to the plan He had to cause them to grow imperceptibly and to appear every year, that their species would not die out. What works of marvellous delicacy are contained in so small a space as the body of a single bee! For, without prophesying the uncertain duration of the universe, it has been about six thousand years since bees have been producing swarms. How many other bees do you think that the first bee which God made – supposing He made only one – bore in its womb, in order to furnish bees up to the present?

ARISTES. Given certain assumptions, that can be easily computed. How many females do you think each queen bee produces in each swarm? That is all we need to ascertain, and the number of years.

THEODORE. Do not delay with this calculation. It would be tiresome. In relation to an infinite number of other animals, however, contemplate what you have just thought about bees. On the basis of this, consider the number and the delicacy of the plants which were in miniature in the first plants and which develop every year to become visible to people.

VI. THEOTIMUS. Let us put aside all this speculation, Theodore. God sufficiently furnishes us with works within our compass, without our tarrying with those which we cannot see. There is no animal or plant which does not, by its wondrous construction, sufficiently indicate that the wisdom of the creator surpasses us infinitely. And each year He produces them in such profusion that His magnificence and greatness must amaze and impress the dullest people. Without going beyond ourselves, in our body we find a machine comprising a thousand springs, all so wisely adjusted to their end, so well connected and subordinated to each other that this suffices to humble and prostrate us before the author of our being. I recently read a book, which deserves examination, on the movement of animals.[*] The author carefully considers the workings of the machine which are required in order to change place. He explains exactly the force of the muscles, the reasons for their placement, all by the principles of geometry and mechanics.

[*] Borelli, *De motu animalium.* [Published in Rome in 1680 by John Alphonso Borelli (1608–79).]

But although he confines himself only to what is easiest to discover in the animal machine, he reveals such art and wisdom in Him who formed it, that he fills the mind of the reader with wonder and surprise.

ARISTES. It is true, Theotimus, that the anatomy of the human body alone, or of the most despised of animals, spreads such light in the mind and strikes it so vividly that one would have to be insensible not to recognize its author.

VII. THEODORE. You are both right. But as for me, what I find most wonderful is that God forms all these excellent works or at least makes them grow and develop before our eyes, by following precisely certain very simple and fertile general laws He has prescribed for Himself. I wonder not so much at trees laden with fruit and flowers, but at their marvellous growth as a result of the laws of nature. A gardener takes an old rope, greases it with a fig, and buries it in a furrow; and some time later I see that all those little seeds we feel between our teeth when we eat figs have broken the ground and have developed roots from one side and a fig-tree nursery from the other. That is what I wonder at! Irrigating the fields as a consequence of the laws of nature and with an element as simple as water, yields an infinity of plants and trees of different natures from the ground. An animal brutally and mechanically couples with another, and thereby perpetuates its species. A fish follows the female and distributes its semen over the eggs she disperses in the water. An area ravaged by hail is entirely replenished some time later, completely covered in plants and its usual riches. Let the wind take away the seeds of a spared area, and with the rain they are spread over areas which have been desolated. All this, and an infinity of effects produced by that law, so simple and natural, that every body must move in the direction of least pressure, is assuredly something at which we cannot sufficiently wonder. Nothing is more beautiful, more magnificent in the universe than this profusion of animals and plants upon which we have just remarked. But, believe me, nothing is more divine than the way in which God fills the world, than the use God is able to make of a law so simple that it seems good for nothing.

ARISTES. I agree with you, Theodore. Let us leave it to the astronomers to measure the size and motion of the stars in order to predict eclipses. Let us leave it to the anatomists to dissect the bodies of animals and plants, in order to observe their mechanics and the connection between their parts. In a word, let us leave it to the physicists to study the detail of nature, in order to wonder at all its marvels. Let us abide principally by the general truths of your metaphysics. It seems to me we have sufficiently revealed the magnificence of the creator in the infinite multitude of His wonderful works; let us follow Him a little in the course of His action.

VIII. THEODORE. You will admire, Aristes, much more than you do now, all the parts of the universe, or rather the infinite wisdom of its author, once you have considered the general rules of providence. For when we examine the work of God without reference to the ways which construct and conserve it, how many defects are seen in it which are obvious to the eye and which sometimes so trouble even the minds of philosophers that they regard this wonderful work either as the necessary effect of a blind nature or as a monstrous blend of creatures both good and bad who derive their being from a God who is both good and wicked. However, when we compare it to the ways by which God must govern it in order to have His conduct bear the character of His attributes, all these defects which disfigure creatures are not referred back to the creator. For if there are defects in His work, if there are monsters and thousands and thousands of disorders, nothing is more certain than that they are not found in His action. You have already grasped this, but you must try to understand it better.

IX. Do you still recall my demonstrating to you that there is a contradiction in any creature being able to move a wisp of straw by its own efficacy?[*]
ARISTES. Yes, Theodore, I remember it and am convinced of it. Only the creator of matter can be its mover.
THEODORE. Thus it is only the creator who can produce any change in the material world, since all the possible modalities of matter consist only in the sensible or insensible shapes of its parts, and since all these shapes have no other cause than motion.
ARISTES. I do not understand very well what you are saying. I fear a surprise.
THEODORE. I have proved to you, Aristes, that matter and extension are but a single thing; remember this.[**] It is on this

[*] Dialogue VII.   [**] Dialogue I, §II; Dialogue III, §§XI, XII.

assumption, or rather on this truth, that I reason. For only extension is required to make a world that is material or at least very similar to the one we inhabit. If now you do not have the same ideas as I, it would be useless to continue speaking together.

ARISTES. I do indeed recall your proving to me that extension is a being or a substance and not a modality of substance, because we can think of it without thinking of anything else. For, in effect, it is evident that anything we can perceive alone is not a way of being, but a being or a substance. Only in this manner can we distinguish substances from their modalities. Of this I am convinced. But is not matter a substance other than extension? This idea continually comes to mind.

THEODORE. It is a different word but it is not a different thing, provided that by 'matter' you understand that out of which the world we inhabit is composed. For surely it is composed of extension, and I do not think you are claiming that the material world is composed of two substances. One of them would be useless, and I think it would be yours, for I do not see that we can make anything very solid from it. How would we make a desk, chairs, or furniture from your matter? A piece of furniture would be very rare and valuable. However, give me extension and there is nothing I cannot make from it by means of motion.

ARISTES. That, Theodore, is what I do not understand very well.

X. THEODORE. Yet that is quite easy provided we judge things by the ideas representing them and do not confine ourselves to the prejudices of the senses. Think, Aristes, of an indefinite extension. If all the parts of this extension retain the same relation of distance among themselves, there will be nothing but a large mass of matter. However, if motion is added and its parts continually change place in respect of each other, then an infinity of forms is introduced, I mean an infinity of shapes and configurations. I call 'shape' the form of a body large enough to be observable, and 'configuration' the shape of the unobservable parts of which large bodies are composed.

ARISTES. Yes, indeed, there are all kinds of shapes and configurations. But perhaps that is not how we get all those different bodies we see. The bodies you produce with your extension alone differ only accidentally; but the majority of those which we see differ perhaps essentially. Earth is not water, a stone is not bread. But it seems to me that with your extension alone you can make only bodies of the same kind.

THEODORE. Here are the prejudices of the senses returning, Aristes. A stone is not bread, true. But, I ask you, is flour wheat? Is bread flour? Are blood, flesh, and bone bread? Or grass? Are these bodies of the same kind or are they different in kind?

ARISTES. Why are you asking me that? Who does not see that bread, flesh, and bone are essentially different bodies?

THEODORE. Because flour is made with wheat, bread with flour, and flesh and bone with bread. If, then, notwithstanding this point, you claim that all bodies are of a different kind, why will you not allow that essentially different bodies can be made with the same extension?

ARISTES. Because your shapes and configurations are accidental to matter and do not change its nature.

THEODORE. True, matter always remains matter, whatever shape we give it; but we can say that a round body is not of the same kind as a square body.

ARISTES. What! If I take some wax and change its shape, will it not be the same wax?

THEODORE. It will be the same wax, the same matter, but we can say that it will not be the same body, for surely what is round is not square. Let us remove the ambiguities. It is essential to the round body that all the parts of its surface be equally distant from the part constituting its center, but it is not essential to it that its inner or unobservable parts have a particular configuration. Likewise it is essential to the wax that the small parts of which it is composed have a particular configuration, but whatever shape we give its mass, we do not change it. Finally, it is essential to matter to be extended, but it is not essential to it to have either a particular shape in its mass or a particular configuration in the unobservable parts composing it. Take note, therefore: what happens to the wheat when it passes through the mill? What happens to the flour when we knead and bake it? It is clear that the situation and configuration of their unobservable parts are changed, as well as the shape of their mass, and I do not grasp how they could undergo a more essential change.

XI. ARISTES. It is claimed, Theodore, that, in addition, a substantial form comes to them.

THEODORE. I am well aware of what is claimed. But I see nothing more accidental to matter than this chimera. What change can it effect on the wheat we grind?

ARISTES. It is that alone which causes it to be flour.

THEODORE. What! Is not well-ground wheat reduced to flour without that?

ARISTES. But perhaps flour and wheat are not essentially different. Perhaps they are two bodies of the same kind.

THEODORE. And are not flour and dough of the same kind? Take note: dough is simply flour and water well mixed together. Do you think that, through proper kneading, we could not make dough without the help of a substantial form?

ARISTES. Yes, but without that we cannot make bread.

THEODORE. Thus, it is a substantial form which changes dough into bread. Here we have it. But when does it come to the dough?

ARISTES. When the bread is baked, well baked.

THEODORE. True. For doughy bread is not, properly speaking, bread. It does not yet have any substantial form other than that of wheat, or of flour, or of dough; for these bodies are of the same kind. However, if the substantial form failed to come, would not well-baked dough be bread? Now, this form comes only when the dough is baked. Let us try, then, to dispense with it. For, after all, it is quite difficult to derive it in connection with the power of matter; we do not know how to get hold of it.

ARISTES. I see indeed, Theodore, that you want to amuse yourself. But let it not be on my account, for I admit to you that I have always considered these so-called forms as fictions of the human mind. Instead, tell me how it is that so many people are given to this view.

THEODORE. Because the senses quite naturally lead them to it. As we have essentially different sensations on the occasion of sensible objects, we are led to believe that these objects differ essentially. And this is true in a sense, for the configurations of the unobservable parts of wax are essentially different from those of water. But as we do not see these tiny parts, their configuration, or their difference, we judge that the masses they compose are substances of different kinds. Now, experience teaches us that in every body there is a common subject, since they can each be made out of one another. We conclude, therefore, that there must be a certain thing which constitutes the specific difference, and it is this that we attribute to the substantial form.

XII. ARISTES. I do indeed understand, Theodore, that this great principle you have proved at such length in our previous discussions is quite necessary, namely, that we must not judge the nature of bodies by the sensations they excite in us, but solely by the idea which represents them and on the basis of which they have all been formed.* Our senses are false witnesses which we must listen to only in respect of the facts. They indicate to us confusedly the relation the bodies surrounding us have to our own body, and this they do sufficiently well for the conservation of life; but there is nothing exact in their testimony. Let us always follow this principle.

THEODORE. Let us follow it, Aristes, and properly understand that all the modalities of extension are and can be but shapes, configurations, observable and unobservable motion, in a word: relations of distance. Thus, an indefinite extension without motion, without change in the relations of distance between its parts, is but a huge mass of unformed matter. When motion is introduced into this matter and moves its parts in an infinity of ways, behold then an infinity of different bodies. For, note, it is impossible for all the parts of this extension to change their relations of distance equally in respect of all the others. Because of this, we can conceive that the parts of extension are moved, and we discover there an infinity of shapes or different bodies. Your head, for example, maintains the same relation of distance to your neck and the other parts of your body, all the parts of which comprise but one body. But as the parts of the air surrounding you move in various ways on your face and on the rest of your body, that air does not comprise a single body with you. Consider each part of the fibers of your body, and conceive how the relation of distance of one particular, determinate part to any of its neighboring parts does not change, or changes very little, and how the relation of distance it has to a certain number of other of its neighboring parts changes constantly. Out of this you construct an infinity of small channels in which the humors circulate. A certain part of fiber in your hand does not move away from another neighboring part of the same fiber, but it constantly changes situation in relation to the spirits, blood, humors and an infinite number of tiny bodies which come into contact

* Dialogues III, IV, V.

with it in passing, and which continually escape through the pores left in our skin by the intertwining of our fibers. This is what causes a particular part or fiber to be just what it is. Thus, keep in mind all the parts of which your fibers are composed. Compare them with one another and with the fluid humors of your body, and you will easily see what I am trying to make you understand.

ARISTES. I am following you, Theodore. Surely nothing is clearer than that all the possible modalities of extension are simply relations of distance, and that it is only through the variety of motion and rest of the parts of matter that this great variety of shapes or different bodies which we admire in the world is produced. When we judge objects through the sensations we have of them, at every turn we find ourselves in a strange predicament. Often we have essentially different sensations of the same objects, and similar sensations of quite different substances. The report of the senses is always obscure and confused. It is necessary to judge things by the ideas representing them. If I consult my senses, then snow, hail, rain, and vapor are bodies of a different kind. However, in consulting the clear and luminous idea of extension I clearly conceive, it seems to me, that a little motion can reduce ice to water and even to vapor, without altering the configuration of the tiny parts of which these bodies are composed. I even think that there is nothing that cannot be made of them by altering their configuration. For as all bodies differ essentially only through the size, configuration, motion, and rest of the unobservable parts of which their masses are composed, it is evident that to produce gold, for example, out of lead or whatever you please, we need simply divide or rather simply join the tiny parts of the lead and give them the size and configuration which are essential to the tiny parts of gold and cause such matter to be gold. We can conceive of this without difficulty. Nonetheless I think that those who seek the philosopher's stone reduce their gold to cinders and smoke, rather than produce something new.

THEODORE. True, Aristes. For who knows the size and configuration of the small parts of this much sought metal? However, even if it were known, who knows how the small parts of the lead or quicksilver are configured? But let us even grant these people working blindly and haphazardly that three parts quicksilver joined together in a certain way make precisely one of those tiny parts out of which gold is composed; I defy them to join these three parts so exactly that they produce no more than one part similar to the parts of gold. Surely the subtle matter found everywhere will in fact prevent them from joining exactly. Perhaps they will end up with mercury; but so badly, so imperfectly, that it will not be able to be exposed to fire without turning to vapor. Even supposing they light upon it in such a way that it undergoes many experiments, what will it be? A new metal, more beautiful, say, than gold, but perhaps quite disdained. The parts of quicksilver will be joined in ratios of four to four, five to five, six to six. But, unfortunately, it was necessary that they be joined only in the ratio of three to three. They will be joined in one way instead of another. Certain gaps will be left between them, which will decrease the metal's weight and will give it a color with which we will be unsatisfied. Bodies, Aristes, are easily changed into other bodies, when it is not required that their unobservable parts alter their configuration. Vapor changes easily into rain, because for this it is enough that the parts decrease their motion and that several be joined together imperfectly. And for a similar reason a cold wind is all that is needed to harden rain into hail. But to change water, for instance, into everything we find in plants, there must be, besides motion, without which nothing happens, molds made expressly to congeal together this highly fluid matter in a certain way.

THEOTIMUS. Very well, Theodore, to what are you confining yourself? You wanted to speak about providence, and you are engaged in questions of physics.

THEODORE. Thank you, Theotimus. Perhaps I have digressed. Nonetheless, it seems to me that everything we have just said is not too remote from our subject. It was necessary for Aristes really to understand that it is by motion that bodies change shape in their masses and change configuration in their unobservable parts. It was necessary, so to speak, to make him sense this truth, and I think that what we have just said is capable of furthering that end. Let us proceed, then, to providence.

XIII. It is surely by means of the sun that God animates the world in which we live. That is how He causes vapors. It is by the motion of vapors that He produces the winds. It is through the contrariety of the winds that He amasses the vapors and turns them into rain; and it is through the rains that He renders our lands fertile. Whether this is or is not entirely as I describe it to you, Aristes, is not important. At least you believe, for instance, that the rain causes the grass to grow, for if it does not rain everything dries up. You believe that a certain herb has the power to purge, another the power to nourish, another to poison. You believe fire softens wax, hardens clay, burns wood, and reduces part of it to ash and finally to glass. In a word, you do not doubt that all bodies possess certain qualities or virtues and that the ordinary providence of God consists in the application of these virtues, by which He produces that variety we admire in His work. Now, these virtues as well as their application consist simply in the efficacy of motion, since it is by means of motion that everything happens. For it is evident that fire burns only by the motion of its parts, that it has the virtue of hardening clay only because, as the parts it scatters in all directions encounter the water in the ground, they expel it by the motion they communicate to it, and so on with the other effects. Thus, fire has force or virtue only by the motion of its parts; and the application of this force to a particular subject arises only from the motion which has transported that subject near the fire. Likewise . . .

ARISTES. What you are saying about fire I extend to all causes and all natural effects. Continue.

XIV. THEODORE. You understand well, then, that ordinary providence is reduced principally to two things: the laws of the communication of motion, since everything happens in bodies by means of motion; and the wise arrangement God introduced into the order of His creatures at the time of their creation, so that His work could be conserved by the natural laws He resolved to follow.

As for the natural laws of motion, God chose the simplest. He willed and still wills now that every body moves or tends to move in a straight line, and that when a body meets other bodies it deviates from the straight line as little as possible; that every body is moved in the direction it is pushed, and that if it is simultaneously pushed by two contrary motions, the greater motion prevails over the weaker one. However, if these two motions are not directly contrary to one another, a body moves along the diagonal line of a parallelogram whose sides have the same proportion as these motions. In fine, God chose the simplest laws based on the single principle that the stronger must prevail over the weaker; and on the condition that there would always be the same quantity of motion in the world from the same direction, I claim that the center of gravity of bodies before and after their impact always remains the same, whether that center is at rest or in motion. I add this condition because experience teaches it to us; beyond which, as God is immutable in His nature, the more uniformity we bestow upon His action, the more we make His conduct bear the character of His attributes.

It is unnecessary, Aristes, to enter any further into the details of these natural laws which God follows in the ordinary course of His providence.* Let them be as you please, it is of little moment right now. You certainly know that God alone moves bodies, that He effects everything in them through motion, that He communicates motion from one to the other only according to certain laws, whatever they might be,** and that the application of these laws arises from the impact of bodies. You know that the impact of bodies is, in virtue of their impenetrability, the occasional or natural cause which determines the efficacy of the general laws. You know that God always acts in a simple and uniform manner; that a moving body always moves in a straight line, but that its impenetrability requires the mover to change; that, nevertheless, it changes as little as possible, either because it always follows the same laws or because the laws it follows are the simplest there are. That is enough concerning the general laws of the communication of motion. Let us proceed to the formation of the universe and to the wise arrangement of its parts which God introduced for all time at the moment of creation, in relation to those general laws; for therein consists the wonder of divine providence. Please, follow me.

XV. I am thinking, Aristes, of a mass of matter without motion. It is simply a block. I want to make a statue out of it. A little motion will soon form it for me. For when we remove the excess, which because of rest constituted a single body with the statue, we are done. I want this statue to have not only the shape of a man, but also his organs and all the parts we do not see. Again, a little motion will form them for me. Because when, for example, the matter surrounding the material from which I want to make the heart is moved, as the remaining matter stays immobile, it is no longer joined with the heart. Thus is the heart

* These natural laws are explained in vol. 3 of the *De la Recherche de la vérité* (Paris: 1700). [*OC* XVII–1 51–143.]
** Dialogue VII.

formed. I can likewise fashion, in principle, the other organs as I conceive them. That is evident. Finally, I want my statue to have not only the organs of a human body, but I also want the mass from which it is made to be changed into flesh and bone, into animal spirits and blood, into a brain, and so on. Again, a little motion will satisfy me. For, assuming that flesh is composed of fibers of a particular configuration intertwined with each other in a particular way, then if it happens that the matter filling the interstices of the fibers of which I am conceiving is moved or no longer has the same relation of distance to the matter of which those fibers are composed, then we have flesh. Likewise, I think that with a little motion the blood, spirits, vessels, and all the rest of the human body can be formed. But what infinitely surpasses the capacity of our mind is knowing which parts need to be removed, which ones we must take away, which ones we must leave.

Let us now suppose that in this machine similar to ours I wish to take a very tiny portion of matter and give it a certain shape, certain organs, a certain configuration in its parts which pleases me. All this will be executed by means of motion, and will never be able to be executed except by motion. For it is evident that a part of matter which constitutes a body with another part, can be separated from it only by motion. Thus, I easily conceive that God can form, in a human body, another body of the same kind which is a thousand or ten thousand times smaller, and in that body another, and so on in the same ratio of a thousand or ten thousand to one. And this He can do at once by giving an infinity of different motions, which He alone knows, to the infinite parts of a certain mass of matter.

ARISTES. What you are telling me about the human body is easy to apply to all the organic bodies of animals and plants.

XVI. THEODORE. Very well then, Aristes. Now conceive of an indefinite mass of matter as large as the universe, from which God wills to fashion a beautiful work, a work which subsists and all of whose beauties are conserved or perpetuated in their species. How will He proceed? Will He first haphazardly remove the parts of matter, in order little by little to form the world out of it by following certain laws; or will He rather form it all at once? Take note: the infinitely perfect Being knows all the consequences of all the motions He can communicate to matter, whatever laws of the communication of motion we assume.

ARISTES. It appears clear to me that God will not remove matter in vain, and since the first impression He can communicate to all its parts is sufficient to produce all kinds of works, surely He will not just decide to form them little by little, by a certain amount of unnecessary motion.

THEOTIMUS. But what will become of the general laws of the communication of motion if God does not use them?

ARISTES. That confuses me somewhat.

THEODORE. What confuses you? These laws as yet dictate nothing; or, rather, they do not exist. For it is the impact of bodies that is the occasional cause of the laws of the communication of motion. Now, without an occasional cause there can be no general law. Thus, before God moved matter, and consequently before bodies could collide with one another, God did not need to and could not follow the general laws of the communication of motion. Moreover, God follows general laws only in order to render His conduct uniform and to make it bear the character of His immutability. Thus, the first step of this conduct, the first motions, cannot and need not be determined by these laws. Finally, an infinity of general laws – which would hardly make them general – would be required to be able to form the organic bodies of plants and animals by following these laws exactly. Thus, the first impression of motion which God initially introduced into matter need not and could not have actually been regulated according to certain general laws; it had to be regulated solely in relation to the beauty of the work God willed to form and had to conserve over time as a consequence of the general laws. Now, this first impression of wisely distributed motion was sufficient to form, in one stroke, the animals and plants which are the most excellent works God made from matter, and all the rest of the universe. That is evident, since all bodies differ from each other only by the shape of their masses and the configuration of their parts, and since motion alone can effect all this, as you have already agreed. Therefore, Aristes, you were right to say that from each mass of matter God made in a stroke what He wanted to form. For although God formed the parts of the universe one after the other, as Scripture seems to teach us, it does not follow that He took any time or followed any general laws in order to bring them, little by little, to their perfection. "And God said, and it was so done."[9] For the first impression of motion was sufficient to produce them in an instant.

[9]   "Dixit, & facta sunt." Malebranche may be speaking elliptically. The reference appears to be to

XVII. THEOTIMUS. That being so, I quite understand how it is a waste of time to try to explain the story of creation which Scripture gives us by means of Cartesian principles or other similar ones.

THEODORE. Surely we are deceived if we claim to prove that God formed the world in following certain general laws of the communication of motion. But we do not waste time examining what must happen to matter as a consequence of the laws of motion. And here is why. Although God formed each part of the universe all at once, He had to have regard for the laws of nature which He desired to follow constantly, in order to make His conduct bear the character of His attributes. For certainly His work could not have been conserved in its beauty had He not proportioned it to the laws of motion. A square sun could not have lasted long; a sun without light would have soon become quite brilliant. You have read, Theotimus, the physics of Mr. Descartes; and someday you will read it, Aristes, for it is well worth it. Thus, I need not explain this any further.

We must now examine what this first impression of motion had to be, by which God at once formed the universe for a certain number of centuries, for it is from this perspective, as it were, that I would have you look and wonder at the infinite wisdom of providence in the arrangement of matter. But I am afraid that your imagination, already perhaps fatigued by the very general matters of which we have just spoken, has left you with insufficient attention to contemplate so vast a subject. For, Aristes, what wisdom is contained in this first step in God's conduct, in this first impression of motion that God will make! What relations, what combinations of relations! Certainly, before this first impression God clearly knew all its consequences and all the combinations of its consequences, not only all the physical combinations, but all the combinations of physics together with morality, and all the combinations of the natural and the supernatural. He compared together all these consequences with all the consequences of all the possible combinations, on all kinds of assumptions. He compared, I say, everything in the plan of making the most excellent work by means of the wisest and most divine ways. He neglected nothing in His action that could be made to bear the character of His attributes; and it is here that He is determined unhesitatingly to take that first step. Try, Aristes,

the first chapter of Genesis, where phrases equivalent to "And God said" and "and it was so done" occur frequently, though never exactly in the form Malebranche gives here.

to see where this first step leads. Note that a grain of matter impelled initially to the right rather than the left, with a weaker or stronger degree of force, could alter everything in the physical, then in the moral; indeed, what am I saying: it could alter everything, even in the supernatural! Therefore, think about the infinite wisdom of Him who compared and regulated everything so well that from the first step He ordered everything toward its end and continues majestically, invariably, always divinely without ever contradicting Himself, without ever repenting, until He assumes possession of that spiritual temple He constructs through Jesus Christ and to which He refers all the stages of His conduct.

ARISTES. True, Theodore, you are right to finish our discussion, for we will soon get lost in such a vast subject.

THEODORE. Think about it, Aristes, for from tomorrow we must become immersed in it.

ARISTES. If we embark on that ocean we shall perish.

THEODORE. No, we shall not perish, provided we do not leave the vessel which is supposed to transport us. Remaining in the church, always subject to its authority, we shall not be shipwrecked if we bump against the rocks lightly. We are made to worship God in the wisdom of His conduct; let us attempt blissfully to lose ourselves in its depths. Never is the human mind better disposed than when in an enforced silence it worships the divine perfections. But that silence of the soul can arise only upon the contemplation of what surpasses us. Courage, then, Aristes; contemplate, admire the general providence of the creator. I have led you to a viewpoint from which you ought to discover an incomprehensible wisdom.

Dialogue XI

Continuation of the same subject. General providence in the arrangement of bodies and in the infinitely infinite combinations of the physical and the moral, the natural and the supernatural.

THEODORE. Have you, Aristes, made any mental effort to compare the first impression of motion God communicated to matter, His first steps in the universe, with the general laws of His ordinary providence and with the various works which had to be conserved and developed through the efficacy of those laws? For it is on the basis of this first impression of motion that we must turn our eyes to God's conduct. That is the viewpoint of general providence, for God never repents nor contradicts Himself. In this regard have you, then, considered the beautiful order of creatures and the simple and uniform conduct of the creator?

ARISTES. Yes, Theodore, but I am too short-sighted. I have discovered much land, but so confusedly that I do not know what to tell you. You have stationed me too high. We discover things from afar, but do not know what we are seeing. You have, as it were, lifted me above the clouds, and my head reels when I look down.

THEODORE. Very well, Aristes, let us descend a little.

THEOTIMUS. But lower down we shall see nothing.

ARISTES. Oh please, Theodore, a little more detail!

THEODORE. Let us descend, Theotimus, since Aristes desires it. But let us three not forget our viewpoint, for soon we shall have to ascend, when our imagination is a little reassured and fortified by detail which is more sensible and more within our reach.

I. Remember our bees from yesterday, Aristes. What a wonderful piece of work this small animal is. How many different organs, what order, what connections, what relations in all its parts! Do not imagine it has fewer than there are in elephants; apparently it has more. Comprehend, then, if you can, the number and the marvellous workings of all the springs of this small machine. It is the feeble action of light that unloosens all these springs. It is the simple presence of objects which determines them and regulates all their movements. Thus, by means of this work which is so exactly formed and so diligently effected, do not judge of the wisdom and foresight of these small animals, for they have none; but judge of the wisdom and foresight of Him who assembled so many springs and ordered them so wisely in relation to so many various objects and different ends. Surely, Aristes, you would be more knowledgeable than philosophers ever were, if you knew exactly the reasons for the construction of the parts of this small animal.

ARISTES. I believe so, Theodore. That surpasses us already. But if such great facility and profound intelligence is required to form a simple fly, how will an infinity of them be produced, all of them contained in one another and all, consequently, ever smaller by a ratio of under one-thousand to one, since a single one of them produces a thousand, and whatever contains is larger than what is contained? That frightens the imagination, yet the mind recognizes the wisdom of the author of such marvels!

THEODORE. Why so, Aristes? If the small bees are organized like the larger ones, whoever conceives a large one can conceive an infinity of small ones contained in each other. It is not, therefore, the multiplicity and the smallness of all these similar animals which ought to enhance your wonder for the wisdom of the creator. But your frightened imagination admires in what is small what we are used to seeing only in what is large.

ARISTES. I believed, Theodore, that I could not wonder too much.

THEODORE. Yes; but one should wonder only with reason. Fear not; if wonder pleases you, you will find much to satisfy you in the multiplicity and smallness of these bees which are contained in one another.

ARISTES. How so, then?

THEODORE. Because they are not all alike.

ARISTES. I quite imagined them so. For what is the probability that the larvae of these flies and the eggs of these larvae have as many organs as the flies themselves, as you claimed yesterday?

II. THEODORE. How poorly you imagined, Aristes! For, quite to the contrary, the larvae possess all the organic parts of the flies. But they possess, beyond this, those parts which are essential to larvae, that is, those which are absolutely necessary for the larvae to be able to search for, devour, and prepare the nourishing juice for the fly which they carry within them and conserve by means of their organs and in the form of larvae.

ARISTES. Well, well! On that account the larvae are more wonderful than the flies; they possess many more organic parts.

THEODORE. Yes, Aristes. And the eggs of the larvae are still more wonderful than the larvae themselves, and so on down the line. So the flies of this year had many more organs a thousand years ago than they do at present. That is a strange paradox. However, take note. It is easy to comprehend that the general laws of the communication of motion are too simple to construct organic bodies.

ARISTES. True, it appears so to me. It is significant that these laws are sufficient to make them grow. There are people who claim that insects come from putrefaction. But if a fly has as many organic parts as an ox, I would rather say that this large animal can be formed from a mound of clay, than maintain that flies are produced from a piece of rotten flesh.[1]

THEODORE. You are right. But since the laws of motion cannot construct bodies composed of an infinity of organs, it is a necessity, therefore, that flies be contained in the larvae from which they hatch. Still, Aristes, do not think that the bee which is still contained in the larva from which it will emerge has the same proportion of size, solidity, and configuration between its parts as it does once it has emerged. For we have often observed that the head of a chicken, for example, when it is in the egg and appears in the form of larvae, is much larger than all the rest of the body, and that the bones assume their consistency only after the other parts. I simply claim that all the organic parts of bees are formed in their larvae, and are so well proportioned to the laws of motion that they can grow through their own construction and through

---

[1] Malebranche is mocking the Aristotelian theory of spontaneous generation of worms, which was partly refuted in the 1688 work *Esperienze intorno alla generazione degl'insetti* (published in Florence) by Tuscan court physician Francesco Redi (1627–97).

the efficacy of these laws, and can assume the shape suitable to their condition, without God intervening anew through extraordinary providence. For it is in this that the incomprehensible wisdom of divine providence consists. This is what can justify providence, although monstrous animals are frequently engendered; for God is not obliged to perform a miracle in order to prevent them from being formed. At the time of creation He constructed animals and plants for future centuries. He established the laws of motion necessary to make them grow. Now He rests, because He does no more than simply follow these laws.

ARISTES. What wisdom in the general providence of the creator!

THEODORE. Would you like us to ascend a little again to our viewpoint, from which we might cast our eye over the marvels of providence?

ARISTES. It seems to me I am there, Theodore. With all the respect of which I am capable I admire and adore the infinite wisdom of the creator in the variety and incomprehensible justice of the various motion He impressed at the outset on that small portion of matter in which He formed, in a single stroke, the bees down through the centuries. Bees! What am I saying? An infinity of larvae we can regard as animals of a different species. And in a tiny space He furnished them with an unobservable nourishment in a thousand ways which escape us. All this occurs in relation to the laws of motion, laws so simple and natural that, although God does everything through them in the ordinary course of His providence, it seems that He affects nothing, that He becomes involved in nothing, in a word, that He rests.

THEODORE. You find, then, Aristes, that this conduct is divine and more excellent than the conduct of a God who at every moment acted by particular volitions, instead of following these general laws; or who, in order to divest Himself of the care of governing His work, had given souls to all the flies, or rather intellects enlightened enough to form their bodies, or at least to guide them according to their needs and to regulate all their labors.

ARISTES. What a comparison!

III. THEODORE. Courage, then, Aristes. Cast your eyes further. In the instant God gave that first impression of motion to the parts of that small portion of matter from which He made bees for all time, or whatever other insect you please, do you think He foresaw that a particular one of these small animals which would hatch in a certain year, on a particular day at a particular hour and under certain circumstances, would also cause someone's eyes to turn toward the object of a criminal passion? Or, indeed, do you think He foresaw it would imprudently come to place itself in the nostrils of a horse and cause it to make a movement fatal for the greatest prince on earth, who is consequently thrown and killed – a death both disastrous and resulting in an infinity of unfortunate consequences? Or, not to combine the physical and the moral, for this entails difficulties whose resolution depends on certain principles I have not explained to you, do you think God foresaw that that insect, through some of its movements, would produce something monstrous or unregulated in the purely material world?

ARISTES. Who doubts that God foresaw all the consequences of that first impression of motion which in an instant formed the entire species of a particular insect in that portion of matter? He even foresaw generally all the consequences of the infinite motions – all different – which He was initially able to bestow upon that same portion of matter. Moreover, He foresaw all the consequences of all the combinations of that portion of matter with all others and their various motions, on all the possible hypotheses involving particular general laws.

THEODORE. Therefore, Aristes, admire and adore the depth of God's wisdom which regulated that first impression of motion on a particular tiny portion of matter, after an infinite number of comparisons of relations, all effected through an eternal act of His intellect. Proceed from this portion of matter to another, and from that to a third. Survey the whole universe, and then in an overview judge the infinitely infinite wisdom which regulated the first impression of motion, by which the entire universe is formed in all its parts and for all time, in such a manner that it is surely the most beautiful work that could be produced in the most general and simplest ways; or, rather, in such a manner that the work and the ways express the perfections God possesses and glories in possessing, better than any other work made in any other way.

ARISTES. What an abyss! What unfathomable depths! What relations and combinations of relations had to be considered in the first impression of matter, in order to create the universe and accommodate it to the general laws of motion which God follows in the ordinary course of His providence! You have brought me to the true viewpoint, from which we discover the infinite wisdom of the creator.

THEODORE. Do you know, Aristes, that as yet you see nothing?

ARISTES. How so nothing?

IV. THEODORE. You see much, Aristes, but it is like nothing in relation to the rest. You have cast your view over the infinitely infinite combinations of the motions of matter. But combine the physical and the moral, the motion of bodies and the volitions of angels and people. Combine, moreover, the natural and the supernatural, and relate all this to Jesus Christ and His church. For since that is the principal of God's designs, it is not likely that in the first impression God communicated to matter He neglected to regulate His action to the relation these motions would be able to have to His great and principal work. Thus, understand what wisdom was required to regulate the first motions of matter, if it is true that the order of nature is subordinate to that of grace; if it is true that death now overtakes us as a consequence of natural laws and that there is nothing miraculous in people being crushed when a house collapses upon them. For you know that our eternity depends on the timely or untimely moment of our death.

ARISTES. Slowly, Theodore. It is God who determines that moment. Our death depends on Him. God alone can give us the gift of perseverance.

V. THEODORE. Who doubts it? Our death depends on God in several respects. It depends on God because it depends on us. For it is in our power to leave a house threatening ruin, and it is God who gave us this power. It depends on God, because it depends on the angels. For God gave the angels the power and the commission of governing the world or the exterior, as it were, of His church. Our timely death depends on God because it depends on Jesus Christ. For in Jesus Christ God gave us a leader who watches over us and who will not countenance death overtaking us in an untimely way, if we ask Him properly for the gift of perseverance. But do you think our death does not also depend on God in the sense that He regulated and produced this first impression of motion, one of the consequences of which is that a certain house would collapse at a particular time in particular circumstances? Everything depends on God because it is He who established all causes, whether free or necessary, and because His foreknowledge is so great that He avails Himself of the former as happily as the latter. For God did not randomly communicate His power to minds; He did this only after having foreseen all the consequences of their motion as well as those of matter. Moreover, everything depends on God because all causes can act only through the efficacy of the divine power. Finally, everything depends on God because through miracles He can interrupt the ordinary course of providence and He never fails to do so when the immutable order of His perfections requires it, that is, when what is due His immutability is of less consideration than what is due His other attributes. But we shall explain all this to you more exactly in what follows. Therefore understand, Aristes, that our salvation is already assured in the chain of causes, whether free or necessary; and that all the effects of general providence are so connected together that the least movement of matter can, in consequence of general laws, contribute to an infinity of considerable events, and that every event depends on an infinity of subordinate causes. Again, wonder at the profundity of God's wisdom which, before He took His initial step, certainly compared the first motions of matter not only with all its natural or necessary consequences but also, much more so, with all the moral and super-natural consequences, on every possible hypothesis.

ARISTES. Surely, Theodore, from the viewpoint at which you have situated me, I discover a wisdom which has no limits. I clearly and distinctly understand that general providence bears the character of an infinite intellect and that it is incomprehensible in a completely different way than imagined by those who have never examined it. *Oh, what profundity in the treasures of God's wisdom and knowledge! How impenetrable His judgments are, how incomprehensible His ways!* A providence founded on an absolute will is much less worthy of the infinitely perfect Being; it bears the character of the divine attributes less than that will which is regulated by the inexhaustible treasures *of wisdom and foreknowledge.*

VI. THEODORE. That is what I wanted to make you see. Let us now enter into some detail, which should refresh your mind and render sensible some of the things you have just been contemplating. Have you ever amused yourself by keeping, in a box, a caterpillar or some other insect commonly believed to transform itself into a butterfly or a fly?

ARISTES. Oh, oh, Theodore! You are suddenly going from the large to the small. You keep coming back to insects.

THEODORE. Because I am pleased we should esteem what everyone despises.

ARISTES. I recall having kept silkworms when I was a child. I took pleasure in watching them spin their cocoons and bury themselves alive in them, in order to revive sometime later.

THEOTIMUS. As for me, Theodore, in a box with some sand I presently have an insect which amuses me, and whose history I know a little. In Latin it is called "Formica-leo." It transforms itself into one of those species of flies which have a very long stomach and are called, I think, "dragonflies."*

THEODORE. I know what it is, Theotimus. But you are wrong to think that it is transformed into a dragonfly.

THEOTIMUS. I have seen it, Theodore; it is an established fact.

THEODORE. And the other day, Theotimus, I saw a mole transformed into a blackbird. How do you think that one animal is transformed into another? It is as difficult for this to occur as it is for insects to be formed from a little flesh.

THEOTIMUS. I understand you, Theodore. The *Formica-leo* is not transformed. It is simply divested of its dress and armature. It loses the horns with which it bores its hole and catches hold of the ants which fall into it. In fact, I have observed these horns in the burrow they make in the sand, and from which they emerge no longer as *Formica-leo*, but as a *dragonfly*, a more magnificent form.

THEODORE. There you have it. The *Formica-leo* and the *dragonfly* are not, properly speaking, two animals of different species. The first contains the second or all the organic parts of which it is composed; note, however, that beyond this it has everything it needs to catch its prey, nourish itself, and prepare suitable nourishment for the other. Now, let us try to imagine the mechanics requisite for the movements which this small animal makes. It only goes backwards in a spiral motion, and always by sinking into the sand; so that, throwing back the sand it takes with its horns with every small movement it makes, it makes a hole terminating in a point, at the bottom of which it hides, its horns always half-open and ready to snatch the ants and other animals unable to overcome the incline

---

* Entomologically, an adult ant lion emerges from the *formica-leo* larva, and not a dragonfly (which belongs to a different species).

of the pit. When its prey escapes and exerts itself sufficiently to make the *Formica-leo* fear losing it, it overwhelms and stuns it by throwing sand on it, thereby rendering the incline of the hole steeper again. Then it seizes its prey, draws it under the sand, sucks its blood and, taking it between its horns, it throws it as far as it can from its hole. Finally, in the finest and most movable sand, it constructs a perfectly round tomb for itself, suitably lines it inside to die in or rather to rest more easily in, and after several weeks is at last seen to emerge in glory in the form of a dragonfly, after having shed several coverings and skins of the *Formica-leo*. Now, how many organic parts are required for all these movements? How many channels are required to carry the blood from which the *Formica-leo* and its dragonfly are nourished? It is clear, then, that this animal, having been stripped of all those parts in its tomb, has far fewer organs when it appears in the form of a fly than when it was seen in the form of *Formica-leo*; unless perhaps we were to maintain that the organs can be constructed and adjusted together as a consequence of the laws of motion. For to suppose that God ordained some intellect to provide for the needs of these insects, to maintain the species and from it always to form new ones, is to render divine providence human, and make it bear the character of a limited intelligence.

ARISTES. Surely, Theodore, there is a greater diversity of organs in the *Formica-leo* than in the fly, and by the same token in the silkworm than in the butterfly. For these worms also shed a rich skin, since they leave a kind of head, a large number of feet, and all the other organs necessary for seeking out, devouring, digesting, and distributing nourishment suitable to the forms of worm and butterfly. Likewise I conceive there is more artistry in the eggs of these worms than in the worms themselves. For supposing the organic parts of the worms to be in the egg, as you say, it is clear that the whole egg contains more artistry than the worm alone, and so on to infinity.

THEODORE. I wish you had read the book by Mr. Malpighi on the silkworm, and what he wrote on the formation of the chicken in the egg.[*] Perhaps you would see that everything I am telling you is not

---

[*] On Bombyce. [Malebranche's reference is to preformation theorist Marcello Malpighi, whose works on chick embryology reported and sketched his microscopic observations of chick embryos through different stages of their development. Cf. *La structure du ver à soie, et la formation du poulet dans l'œuf* (1686). The reference to the Bombyce is to Malpighi's work on the bombycid, the moth or larva of the Bombycidae family of lepidopterous insects, which includes the silkworm of the genus Bombyx.]

without foundation. Yes, Aristes, the egg is the work of an infinite intellect. People find nothing in the egg of a silkworm; and in the egg of a chicken they see only the white and the yolk and perhaps the cords, which again they take for the embryo of the chicken. But . . .

ARISTES. What, the embryo of the chicken! Is that not what we find when we first open the egg? It is white, somewhat hard, and we do not eat it willingly.

THEODORE. No, Aristes, that is one of the cords which serves to hold the yolk so suspended in the white that, however we turn and turn the egg again, the less heavy side of the yolk where the small chicken is always faces up toward the warm stomach of the hen, for that is necessary to make it hatch. There are two of these cords attached on one side to the top of the egg and on the other to the yolk, one at each end.

ARISTES. That is a wonderful mechanism.

THEODORE. There is not much intelligence in it. But you can always see from this that more artistry and skill is required to form the egg and everything it contains, than is required to form the chicken alone, since the egg contains the chicken and furthermore involves its own particular structure.

VII. Please, now, conceive if you can what the present structure must be of the organs of the eggs or worms which, as a consequence of the laws of motion, will be butterflies in ten thousand years. Admire the variety of the organs of all the worms or of all the eggs contained in one another for all that time. Try to imagine what the nourishment could be on which today's worms or butterflies were sustained six thousand years ago. There is a great difference between the form of the dragonfly and that of the *Formica-leo*; but perhaps there is no less difference between the *Formica-leo* and the egg which contains it, and so on. The silkworm is nourished by the leaves of the mulberry tree, but the tiny worm contained in the egg is nourished by nothing; it has everything it needs next to it. True, it does not always eat. But it conserves itself without eating, and for six thousand years has been conserving itself. We find it strange that certain animals spend the winter without nourishment. What a marvel it is, then, that silkworms organize their nourishment so exactly, that they lack it precisely only when they are strong enough to break out of their prison and when the mulberry trees have sprouted tender leaves to nourish them anew.

For example, how wonderful providence is to have enclosed in the eggs from which chickens hatch, everything needed to make them grow and even to nourish them for the first days after they have hatched. For as they still do not know how to eat and they drop everything they peck at, the yolk of the egg, of which half has not been consumed and remains in their stomach, nourishes and fortifies them. But this same providence is still more evident in those neglected eggs which insects spread everywhere. The hen must incubate its eggs itself, or human intervention must come to the rescue. But the eggs of insects, even though they are not incubated, do not fail to hatch quite successfully. By its heat, the sun animates them, as it were, to devour their food at the same time it prepares new food for them, and when the worms break free from their prison, they find themselves in the midst of an abundance of young buds or tender leaves suited to their needs. The insect which gave birth to them took care to put them in a place suitable for them, and left the rest to the more general order of providence. One insect lays its eggs under a leaf which is folded up and attached to a branch, for fear it will fall in winter. Another fixes them in a secure place next to their food. The dragonfly *Formica-leo* goes to hide them in the sand, sheltered from the rain. Most of them spread through the water. In a word, they put them all in places where nothing is wanting for them, not through a particular intellect which guides them, but through the disposition of the parts composing their mechanism and as a result of the general laws of the communication of motion.

ARISTES. That is incomprehensible.

THEODORE. True. But it is good to understand clearly that God's providence is absolutely incomprehensible.

VIII. THEOTIMUS. I must, Theodore, tell you about an experiment I undertook. One summer's day I took a thick piece of meat which I enclosed in a bottle, and I covered it with a piece of gauze. I noted that various flies came to lay their eggs or larvae on this gauze, and when they hatched they ate through the gauze and fell onto the meat, which they devoured in a short time. But as that smelled too bad, I threw it all away.

THEODORE. That is how flies come from putrefaction. They deposit their larvae on the meat and immediately fly away. These larvae eat and the flesh putrefies. After those larvae have eaten well, they enclose themselves in their cocoons and leave them as flies; and on this basis ordinary people believe insects come from putrefaction.

THEOTIMUS. What you are saying is certain. For I have enclosed flesh several times in a hermetically sealed bottle where no flies have been, and I have never found larvae.

ARISTES. But how, then, can it be that we find large ones in all kinds of fruits?

THEODORE. We find large ones, but they entered the fruits as small ones. Look closely, on the skin you will discover either a small hole or its scar. But, please, let us not dwell on the proofs people proffer that there are animals which come from putrefaction. For these proofs are so weak that they do not deserve any reply. We find mice in a newly constructed vessel, or in a place where there were none. Therefore, this animal must have been engendered by some putrefaction. As if these animals were prohibited from attending to their needs at night, from moving on planks and ropes onto small boats and from there onto large ships, or as if vessels could be constructed elsewhere than on shore. I cannot understand how such a large number of people of good sense have been able to commit such a blatant and palpable error for similar reasons. For what is more incomprehensible than an animal forming itself naturally out of a little rotten meat? It is infinitely easier to conceive of a piece of rusty iron being turned into a perfectly good watch; for there are infinitely more parts of greater delicacy in a mouse, than in the most complex clock.

ARISTES. Surely we do not understand how a machine composed of an infinity of different organs perfectly well harmonized together and ordered to different ends, is simply the effect of that law, so simple and natural, that every body must be moved in the direction of least pressure; for that law is much better suited to destroy than to form this machine. But we understand no better how animals of the same species which succeed one another were all contained in the first one.

THEODORE. If we do not understand how that is the case, at least we understand that it is not impossible, since matter is infinitely divisible. But we shall never comprehend how the laws of motion are able to construct bodies composed of an infinity of organs. We have enough trouble conceiving how these laws can, little by little, make them grow. What we clearly conceive is how they can destroy them in a thousand ways. We do not understand how the union of two sexes can be the cause of fecundity, but we understand well that it is not impossible, supposing bodies to be formed already. But that this union is the cause of the organization of the parts of animals, and of a particular animal, is surely something we shall never understand.

ARISTES. Still, I have heard that Mr. Descartes began a treatise on the *Formation of the Foetus*,[2] in which he claims to explain how an animal can be formed from the mixture of the seed of the two sexes.

THEODORE. The sketch by this philosopher can help us understand how the laws of motion suffice to cause the parts of animals to grow little by little. But that these laws are able to form them and connect them all together, is something no one will ever prove. Apparently even Mr. Descartes recognized this himself, for he did not press his ingenious conjectures very far.

ARISTES. His enterprise was a little foolhardy.

THEODORE. Very foolhardy, if he planned to explain the construction of animals as God has made them, for they possess an infinity of parts that need to be known before we look for the causes of their formation. But apparently he did not think of this. For we would not be wise were we to wish to explain exactly how a watchmaker makes a watch, without knowing in advance what parts comprise this work.

ARISTES. Perhaps this philosopher would have done better to explain the generation of plants rather than animals by the laws of motion.

IX. THEODORE. Not at all. That undertaking would have been equally impossible. If seeds do not contain in miniature what we see enlarged in plants, general laws could never render them fertile.

ARISTES. Plants in seeds, an apple tree in a pip! There is always some difficulty believing this, although indeed we know that matter is infinitely divisible.

THEOTIMUS. I tried an experiment which contributed much to persuade me of it. Nonetheless it is not the case that I believe that the apple tree, for example, which is in the germ of the pip, has the same proportions of size and other qualities between its branches, leaves, and fruit, as large trees have; and surely Theodore does not claim this either. I maintain simply that all the organic parts of the apple tree are formed,

---

[2] Descartes, *On Man (L'Homme)* (AT IX).

and are so well proportioned to the laws of motion that through their own construction and the efficacy of these laws they can grow without the assistance of a particular providence.

ARISTES. I understand your opinion quite well; tell us about your experiment.

THEOTIMUS. I took, Aristes, about twenty of the largest beans.* I opened two or three of them and noted that inside they were composed of two parts which separated easily and which, I learned, are called their "lobes"; that the germ was attached to each of these lobes; that on one side it terminated in a point directed outwards, and on the other it was hidden between the lobes. That is what I saw at first. I sowed the other beans to make them germinate and to see how they grow. Two days later I began to open them. I continued for about fifteen days, and I noticed distinctly that the root was contained in that part of the germ which is on the outside and terminates in a point; that the plant was contained in the other part of the germ which passes between the two lobes; that the root was itself a plant which had its roots in the substance of the two lobes of the bean from which it drew its nourishment; that when it had sprouted in the ground as plants in the air, it furnished the plant abundantly with the necessary juice; that, in the majority of the seeds, in the course of its growth the plant passed between the lobes which, after having furthered the growth of the root, changed into leaves and protected the plant from the injuries of the air. Thus I was persuaded that the germ of the bean contained the root of the plant and the plant itself, and that the lobes of the bean were the foundation in which this tiny plant had already been sown and already had its roots. Take some of these large green beans, Aristes, which we eat at the beginning of the summer. Open them carefully. Consider them attentively. Without a microscope you will see a part of what I have just told you. You will discover even the first leaves of the plant in that small part of the germ folded up between the two lobes.

ARISTES. I can well believe all that. But how this seed contains the plant which we shall see in eight years is what is difficult to imagine and what your experiment does not prove.

THEOTIMUS. True. But we see already that the plant is in the

---

* Cf. *The Anatomy of Plants*, by Mr. Grew. Cf. Mr. Malpighi. [Published in London in 1682 by Nehemiah Grew (1641–1712). The reference to Malpighi is to *Anatome plantarum* (London, 1675).]

seed. Without the assistance of a microscope we see that even in winter the tulip is in its bulb. We cannot actually see every part of the plant in the seed.

Very well, Aristes, we must try to imagine them. We cannot imagine how the plants which will emerge in one hundred years are in the seed. We may try to conceive it. At least it can be conceived. But we do not see how the plants are formed solely as a consequence of the general laws of the communication of motion. We cannot imagine how this could occur. Still less can we conceive it. What reasons can we have, then, for holding this, and for denying what Theodore has just told us?

ARISTES. I would be strongly inclined to believe that God conserves animals and plants by particular volitions if Theodore had not pointed out to me that to deprive providence of its generality and simplicity would be to render it human and have it bear the character of a limited intellect and of a particular cause. Thus, we must be disabused of this idea and believe that God, by means of the first impression of motion He communicated to matter, divided it so wisely that in a stroke He formed the animals and plants for all time. That is possible, since matter is infinitely divisible. And it happened this way as this conduct is more worthy of the infinitely perfect Being than any other.

THEOTIMUS. Add to this, Aristes, that Scripture teaches us that God now rests and that initially He made not only the plants for the first year of creation, but also the seed for all others: "Let the earth bring forth the green herb, and such as may seed, and the fruit tree yielding fruit after its kind, *which may have seed in itself* upon the earth."[*] These last words, "which may have seed in itself," joined to these, "and he rested on the seventh day from all his work which he had done,"[**] indicate, it seems to me, that to conserve His creatures God no longer acts as He did when He formed them. Now, He acts only in two ways, either by particular or by general laws. Thus, at present He does no more than simply follow His laws, unless there are significant reasons which require Him to interrupt the course of His providence, reasons which I do not believe you can find in the needs of animals or plants.

X. ARISTES. Undoubtedly not. For if there were less of them by half, there would be only too many. For I ask you, Theodore, to what end are there so many plants useless to our ends, so many insects which

[*] Genesis 1[: 11].   [**] [Genesis] 2: 2.

bother us? These small animals are the work of an infinite intellect, I grant it. But this is just what raises the difficulty. For why are works formed to nourish the swallows and devour our buds? Is it because the world would not be as perfect as it is, Theodore, if the caterpillars and may-bugs did not come to strip the trees of their fruits and leaves?

THEODORE. If, Aristes, you judge the works of God solely in relation to yourself, you will soon blaspheme against providence; you will soon pass strange judgments on the wisdom of the creator.

ARISTES. But how so! Is it not for human beings that God made everything?

THEODORE. Yes, Aristes, for that man under whose feet God subjected everything without exception; for that man of whom St. Paul speaks in the second chapter of the letter to the Hebrews.[3] God made everything for His Son, everything for His church, and His church for Him. But if He made fleas for humans, that is surely to bite and punish them. Most animals have their particular vermin. But people have this advantage over them, that for them there are several species of vermin, so true it is that God made everything for them. To devour their wheat God made locusts. To fertilize their lands He practically provided wings for the seeds of thistles. To wither all their fruits He created insects of an infinity of species. In this sense, if God did not make everything for humans, He did not stop far from doing so.

Take note, Aristes, God's foreknowledge is infinite. He must regulate all His plans according to it. Before giving matter that initial impression of motion which forms the universe for all time, He clearly knew all the consequences of all the possible combinations of the physical and the moral, on all kinds of hypotheses. He foresaw that under particular circumstances man would sin and that his sin would be communicated to his entire posterity as a consequence of the laws of the union of the soul and the body.* Thus, since He willed to permit him this fatal sin, He had to make use of His foreknowledge and combine the physical with the moral so wisely that all His works would effect between themselves the most beautiful harmony possible for all time. And this marvellous harmony consists in part in that order of justice by which creatures revolt against man, as it were, and punish him for his

---

[3] Hebrews 2: 8–9.

* *De la Recherche de la vérité*, Bk. II, Ch. 7 [*OC* I 304–9], and the Elucidation [VIII] of that same Chapter [*OC* III 71–118].

disobedience, because man revolted against the creator, which God foresaw would happen.* That is why there are so many different animals at war with us.

XI. ARISTES. What! Before man sinned, God had already prepared the instruments of His vengeance? For you know that man was created only after everything else. That seems very harsh to me.

THEODORE. Before his sin man had no enemies; his body and everything surrounding it was subject to him. He did not suffer pain against his will. It was just that God protected him by a particular providence, or committed him to the care of some guardian angel to prevent the grave consequences of the general laws of the communication of motion. Had he preserved his innocence, God would always have shown him the same consideration, for He never fails to render justice to His creatures. What! Do you not hold that God makes use of His foreknowledge, and chooses the wisest combination possible between the physical and the moral? Would you have an infinitely perfect Being not make His conduct bear the character of His wisdom, or have Him make and test man before making those creatures which bother us; or, finally, would you have Him change and reform His work after the sin of Adam? God, Aristes, never repents nor contradicts Himself. The first step He makes is governed by the foreknowledge of everything that must follow it. What am I saying! God is determined to take that first step only after He has compared it not simply with everything that must follow it, but again with an infinity of other first steps on an infinity of other hypotheses and all kinds of other combinations of the physical and of the moral, and of the natural and the supernatural.

Once again, Aristes, God foresaw that under particular circumstances man would revolt. After having compared everything, He thought He should permit sin.** I say "permit." For He did not necessitate man to commit it. Thus, through a wise combination of the physical and the moral He had to make His action bear the marks of His foreknowledge. But, you say, He thereby prepared the instruments of His vengeance before sin. Why not, since He foresaw that sin and willed to punish it? Had God made innocent people unhappy, and employed these instru-

---

* Ecclesiasticus 39: 35.
** For the reasons for God's permission of sin, cf. the *Conversations chrétiennes*, pp. 63ff. of the Paris edition of 1702 [*OC* IV 45f.].

ments prior to sin, we would have grounds for complaint. But is a father forbidden to keep rods ready to punish his children, especially when he foresees that they will not fail to disobey him? May he not even show them those threatening rods, to hold them to their duty? Can we doubt that bears and lions were created before sin? And is it not sufficient to believe that those cruel beasts, which God now uses to punish us, respected in Adam his innocence and divine majesty? However, if you find it bad that prior to the commission of sin God prepared the instruments for punishing it, console yourself. For by His foreknowledge He also found the remedy for evil, before it arose. Certainly, before the fall of the first man, God already had the plan to sanctify His church through Jesus Christ. For St. Paul teaches us that, in their marriage prior to sin, Adam and Eve were the illustration of Jesus Christ and His church: "This is a great sacrament; but I speak in Christ and in the church;"* the first Adam being, up to his sin, the illustration of the second, the "figure of him who was to come."** Because the foreknowledge of God is infinite, Aristes, it regulated everything. God permitted sin. Why? Because He foresaw that His work, restored in a particular way, would be worth more than the same work in its original construction. He established the general laws which would cause freezing and hail in the fields. He created cruel beasts and an infinity of very bothersome animals. Why all this? Because He foresaw sin. He established an infinity of marvellous relations between all His works; He represented Jesus Christ and His church in a thousand ways. This is an effect and a certain indication of His foreknowledge and wisdom. Thus, do not find fault with God's having used His foreknowledge and having from the outset wisely combined the physical and the moral, not for the brief time when the first man preserved his innocence, but in relation to him and to all his children as they would be to the end of time. Adam could not complain that the animals ate one another, rendering to him, as to their sovereign, the respect due to him. Rather, he was to learn thereby that they were only brutes incapable of reason, and that God had distinguished him among all His creatures.

XII. ARISTES. I understand what you are telling me. God had good reasons to create large animals capable of punishing us. But why are there so many small insects which do us neither good nor harm, and

* Ephesians 5[: 32]. ** Romans 5[: 14].

whose mechanism is perhaps more marvellous than that of the large animals, a mechanism hidden from our eyes and which does not teach us the wisdom of the creator?

THEODORE. Without stopping to prove to you that there is no animal, however small, which cannot in one way or another have some relation to us, I reply that the principal design of God in the formation of these small insects was not to do us some good or harm by them, but to adorn the universe with works worthy of His wisdom and other attributes. Ordinary people despise insects, but there are those who do study them. Apparently even angels admire them. But even if all intellects neglected them, that these small works express the divine perfections and render the universe more perfect in itself, although less comfortable for sinners, is sufficient for God to create them, assuming He can conserve them without multiplying His ways. For God surely made the most perfect work through the most general and simplest ways. He foresaw that the laws of motion would suffice to conserve in the world whatever species of insect you please. He willed to draw all possible applications from His laws, in order to render His work more complete. Thus, first He formed the entire species of that insect, by means of a wonderful division of a certain portion of matter. For we must indeed always keep in mind that it is by motion that everything happens in bodies, and that in the first determination of motion it was an issue of indifference to God whether He moved the parts of matter one way or another, as there were no general laws of the communication of motion before bodies collided with one another.[*]

ARISTES. I can conceive that, Theodore. A world full of an infinity of animals small and large is more beautiful and better indicates intelligence than another where there are no insects. Now, such a world costs God no more than another, as it were, or does not demand a more composite and more particular providence, and consequently bears the character of divine immutability as much as any other. Thus, we need not be surprised that God has made such a large number of insects.

XIII. THEODORE. What you are saying here is general, Aristes, and does not exclude an infinity of reasons which God had to make the world such as it is.

[*] Dialogue X, §XVII.

ARISTES. I must tell you, Theodore, of a thought which came to mind when you were telling me about the apparent transformation of insects. Worms crawl on the ground. They lead there a sad and humiliating life. They make a tomb for themselves from which they depart in glory. I imagined to myself that God thereby willed to represent the life, death, and resurrection of His Son, and even of all Christians.

THEODORE. I am pleased, Aristes, that this thought has entered your mind. For although it appears quite solid to me, I would not have dared suggest it to you.

ARISTES. Why not?

THEODORE. Because there is something base about it which displeases the imagination. Aside from that, this simple word 'worm' or 'insect,' combined with the lofty idea we ought to have of the savior, can excite mockery. For I think you know that the ridiculous consists in the conjunction of the small and the great.

ARISTES. Yes, but what appears ridiculous to the imagination is often quite reasonable and correct. For we often scorn what we do not know.

THEODORE. True, Aristes. The lily of the field which we neglect is more magnificently adorned than Solomon in all his glory. Jesus Christ did not fear mockery when He advanced that paradox. The imagination is content as well as reason when we compare the magnificence of King Solomon to the glory of Jesus Christ resurrected. But it is not too satisfied when in the beauty of the lilies we seek a representation of the savior. Still, the magnificence of Solomon was simply the work of the hands of people, but it is God who gave the flowers all their ornaments.

ARISTES. You believe, then, Theodore, that God represented Jesus Christ in the plants as well as in the insects?

THEODORE. I believe, Theodore, that God related everything to Jesus Christ in a thousand different ways, and that not only creatures express the divine perfections, but they are also as much as possible emblems of His beloved Son. The seed we sow must die, as it were, in order to be resuscitated and bear its fruit.

I find it is a natural representation of Jesus Christ, who died in order to be gloriously resurrected: "unless the grain of wheat falling into the ground die, itself remaineth alone. But if it die, it bringeth forth much fruit."[*]

* John 12: 24.

212

THEOTIMUS. We can use anything we wish to make comparisons. But it does not follow from this that God willed to represent Jesus Christ by all those things which have some arbitrary relation to Him.

THEODORE. If I did not know, Theotimus, that the principal designs of God are Jesus Christ and His church;* that nothing pleases God except through Jesus Christ; that it is in and through Jesus Christ that the universe subsists, because it is only He who sanctifies it, who elevates it from its profane state, who renders it divine; I would regard what I take for natural representations as arbitrary and thoroughly base comparisons. Yes, Theotimus, I believe that God had Jesus Christ so much in view in the formation of the universe, that what is perhaps most wonderful in providence is the relation it constantly establishes between the natural and the supernatural, between what occurs in the world and what happens to the church of Jesus Christ.

XIV. ARISTES. Surely, Theotimus, that God willed to represent Jesus Christ by the changes in insects is something that strikes us as obvious. A worm is a contemptible and impotent creature – witness Jesus scorned: "But I am a worm, and no man: the reproach of men, and the outcast of the people."** See Him charged with our infirmities and weakness: "Surely he hath borne our infirmities."† A worm envelops itself in its tomb and revives some time later without being corrupted. Jesus Christ dies and is resurrected without his body having been subject to corruption.‡ "Neither did his flesh see corruption." The worm is resurrected into a completely spiritual body, as it were. It does not crawl, it flies. It is no longer nourished on putrefaction, it drinks from flowers alone. No longer is there anything contemptible about it; nothing could be more magnificently adorned. Likewise the resurrected Jesus Christ is filled with glory. He is raised to the heavens. He does not crawl, as it were, from village to village in Judaea. He is no longer subject to the weariness and other infirmities of His laborious life. He governs all nations and can break them "like a potter's vessel," as Scripture says.§ He has been given sovereign power in heaven and on earth. Can we say this comparison is arbitrary? Surely it is natural.

---

* Dialogue IX, §VI.   ** Psalm 21[: 7].   † Isaiah 53[: 4].
‡ Acts 2: 21 [Malebranche's reference should be to Acts 2: 31].
§ Psalm 110 [The reference should be to Psalm 2: 9.]

THEODORE. You are forgetting, Aristes, parallels too exact to be neglected.

ARISTES. What are they?

THEODORE. Before their transformation these worms are always growing. But flies, butterflies and in general everything that flies after having been a worm, everything that has been transformed, always remains in the same state.

ARISTES. That is because on earth we can continually merit, and in heaven we remain what we are.

THEODORE. I have observed that insects do not reproduce unless they are resuscitated and, so to say, glorified.

ARISTES. You are right. This is because Jesus Christ sent the Holy Spirit to His church, He rendered it fruitful, only after His Resurrection and entrance into the possession of His glory. "For as yet the spirit was not given," says St. John, "because Jesus was not yet glorified."* And, as Jesus Christ says Himself: "It is expedient to you that I go: for if I go not, the Paraclete will not come to you; but if I go, I will send him to you."** I am no longer surprised that God made such a large number of insects.

THEODORE. If God is pleased in His work, Theotimus, it is because everywhere He sees His beloved Son. For we are ourselves pleasing to God only insofar as we are expressions of Jesus Christ. Matter, by the modalities of which it is capable, cannot exactly express the internal dispositions of the blessed soul of Jesus, His love, His humility, His patience. But it can imitate the various states in which His body exists quite well. And I think that the arrangement of matter which represents Jesus Christ and His church does more honor to the love of the Father for the Son, than any other arrangement honoring His wisdom and other attributes.

ARISTES. Perhaps it is even the case that there is more art and intelligence in the dispositions of matter suited to represent Jesus Christ. For when a living animal fashions a tomb for itself and encloses itself inside in order to emerge from it in glory, can we imagine a more wonderful mechanism than that by which these motions are executed?

THEOTIMUS. I share your views entirely. And I believe, moreover, Theodore, that by means of the dispositions of the body God even

* [John] 7: 39.   ** John 16: 7.

represented the dispositions of the holy soul of Jesus, and principally the surplus of His love for His church. For St. Paul teaches us that this violent passion of love which causes us to leave our father and mother for our wife, is a representation of the surplus of the love of Jesus Christ for His bride.* Now, although animals, strictly speaking, are incapable of love, they express this great passion by their movements and conserve their species a little like people. Thus, they naturally represent that violent love of Jesus Christ, which led him to spill His blood for His church. In effect, in order strongly and vividly to express the folly of the Cross, the annihilation of the Son of God, the surplus of His love for people, a blind and foolish passion was required, as it were, a passion which knows no measure.

ARISTES. Let us wonder at the incomprehensible wisdom of the creator in the marvellous relations He established between His works, and let us not view as useless those creatures capable of doing us neither good nor evil. They render God's work more perfect. They express the divine perfections. They represent Jesus Christ. That is what constitutes their excellence and beauty.

THEODORE. Let us admire them, Aristes. But as God loves His creatures only in proportion to the relation they have to His perfections, only insofar as they are expressions of His Son, let us be perfect as our heavenly Father is perfect, and form ourselves on the model He gave us in His Son. It is not enough for Christians to represent Jesus Christ as animals and material beings do, nor even as Solomon does through the trappings of a brilliant glory. We must imitate His virtues, those He practised in His humiliating and arduous life, those which suit us as far as we crawl on the earth, knowing well that a new life is reserved for us in heaven, from where we await our glorious transformation. "But our conversation is in heaven," says St. Paul, "from whence also we look for the savior, our Lord Jesus Christ, who will reform the body of our lowness, made like to the body of his glory."**

* Ephesians 5[: 31–2].   ** Philippians 3: 20–1.

Dialogue XII

Divine providence in the laws of the union of the soul and body, and how through these laws God unites us to all His works. The laws of the union of the mind with Reason. By these two kinds of law societies are formed. How God distributes temporal goods to people through the angels, and inner grace and all kinds of goods through Jesus Christ. The generality of providence.

ARISTES. Ah, Theodore! How wonderful God is in His works! How profound are His designs! What relations, what combinations of relations had to be compared in order to give matter that first impression which formed the universe with all its parts, not for a moment, but for all time! What wisdom in the subordination of causes, in the series of effects, in the union of all the bodies composing the world, in the infinite combinations not only of the physical and the physical, but of the physical and the moral, and of both and the supernatural!

THEODORE. If the simple arrangement of matter, if the necessary effects of certain very simple and very general laws of motion appear to us to be something so marvellous, what are we to think of the various societies established and conserved as a consequence of the laws of the union of the soul and the body? How are we to judge the Jewish people and their religion, and finally the church of Jesus Christ? What should we think, my dear Aristes, of the celestial Jerusalem, if we had a clear idea of the nature of the materials from which that holy city will be constructed, and were able to judge the order and harmony of all the parts composing it? For, after all, if God made so magnificent a world with the vilest creatures, with matter, what kind of work will the temple of the true Solomon be, which will be constructed with intellects alone? It is the impact of bodies which determines the efficacy of natural laws, and this occasional cause, as completely blind and simple as it is, produces an infinity of wonderful works by the wisdom of the providence of the creator. Thus, Aristes, what will be the beauty of God's house, given that it is an intellectual nature enlightened by eternal wisdom and subsisting in that same wisdom; given that it is Jesus Christ, as I shall soon explain, who determines the efficacy of the supernatural laws by which God executes this great work? How magnificent this temple of the true Solomon will be! Would it not be more perfect than this universe, in the same way that minds are more noble than bodies and the occasional cause of the order of grace is more excellent than that which determines the efficacy of natural laws? Surely God is always alike unto Himself. His wisdom is not exhausted by the marvels He has effected. Undoubtedly He will derive from spiritual nature beauties which will infinitely surpass everything He has made from matter. What do you think of this, my dear Aristes?

ARISTES. I think, Theodore, that you enjoy rushing me from one abyss to another.

THEODORE. Yes, from profound abysses to others even more profound. Do you want to consider only the beauties of this visible world, only the general providence of the creator in the division of matter, in the formation and arrangement of bodies? This earth we inhabit is made only for the societies formed on it. If people are capable of forming societies together, it is to serve God in a single religion. Everything is naturally related to the church of Jesus Christ, to the spiritual temple God is to inhabit eternally. Thus, we need not dwell on this first abyss of God's providence concerning the division of matter and the arrangement of bodies. We must leave there in order to enter into a second abyss, and from there into a third, until we have arrived where everything ends and where God relates all things. For it is not sufficient to believe and to say that God's providence is incomprehensible; we must know it, we must comprehend it. And to assure ourselves properly that it is incomprehensible in every way, we must attempt to grasp it in every sense, and follow it everywhere.

ARISTES. But we shall never exhaust the scope of providence even if we follow it to heaven.

THEODORE. Yes, if we follow it that far. But soon we shall lose sight of it. We shall in fact be obliged, Aristes, to pass very lightly over what should detain us most, be it the magnificence of the work or the wisdom of its action. For God's providence over His church is an abyss in which even the mind enlightened by faith discovers almost nothing. But let us begin our subject.

I. You know, Aristes, that man is composed of two substances, mind and body, whose modalities are reciprocal as a consequence of the general laws which are causes of the union of these two natures; and you are aware of the fact that these laws are but the constant and ever efficacious volitions of the creator. Let us look a little at the wisdom of these laws.

The moment we light a torch or the sun rises, light is spread in all directions, or rather it pushes the matter surrounding it in all directions. As the surfaces of bodies are variously disposed, they reflect light variously, or rather they diversely modify the pressure the sun causes. (Imagine this as you please; it does not matter at the moment. It is likely that these modifications of pressure consist only in the vibrations or jolts which the subtle matter receives through that which grazes it by constantly gliding over the surface of the bodies between it and those same bodies.) All these vibrations or modifications of pressure, alternatively faster or slower, are extended or communicated in a circle instantly in all directions, because everything is a plenum. Thus, once we open our eyes, all the rays of light which are reflected from the surface of bodies and enter through the pupil, are scattered in the eye's humors in order to be collected together on the optic nerve. (The eye's mechanism is a wonderful thing considered in relation to the action of light, but we should not dwell on that. If you want to study this matter, you can consult the *Dioptrics* of Mr. Descartes.)[1] The optic nerve is thus affected in several different ways by the various vibrations of pressure of the matter which reaches it freely; and the disturbance of this nerve is communicated to that part of the brain to which the soul is closely united. Whence it happens, as a consequence of the union of the soul and body:

---

[1] AT VI.

II. 1. That we are informed of the presence of bodies. For although bodies are invisible by themselves, the sensation of color which we have in us even despite ourselves on their occasion, persuades us that we see them themselves, because God's operation in us contains nothing sensible. And as colors touch us lightly, instead of regarding them as sensations which belong to us, we attribute them to objects. Thus, we judge that objects exist and are white and black, red and blue, in a word, however we see them.

2. Although the differences in the light reflected from objects consist only in faster or slower vibrations of pressure, nonetheless the sensations of color which correspond to these vibrations or modifications of light possess essential differences, so that in that way we more easily distinguish objects from one another.

3. Thus, by the sensible differences between colors which bound precisely the intelligible parts we find in the idea of space or extension, in a stroke we discover an infinity of different objects, their size, their shape, their situation, their motion, or their rest. We discover all this very precisely in relation to the conservation of life, but otherwise quite confusedly and quite imperfectly. For we must always remember that the senses are not given to us to discover the truth or the exact relations between objects, but to conserve our body and everything that can be useful for it. As everything we see, for example, is not always either good or bad for our health, and as often two different objects can reflect light in the same way (for how many bodies are equally white or black), the sensations of color hardly touch or affect us. They help us distinguish objects rather than unite us to or separate us from them. It is to those objects that we relate these sensations, and not to the eyes which receive the impression of light. For by a kind of natural judgment which is not free, we always refer sensations to what most suits the good of the body. We refer the pain of a prick not to the thorn but to the pricked finger. We refer heat, smell, and taste both to the organs and to the objects. As for color, we refer it to objects alone. It is clear that all this must be the case for the good of the body, and it is not necessary for me to explain it to you.

III. That, Aristes, is what appears most simple and more general in the sensations of colors. Let us briefly look at how all this happens. For it seems to me that an infinite wisdom is required to regulate that detail of colors in such a way that objects near or distant are seen approximately according to their size. When I say "distant," I do not mean they are excessively so, for when bodies are so small or so distant that they can no longer do us either good or evil, they escape us.

ARISTES. Surely, Theodore, an infinite wisdom is required to effect, at every blink of the eye, this distribution of colors over the idea which I have of space, so that a new world is formed in my soul, as it were, a world which is related closely enough to the one in which we exist. But I doubt God is so exact in the sensations He gives us, for I know well that the sun does not diminish in proportion as it moves off the horizon, and yet it appears smaller to me.

THEODORE. But at least you are quite certain that God is always exact in making you see the sun as that much smaller as it moves further off the horizon. This exactitude, Aristes, signifies something.

ARISTES. I believe so. But how does it happen?

THEODORE. It happens because God, as a consequence of these laws, instantly gives us the sensations of color which we would give to ourselves if we knew optics in a divine manner and understood precisely all the relations obtaining between the shapes of the bodies which are projected to the back of our eyes. For God determines to act in our soul in a particular way only through the changes which happen in our body. He acts in the soul only through the knowledge He has of what is happening in our organs, as if He knew nothing of what is happening externally. That is the principle; let us follow it.

The more distant a body, the smaller the image traced at the back of the eye. Now, when the sun rises or sets, it appears further from us than it does at noon, not only because we observe a lot of land between us and the horizon where it is then, but also because the sky appears like a flattened spheroid.[*] Thus, the image of the rising sun should be smaller at the back of our eyes than that of the risen sun. Yet it is equal, or almost equal. Thus, the sun must appear larger when it is near the horizon than when it is well above it.

THEOTIMUS. I carried out an experiment which demonstrates what you are saying, namely, that the reason why the sun appears to change size arises from the fact that it appears noticeably to change its distance. I took a piece of glass which I covered in smoke in such a way

* Cf. my *Réponse à M. Regis* [*OC* XVII–1 257–320].

that, looking through it, I would see only the sun.[*] And I noticed that this apparent size disappeared every time I looked through that glass, because since the smoke eclipsed all the other objects between us and the horizon, by using my senses I no longer saw a distance beyond which I could place the sun.

ARISTES. Would that not be because the glass, obscured by the smoke, lets only a few rays into the eye?

THEOTIMUS. No, Aristes. For whether I looked at it with or without the glass, I always saw the sun as being equal in size when it was far above the horizon.

ARISTES. That is conclusive.

IV. THEODORE. Therefore take note, Aristes, that although you are persuaded that the sun is no smaller at noon than in the evening, nonetheless you see it as much smaller. And from this fact judge that the sensation of the luminous circle which represents that star to you is fixed exactly to a certain size only in relation to the colors of all the objects we see between us and it since, using our senses, it is the sight of these objects which makes us see it as distant. Again, judge from this fact that all the apparent sizes not only of the sun, but generally of everything we see, must all be regulated by reasoning similar to what I have just provided, in order to explain to you the various appearances of the size of the sun. And understand, if you can, the wisdom of the creator who, as soon as you open your eyes, unhesitatingly gives you an infinity of various sensations of color of an infinity of objects, sensations which indicate their difference and size for you not in proportion to the difference and size of the images traced at the back of the eye, but – what is noteworthy – determined by the most exact possible reasonings of optics.

ARISTES. In this I do not wonder so much at the wisdom, exactitude, and uniformity of the creator, as at the stupidity or the pride of those philosophers who imagine that the soul itself forms the ideas of all the objects surrounding us. Nonetheless I grant that, once our eyes are open, an infinite wisdom is necessary to produce that distribution of colors which partially reveals to us how the world is. But I would prefer that our senses never deceived us, at least not in matters of consequence nor in too striking a manner. The other day, as I moved down the river

[*] This is done by passing the glass through the flame of a candle.

very quickly, it seemed to me that the trees on the shore moved, and I have a friend who often sees everything turning in front of him, so that he cannot keep standing. These illusions are quite striking and bothersome.

V. THEODORE. God could not do anything better, Aristes, in willing to act in us as a consequence of certain general laws. For recall the principle I have just told you. The occasional causes of what must happen to the soul can be found only in what happens to the body, since it is the soul and the body which God willed to unite together. Thus, God can determine to act in our soul in a particular way only by the various changes that occur in our body. He may act in our soul not insofar as He knows what is happening outside of it, but insofar as He knows nothing of what surrounds us, only through the knowledge He has of what is happening in our organs. Once again, Aristes, that is the principle. Imagine that your soul knows exactly everything new that happens in its body, and that it gives itself all the most suitable sensations possible for the preservation of life. That will be exactly what God does in the soul.

You are walking, then, and your soul has an inner feeling of the movements taking place in your body. Thus, although the traces of objects change place in your eyes, your soul sees these objects as stationary. But you are on a boat. You have no sensation of being transported, since the motion of the boat alters nothing in your body which could inform you of this. Thus, you will see the entire shore in motion, since the images of the objects continually change place in your eyes.

Likewise when you bow your head, you turn your eyes and, if you wish, you look at a steeple from between your legs. You should not see it reversed top to bottom. For although the image of that steeple is reversed in your eyes, or rather in your brain, for objects are always represented inversely at the back of the eye, your soul knows the disposition of your body by the change that disposition makes in your brain, and therefore it should judge that the steeple is upright. Now, once again, as a consequence of the laws of the union of the soul and the body, God gives us all the sensations of objects, in the same way our soul would give them to itself if it reasoned precisely from the knowledge it would have of everything that happens in the body or in the principal part of the brain. Note, however, that the knowledge we have of the nature of the size or situation of objects does not help us at all in correcting our sensations, unless this knowledge is sensible and is presently produced by some change presently occurring in the brain. For although I know that the sun is not larger in the evening and the morning than at noon, I continue to see it as larger. Although the shore is stationary, nonetheless it appears to me to move. Although I know that a particular medicine is quite good for me, still I find it tastes terrible, and so on with the other sensations. For God regulates the sensations He gives us only on the basis of the action of the occasional cause He has established for that purpose, that is, on the basis of the changes of the principal part of our body to which our soul is immediately united. Now, sometimes it happens that the course of spirits is either so impetuous or so irregular that it prevents the present change in the disposition of the nerves and muscles from being communicated to that principal part of the brain. And then everything is inverted: we see two objects for one; we can no longer preserve our balance to remain upright, and perhaps that is what happens to your friend. But what do you want? The laws of the union of the soul and body are infinitely wise and are always followed precisely; but the occasional cause which determines the efficacy of those laws often fails our needs, because the laws of the communication of motion are no longer subject to our volitions.

ARISTES. What order and wisdom there are in the laws of the union of the soul and the body! From the moment our eyes are open we see an infinity of different objects and their different relations, without any effort on our part. Surely nothing is more marvellous, although no one reflects on it.

VI. THEODORE. God does not only reveal His works to us in this way, but He unites us to them in thousands and thousands of ways. If I see, for instance, a child about to fall, the sight alone – the simple disturbance of the optic nerve – will trigger certain springs in my brain which make me move forward to help it and cry out for others to help it; and at the same time my soul will be touched and moved, as it should be, for the good of the human species. If I look at a man's face, I understand whether he is sad or happy, whether he esteems or despises me, whether he wishes me good or evil; all of which I understand by certain movements of the eyes and lips which have no relation to what they signify. For when a dog bares its teeth at me I conclude it is angry. But even though a man shows me his teeth, I do not think he wants to bite me. The laugh of a person instills trust in me, and that of a dog makes me afraid. Painters who wish to express passions find themselves quite confused. Often they take one look or grimace for another. But when people are animated by a certain passion, all those who observe them really notice it, although perhaps they do not notice whether their lips are raised or lowered, whether their nose curves out or in, whether their eyes are open or closed. This is because God unites us together by the laws of the union of the soul and the body, not only people with people, but every creature with all those which are useful to it, each one in its own way. For if, for example, I see my dog trying to please me, that is, wagging its tail, arching its back, lowering its head, this sight connects me to it and produces not only a kind of friendship in my soul but also certain movements in my body which also bind the dog to me in return. That is what produces people's passion for their dog and a dog's loyalty to its master. This is because a little light triggers certain springs in the two machines composed by the wisdom of the creator, in such a way that they can be mutually conserved. That is common to both; but humans, beyond the mechanism of their body, possess a soul and consequently sensations and movements which correspond to the changes occurring in their body, whereas the dog is but a mere machine, whose movements, regulated toward their end, should cause us to wonder at the infinite intelligence of Him who constructed it.

ARISTES. I understand, Theodore, that the laws of the union of the soul and body do not serve to unite our mind simply to a certain portion of matter, but also to the rest of the universe; nonetheless to certain parts much more than to others, according as they are more necessary to us. My soul is spread, as it were, in my body through pleasure and pain. It goes outside it by other, less vivid sensations. But through light and colors it is spread everywhere, even as far as the heavens. It even takes an interest in what happens there. It examines the movements of the heavens. It is distressed by or rejoices in the phenomena it observes there and it relates everything to itself, as if it had a right to all creatures. What a marvellous series of connections this is!

VII. THEODORE. Consider rather the consequences of these laws in the establishment of societies, in the education of children, in the advance of the sciences, in the formation of the church. How do you know me? You see only my face, simply a certain arrangement of matter visible through color alone. I move the air by my words. That air strikes your ear, and you know what I am thinking. We do not train children merely like horses and dogs; we also inspire the sentiments of honor and probity in them. In your books you have the opinions of the philosophers and the history of the ages. But without the laws of the union of the soul and the body, your entire library would be no more than black and white paper. Follow these laws in religion. How are you a Christian? It is because you are not deaf. It is through our ears that faith is spread into our hearts. It is by means of miracles that we have seen that we are certain of what we do not see. It is through the power these laws give us that the minister of Jesus Christ can move his tongue to preach the Gospel and absolve us of our sins. It is evident that these laws are of utmost importance in religion, morals, the sciences, society, and for the public and the private good. Thus it is one of the most important ways of which God avails Himself in the ordinary course of His providence, for the conservation of the universe and the execution of His plans.

VIII. Now, I ask you, how many relations and combinations of relations were required to establish these wonderful laws and to apply them to their effects in such a way that all the consequences of these laws were the best and most worthy of God which are possible. Do not consider simply these laws in relation to the conservation of the human species. That is already infinitely beyond us. Courage! Compare them with all the things to which they are related, however contemptible they appear to you. Why, for example, do wheat and barley not have, like thistles and sowthistles, tiny wings for the wind to carry and spread them over the fields? Has not God foreseen that people who clear their lands of thistles would take sufficient care to sow wheat there? How is it that a dog has such a keen sense of smell for the odors which animals emit, yet it cannot smell flowers? Is it not because God foresaw that people and this animal would go hunting together? If, in creating plants and animals, God had regard for the use to which people would put the power they have as a consequence of the laws of the soul and body, surely He would have omitted nothing in insuring that these laws had advantageous consequences for society and for religion. Thus, judge the incomprehensible wisdom of God's providence in the establishment of these laws as you judged it in the first impression of motion which He communicated to matter when He formed the universe.

ARISTES. My mind gets lost in these kinds of reflections.

THEOTIMUS. True, but it does not fail to understand that the wisdom of God in His general providence is incomprehensible in every way.

IX. THEODORE. Let us continue, then. The human mind is united to the human body in such a way that through the body it is connected to everything surrounding it, not only to observable objects, but to invisible substances; for people are attached and connected together through the mind as well as the body, all as a consequence of the general laws which God employs to govern the world. And this is the marvel of providence. The human mind is also united to God, to eternal Wisdom, to the universal Reason which enlightens all intellects. And it is also united to Him through the general laws of which our attention is the occasional cause which determines their efficacy. The disturbances excited in my brain are the occasional or natural cause of my sensations. But the occasional cause of the presence of ideas to my mind is my attention. I think about what I will. It is up to me to examine the subject we are speaking about, or any other. But it is not up to me to feel pleasure, to hear music, to see one particular color alone. This is because we are not made to know the relations that obtain between our body and sensible objects. For it would not be fitting that, in order to conserve its life, the soul be required to attend to everything capable of making us lose it. It had to discern this by the short and sure proof of instinct or sensation, so that it could fully occupy itself with fulfilling its duties to God and seeking the true goods, the goods of the mind. It is true that at present our sensations introduce discord and confusion into our ideas, and that thus we do not always think on what we will. But this is a result of sin; and if God permitted this sin, it is because He knew well that it would provide the occasion for the sacrifice of Jesus Christ, from which He derives more glory than from the perseverance of the first man. In any case, as Adam had all the assistance necessary to persevere, God need not have given him those prevenient graces which are well-suited only for a weak and languid nature. However, this is not the time to examine the reasons why God permitted sin.

X. It is, then, our attention that is the occasional and natural cause of the presence of ideas to our mind, as a consequence of the general laws of its union with universal Reason. And God had to establish it in this way in the plan He had to make us perfectly free and capable of deserving heaven. For it is clear that if the first man had not existed as the master of his ideas by means of his attention, his distraction would not have been voluntary, a distraction which was the primary cause of his disobedience. As we are able to love only by love of the good, we always determine ourselves according to what appears best to us at the time we determine ourselves. Thus, were we in no way masters of our attention, or were our attention not the natural cause of our ideas, we would be neither free nor in a position to be worthy. For we would be unable even to suspend our consent, since we would not have the power to consider reasons capable of leading us to suspend it. Now, God willed that we be free, not simply because this quality is necessary for us to merit heaven, for which we are all created, but also because He willed to make the wisdom of His providence and His nature as seer into hearts shine forth, by availing Himself as readily of free causes as of necessary causes in the execution of His designs.

For you should know that God forms all societies, governs all nations, the Jewish people, the present-day church, the future church, by the general laws of the union of minds with His eternal wisdom. It is through the aid of that wisdom that sovereigns rule beneficently and establish excellent laws: "By me kings reign, and lawgivers decree just things."[*] It is even by consulting wisdom that the wicked succeed in their pernicious designs. For as a consequence of the general laws we can press the light of Reason into the service of injustice. If a good bishop watches over his flock, if he sanctifies it, if God uses him to elect certain people to the ranks of the predestined, it is in part because this minister of Jesus Christ consults Reason by his attention to the order of his duties. And if, on the contrary, wretches corrupt the mind and heart of those who are subject to their rule, if God allows them to be the cause of people's ruin, that is in part because these ministers of the devil abuse the lights they receive from God as a consequence of natural laws.

[*] Proverbs 8: 15.

Angels, all the blessed spirits, and even the sacred humanity of Jesus Christ, albeit in a different way, are all united to eternal wisdom. Their attention is the occasional or natural cause of their knowledge. Now, Jesus Christ governs souls, and the angels have power over body. God uses Jesus Christ to sanctify His church, as He used the angels to lead the Jewish people. Thus, since all the blessed spirits always consult the eternal wisdom much more than we do, in order to do nothing that does not conform to order, it is clear that God uses the general laws of the union of minds and Reason in order to execute all the plans He entrusted to intelligent natures. He even employs the malice of demons and the use which He certainly foresees they will make of the natural lights remaining in them. This is not because God acts by particular volitions at every moment, but because He established certain laws in certain circumstances only through the knowledge of the marvellous effects to follow from them, for His foreknowledge has no limits and is the rule of His providence.

XI. ARISTES. It seems to me, Theodore, that you are considering the wisdom of providence only in the establishment of the general laws and in the series of causes with their effects, leaving all creatures to act according to their own nature, the free ones freely and the necessary ones according to the power they have as a consequence of the general laws. You want me to wonder at and adore the impenetrable depth of God's foreknowledge in the infinitely infinite combinations He had to effect in order to choose between an infinity of ways of producing the universe, which He had to follow to act in the most divine way possible. Surely, Theodore, that is the most beautiful aspect of providence, but it is not the most pleasing. This infinite foreknowledge is the foundation of that generality and that uniformity of conduct which bears the character of the wisdom and immutability of God; but it does not, it seems to me, bear the character either of His goodness toward people or of the severity of His justice against the wicked. It is not possible for God either to avenge us through a general providence against those who do us some injustice, or to provide for all our needs. And what means do we have of being content when we lack something? Thus, Theodore, I wonder at your providence, but I am not quite satisfied with it. It is excellent for God, but not too good for us, for I hold that God provides for all His creatures.

THEODORE. He provides for them, Aristes, quite abundantly. Do you want me to lay out the blessings of the creator?

ARISTES. I know that every day God gives us a thousand goods.

THEODORE. What more do you want?

ARISTES. To lack nothing. God made all the creatures for us, but some people have no bread. A providence which would furnish all equal natures equally or which would distribute good and evil exactly according to merit would be a true providence. To what end this infinite number of stars? What is it to us that the movements of the heavens are so well regulated? Would that God left all that and thought a little more about us. The earth is desolated by the injustice and malignity of its inhabitants. Yet God does not make Himself feared; it seems that He does not interfere in the details of our affairs. The simplicity and generality of His ways causes this thought to occur to me.

THEODORE. I understand you, Aristes. You assume the position of those who do not want providence and who believe that here below it is chance that makes and rules everything. And I understand that you would thereby oppose the generality and uniformity of God's conduct in the government of the world, because that conduct is accommodated neither to our needs nor to our inclinations. However, please note that I am reasoning on the basis of established facts and on the basis of the idea of the infinitely perfect Being. For after all the sun rises indifferently over the good and the wicked. It often scorches the lands of good people while rendering those of impious people fruitful. In short, people are not wretched insofar as they are criminal. This is what must be reconciled with a providence worthy of the infinitely perfect Being.

Hail, Aristes, ravages the harvest of a good person. Either this disagreeable effect is a natural result of general laws, or God produces it by a particular providence. If God produces this effect by a particular providence, then far from providing for all, He positively wills and even brings it about that the most virtuous person in the land goes without bread. It is better, then, to maintain that this grievous effect is a natural consequence of general laws. And that is what we commonly mean when we say that God permitted a particular misfortune. Moreover, you agree that governing the world by general laws is beautiful and sublime conduct which is worthy of the divine attributes. You claim only that it does not sufficiently bear the character both of the paternal goodness of God toward the good, and of the severity of His justice toward the wicked. This is because you do not consider the misery of good people and the prosperity of the impious. For, things being as you see they are, I submit to you that a particular providence of God would not in the least bear the character of His goodness and justice, since quite often the just are overwhelmed by evils and the wretched are showered with goods. However, supposing God's conduct has to bear the character of His wisdom as well as His goodness and justice, although at present the goods and evils are not proportioned to people's merits, I do not find any harshness in His general providence. For in the first place I submit to you that, from an infinity of possible combinations of causes with their effects, God chose that which most felicitously reconciled the physical and the moral. And I submit that the hail which it was foreseen would fall on the land of a particular good person, was not for God one of the motives for making His choice; but rather that hail which He foresaw would fall on the land of a wicked person. I say, one of His "motives." Note the signification of this term. For if God afflicts the just it is because He wants to test them and have them deserve their reward. In truth, that is His motive. In the second place, I reply that as all people are sinners, they do not deserve that God should depart from the simplicity and generality of His ways, in order at present to proportion goods and evils to their merits and demerits; that sooner or later God will render to people according to their deeds, at least on the day He will come to judge the living and the dead, and that He will establish general laws to punish them, which will last an eternity.

XII. Still, Aristes, do not think I am claiming that God never acts by particular volitions and that at present He only follows the natural laws He established initially. I am claiming simply that God never departs from the simplicity of His ways or the uniformity of His conduct without serious reasons. For the more general providence is, the more it bears the character of the divine attributes.

ARISTES. But when does He have these important reasons? Perhaps He never has them.

THEODORE. God has these important reasons when the glory He derives from the perfection of His work counterbalances that which He receives from the uniformity of His conduct. He has these serious reasons when what He owes to His immutability is equal to or of less consideration than what He owes to another one of His attributes in particular. In a word, He has these reasons when He acts as much or more according His nature by departing from the general laws He has prescribed for Himself than by following them. For God always acts according to what He is. He inviolably follows the immutable order of His own perfections, because it is in His own substance that He finds His law, and because He cannot prevent Himself from doing justice to Himself or from acting for His glory, in the sense in which I explained to you the other day.* If you ask me when it happens that God acts as much or more according to what He is by departing from His general laws, than by following them, I reply that I know nothing of this. But I do indeed know that sometimes it happens. I know that, I say, because faith teaches it to me. For Reason, which shows me that it is possible, does not assure me that it actually happens.

ARISTES. I understand your thought, Theodore, and I see nothing more in conformity with Reason and even with experience. For in fact we observe, through all the effects known to us, that they have their natural causes, and that thus God governs the world according to general laws He established for that purpose.

XIII. THEOTIMUS. True. But still Scripture is replete with miracles which God performed in favor of the Jewish people, and I do not think He neglects His church so much that He does not depart from the generality of His conduct in its favor.

THEODORE. Surely, Theotimus, God performs infinitely more miracles for His church than for the synagogue. The Jewish people were accustomed to seeing what we call miracles. There had to be a prodigious quantity of them as the abundance of their lands and the prosperity of their forces were bound to their exacting observance of the commandments of the law. For it is unlikely that the physical and the moral could accord so exactly that Judaea was always fertile in proportion as its inhabitants were good people. Thus, there is an infinity of miracles among the Jews.** But I believe many more happen among us, not in order to adjust temporal goods and evils to our deeds, but to distribute to us gratuitously the true goods or aid necessary to acquire

* Cf. Dialogue IX.
** By "miracle," I mean the effects which depend on general laws which are not known to us naturally. Cf. the *II. Lettre* of my *Réponse au I. Volume des Réflexions Philosophiques & Théologiques de M. Arnauld* [*OC* VIII 693–750].

them, all of which nevertheless happens without God at every instant departing from the generality of His conduct. This is what I must explain to you, for it is surely what is most wonderful in providence.

XIV. As human beings are composites of mind and body, they require two kinds of goods, those of the mind and those of the body. God also abundantly provided them with these goods, through the establishment of the general laws about which I have been speaking to you until now. For not only was the first man initially placed in the earthly paradise where he found fruits in abundance and one among them capable of rendering him immortal, but his body was as yet so well formed and so subject to his mind, that as a consequence of general laws He could enjoy all those goods without deviating from the true good. On the other side he was united to sovereign Reason, and his attention, over which he was the absolute master, was the natural or occasional cause of his knowledge. His sensations never disturbed his ideas despite himself. For he was exempt from that concupiscence which incessantly solicits the mind to renounce Reason to follow the passions. He was, then, well provided for in mind and body. For he clearly knew the true good, and could not lose it. He sensed the goods of the body and could enjoy them. All this as a consequence of the general laws of the mind's union with the body on the one hand and with universal Reason on the other, without these two unions harming one another, because the body was subject to the mind.

But, having sinned, man suddenly found himself quite poorly provided with these two kinds of goods. For since order, which is the law God inviolably follows, does not permit there to be exceptions at every moment to the general laws of the communication of motion in favor of a rebel, it is necessary that the action of objects is communicated to the principal part of the brain and that the mind itself is affected by them as a consequence of the laws of the union of the soul and body. Now the mind, disturbed despite itself by hunger, thirst, weariness, pain, a thousand different passions, can neither love nor seek as is necessary the true goods; and instead of peaceably enjoying those of the body, the slightest deprivation renders it unhappy. Thus, man, a rebel against God, having lost the authority he had over his body, by the loss of this power finds himself deprived of the goods with which providence had provided him. Let us see briefly how God will draw him from this unhappy condition, without doing anything against the order of justice and without changing the general laws He has established.

XV. Prior to sin the human being was and had to be subject only to God. For the angels had no authority naturally over minds which are equal to them. They have power only over bodies, inferior substances. Now, as Adam was the master of what happened in the principal part of his brain, even when the demons were able to disrupt the economy of his body through the action of objects or otherwise, they could neither unsettle him nor render him unhappy. But having lost almost all the power he had over his body, for there was still as much of it left for him as was necessary to conserve the human species which God did not wish to destroy because of the redeemer, he found himself necessarily subjected to angelic nature, which could now disquiet and tempt him by producing traces in his body suitable to excite unpleasant thoughts in his mind. Since God then saw him as a sinner, as it were, at the discretion of the devil and surrounded by an infinity of creatures capable of killing us, deprived as he was of all help, He subjected him to the conduct of the angels, not only him but also all his posterity and principally the nation of which the Messiah was to be born. Thus you see that, although they are sinners, God distributes temporal goods to people not through a blind providence but through the action of an intelligent nature. As for the goods of the mind or that inner grace which counterbalances the efforts of concupiscence and delivers us from the captivity of sin, you know that God gives them to us through the sovereign priest of true goods, our savior Jesus Christ.

Surely, Aristes, this conduct of God is admirable. By their sin human beings become the slaves of the devil, the most wicked of creatures, and they depend on the body, the vilest of substances. God subjects us to the angels both out of justice and out of goodness. In this way He protects us against the demons and He proportions the temporal goods and evils to our good and evil deeds. Note, however, He alters nothing in the general laws of motion, nor even in those of the union of the mind with the body and with universal Reason. For, after all, in the sovereign power which God gave Jesus Christ as man over all things generally, and in the power the angels have over what concerns temporal goods and evils, God departs as little as possible from the simplicity of His ways and the generality of His providence, because He communicates His power to creatures only through the establishment of certain general laws. Please, follow me.

XVI. The power angels have is over bodies only. For if they act on our minds, it is because of the union of the soul and body. Now, nothing happens in the body except through movement, and it is a contradiction to suppose that angels could produce it as true causes.[*] Thus, the power of angels over bodies and consequently over us derives only from a general law which God has made for Himself, to move bodies at the will of angels. God does not, then, depart from the generality of His providence when He employs the ministry of angels to govern nations, since angels act only through the efficacy of and as a consequence of a general law.

We must say the same thing about Jesus Christ as man, as leader of the church, as sovereign priest of true goods. His power is infinitely greater than that of the angels. It extends to everything, even to minds and to hearts. However, it is through His intercession that our mediator exercises His power: "He is always living to make intercession for us;"[**] it is through desires ever efficacious because they are always granted: "And I knew that thou hearest me always."[†] In truth, it is not through a moral intercession like that of one person interceding on behalf of another, but through an intercession which is powerful and ever unfailing in virtue of the general law God established to refuse His Son nothing, through an intercession similar to that of the practical desires we form to move our arm, to walk, or to speak. For all the desires of creatures are powerless in themselves; they are efficacious only by the divine power; they do not act independently; they are, fundamentally, only prayers. But as God is immutable in His conduct and follows exactly the laws He has established, we have the power to move our arm, and the leader of the church has the power to sanctify it, because God established the laws of the union of body and soul to our advantage, and because He promised His Son to grant all His desires, according to the words of Jesus Christ Himself: "And I knew that thou hearest me always;"[‡] "And I will ask the Father, and he shall give you another Paraclete;"[§] "All power is given to me in heaven and on earth;"[¶] and, according to what His Father said to Him after His resurrection, as

---

[*] Dialogue VII, §vi, etc. [**] Hebrews 7: 25. [†] John 11: 42. [‡] John 11: 42.
[§] John 14: 16. [¶] Matthew 28[: 18].

explained by St. Peter and St. Paul: "Thou art my Son, this day have I begotten thee;"[*] "Ask of me, and I will give them the Gentiles for thy inheritance ..."[**]

XVII. ARISTES. I am persuaded, Theodore, that creatures do not have their own efficacy and that God communicates His power to them only through the establishment of certain general laws. I have the power to move my arm, but it is in consequence of the general laws of the union of the soul and body; and as God is immutable, He is steadfast in His decrees. God gave the angel leading the Jewish people the power to punish and reward them, because He willed that that angel's volitions be followed by their effects. With this I agree. But it is God Himself who ordained this minister to do everything he had to do. God gave Jesus Christ a sovereign power. But He prescribed for Him everything He must do. It is not God who obeys the angels, it is the angels who obey God. And Jesus Christ teaches us that He told us nothing by Himself and that His Father indicated to Him everything He was to tell us. Jesus Christ intercedes, but for those whom His Father has predestined. He disposes of everything in His Father's house, but He disposes of nothing on His own. In this way God departs from the generality of His providence. For although He executes the volitions of Jesus Christ and the angels as a consequence of general laws, He forms all their volitions in them, and He does this by particular inspirations. There is no general law for that.

THEODORE. Are you quite certain, Aristes? Assuredly, if God ordains particularly that the holy soul of the savior and the angels should form all the desires they have in respect of us, God thereby departs from the generality of His providence.[†] However, I ask you, do you think that the angel leading the Jewish people needed much light to govern them, and that the true Solomon had to be united in a particular way to eternal wisdom, in order to succeed in the construction of His great work?

ARISTES. Yes, certainly.

THEODORE. Why so? The most stupid and least enlightened mind can succeed as well as the wisest of people, if it is shown everything it

[*] Acts 13: 33. Cf. Hebrews 5: 5.   [**] Psalm 2 [: 8 in the Douay-Rheims version].
[†] All this is explained at quite some length in my *Réponses à M. Arnauld*, principally in the *Réponse* to his *Dissertation* [*OC* VII 469–615] and in my first letter concerning the third volume of the *Réflexions* [*OC* VIII 791–890].

must do and the way it must do it, especially if everything to be done consists simply in forming certain desires in particular circumstances. Now, according to you, neither the angel leading the people nor even Jesus Christ desired anything His Father did not ordain in detail. I do not see, then, that He required an extraordinary wisdom for His work. But, further, please tell me what this sovereign power consists in, which Jesus Christ has received.

ARISTES. That all His desires are fulfilled.

THEODORE. But, Aristes, if Jesus Christ can desire nothing except by an express order of His Father, if His desires are not in His power, how will He be capable of receiving any true power? You have the power to move your arm, but that is because it depends on you to will or not to will to move it. Cease being the master of your volitions, and in virtue of that alone you lose all your powers. Is this not evident? Please take care, then, not to offend the wisdom of the savior, and not to deprive Him of His power. Do not divest Him of the glory He should derive from the part He has in the construction of the eternal temple. If He had no other part than to form the powerless desires commanded by particular decrees, His work would not, it seems to me, do Him much honor.

XVIII. ARISTES. No, Theodore. But God derives even more from it.

THEODORE. For God should derive much more glory from the magnificence of the eternal temple than the wise Solomon who constructs it. But let us consider it a little. Let us compare the two principal orders of divine providence together, in order to identify which one is the more worthy of the divine attributes. According to the first, God initially forms a particular design independently of the ways of executing it. He chooses its architect. He imbues Him with wisdom and intelligence. Beyond this He shows Him in detail all the desires He is to form, and all the circumstances of these desires. And, finally, He Himself very precisely executes all the desires He ordered formed. There is the idea you have of God's conduct, since you would have Him form all the desires of the sacred soul of Jesus Christ by particular volitions. And here is the idea I have of it.* I believe that God, having through His infinite foreknowledge foreseen all the effects of all the possible laws He could establish, united His Word to a particular

---

    * Cf. Dialogue IX, §§ x–xii.

human nature, and that in certain circumstances the work which resulted from this union would do Him greater honor than any other work produced in any other way. As God once again foresaw that by acting through the sacred humanity of our mediator in very simple and very general ways – I mean, in the ways most worthy of the divine attributes – it would make such use of His power or form such a chain of desires with perfect freedom (for God allows free causes to act freely) that, with these desires granted and worthy of being granted because of His sacrifice, the future church to be formed from this would be fuller and more perfect than if God had chosen any other nature in any other circumstance.

Please compare, then, the idea you have of providence with mine. Which of the two indicates more wisdom and foreknowledge? Mine bears the character of the most inscrutable quality of the divinity, which is the foresight of the free acts of creatures in all kinds of circumstances. According to mine, God employs free causes as readily as necessary causes for the execution of His plans. According to mine, God does not blindly form His wise plans. Before forming them, speaking humanly, He compares all possible works with all possible means of executing them. According to my idea, God must derive an infinite glory from the wisdom of His conduct; but His glory detracts nothing from that of the free causes to whom He communicates His power without depriving them of their freedom. God gives them part of the glory of His work and of theirs, by letting them act freely according to their nature; and in this way He augments His own. For it is infinitely more difficult to execute His plans securely through free causes than through necessary causes, causes either necessitated or invincibly determined by express decrees and invincible impressions.

ARISTES. I agree, Theodore, that there is more wisdom, and that God and even the sacred humanity of our mediator derive more glory according to this idea of providence, than according to any other.

THEODORE. You could add that according to this idea, we understand quite well how Jesus Christ did not receive a sovereign power over all nations in vain, and why His sacred humanity had to be united to eternal wisdom, so that He might favorably execute His work. But it is enough that you agree that one of these two orders of providence is wiser than the other; for one would have to be very impious to attribute to God the order which appears the least worthy of His attributes.

XIX. ARISTES. I submit, Theodore. But please explain to me how it is that Jesus Christ Himself says that He is faithfully executing the volitions of His Father. "For I do always the things that please him," He says.* And, in another place: "For I have not spoken of myself; but the Father who sent me, he commanded me what I should say, and what I should speak. And I know that his commandment is life everlasting. The things therefore that I speak, even as the Father said unto me, so do I speak."** How do we reconcile these passages, and a number of other similar ones, with the view that God does not form all the desires of the human will of Jesus Christ by particular volitions? This somewhat troubles me.

THEODORE. I confess, Aristes, I simply do not understand how these passages can trouble you. What! Are you not aware that the divine Word, in which the sacred humanity of the savior subsists, is the living law of the eternal Father, and that it is even a contradiction that the human will of Jesus Christ should ever deviate from that law? Tell me, please, when you give alms, are you not certain that you do the will of God; and if you were really assured that you always did good works, could you not say, without fear, "for I do always the things that please him"?

ARISTES. True. But there would always be a considerable difference.

THEODORE. Quite considerable, certainly. For how do we know we do God's will in giving alms? Perhaps it is because we have read in the written law that God commands us to help the wretched; or because in entering into ourselves to consult the divine law we have found in that eternal code, as St. Augustine calls it, that such is the will of the infinitely perfect Being. Thus, Aristes, understand that the divine Word is the law of God Himself, and the inviolable rule of His volitions. Therein are found all the divine commandments. "But in the only-begotten Word of the Father every commandment exists," says St. Augustine.† Understand that all minds, some more, some less, possess the freedom to consult this law. Comprehend that their attention is the

---

* John 8: 29.   ** John 12: 49, 50.

† *Confessiones*, Bk. 13, Ch. 15. "The command of the Father Himself is the Son. How then is He not the command of the Father, He who is the word of the Father?" (*Sermones* 140.) *De Verbis Evangelium* VI. [The reference to the *Confessions* appears to be mistaken; the excerpt can be found in Augustine's *In Iohannis evangelium tractatus* 47, §14, trans. John Rettig, *The Fathers of the Church* (Washington, D.C., Catholic University of America Press, 1993), vol. 88, p. 227.]

occasional cause which explains all its divine commandments to them as
a result of the general laws of their union with Reason. Know that we
can do nothing that is not pleasing to God when we observe exactly
what we find written there. Above all, know that the sacred humanity of
the savior is more closely united to that law than the most enlightened
of intellects, and that it is through that humanity that God willed to
explain its obscurities to us. Note, however, that He did not deprive
Him of His freedom or of the power to dispose of that attention which
is the occasional cause of all our knowledge. For, although under the
direction of the Word, surely the blessed soul of Jesus has the power to
think what it pleases in order to execute the work for which God chose
it, since for the execution of His designs God, in His capacity as seer
into hearts, employs free causes as readily as necessary causes.[*]

XX. Nonetheless, Aristes, do not think that God never departs from
the generality of His conduct in respect of the humanity of Jesus Christ,
and that He forms the desires of that blessed soul only as a consequence
of the general laws of the union it has with the Word. When God
foresees that our mediator must, from an infinity of good works He
discovers in the Word as a consequence of His attention, make that
choice whose results are the best possible, then God, who never deviates
from the simplicity of His ways without reason, does not determine
Him through particular volitions to do what He will in any event do
through the use of His freedom in consequence of general laws. When,
however, because of the infinite and infinitely infinite combinations of
all the effects which are or will be the results of His desires, the blessed
soul of the savior actually could, from among several good works (for
He can choose only good works), choose those which appear the best
and whose results would nevertheless be less advantageous for His
work; then, if God derives more glory from the beauty of the work than
from the simplicity of His ways, He departs from this simplicity and
acts in a particular and extraordinary way in the humanity of the savior,
in order that it might will precisely what will honor Him most. But
although He acts in the savior's humanity in this way, I believe He
never determines it by invincible impressions of sensation, however

[*] Cf. the first *Lettre touchant le II. & le III. Volume des Reflexions de M. Arnauld* [*OC* VIII
791–890], and the *Réponse* to his *Dissertation* [*OC* VII 469–615], and the first letter I wrote [*OC*
IX 991–1000] concerning his [letter of 30 April, 1694].

infallible they are, so that it has the greatest possible part in the glory of His work. For that conduct which does honor to the freedom and power of Jesus Christ is still more glorious to God than any other, since it expresses His nature as seer into hearts and is excellent testimony to His knowledge of how to employ free causes as readily as necessary causes for the execution of His plans.

ARISTES. I understand your thought perfectly, Theodore. You hold that God never departs from the simplicity and generality of His ways without important reasons, so that His providence does not resemble that of limited intellects. You would have His foreknowledge be the foundation of the predestination even of Jesus Christ, and would have it that if He unites His Word to a particular nature in certain circumstances, this is because He foresees that the work which would follow from that predestination, which is the cause and foundation of the predestination of all the elect as a consequence of the general laws comprising the order of grace – that that work, I say, would be the most excellent which could be produced by the most divine ways. You would have it that the work and the ways joined together are more worthy of God than any other work produced in any other way.

XXI. THEODORE. Yes, Aristes, by this principle I mean that God can act only for Himself, only by the love He bears Himself, only through His will which is not, as in us, an impression which comes to Him from elsewhere and leads Him elsewhere. In a word, He can act only for His glory, only to express the divine perfections which He invincibly loves, which He glories in possessing, and in which He revels in the necessity of His Being. He wills that by its beauty and magnificence His work bears the character of His excellence and greatness, and that His ways do not contradict His infinite wisdom and His immutability. If there are faults in His work, monsters among bodies, and an infinity of sinners and damned, this is because there cannot be faults in His conduct; it is because He must not form His plans independently of His ways. For the beauty of the universe and for the salvation of men, God made everything He can make, not absolutely, but in acting as He must act, acting for His glory according to everything He is. He loves all things in proportion as they are lovable. He wills the beauty of His work and that all men be saved, He wills the conversion of all sinners. But He loves His wisdom more, He loves it invincibly, He follows it inviolably. The immutable order of His divine perfections: therein lies His law and the rule of His conduct, a law which does not prohibit Him from loving us and from willing that all His creatures be just, holy, happy, and perfect, but a law which does not allow Him for a moment to depart from the generality of His ways for sinners. His providence sufficiently bears the marks of His goodness toward people. Let us grant that, let us rejoice that it also expresses His other attributes.

THEOTIMUS. Well then, Aristes, what do you think of divine providence?

ARISTES. I adore it, and submit myself to it.

THEODORE. Infinite discussions would be required, Aristes, to make you consider all the beauties of this adorable providence and to notice its principal traits in what we see happen every day. But I have sufficiently explained this principle to you, it seems to me. Follow it closely, and you will surely understand that all those contradictions which constitute a pitiable triumph for the enemies of providence are so many proofs which demonstrate what I have just told you.

Dialogue XIII

We must not criticize the ordinary way of speaking about providence. The principal general laws by which God governs the world. God's providence in the infallibility He preserves for His church.

I. ARISTES. Ah, Theodore! How beautiful and noble the idea of providence you have given me appears! But, further, how fertile and luminous it is, how suited to silencing the freethinkers and the impious! Never has a principle had more advantageous consequences for religion and morality. What light is spread by this wonderful principle, what difficulties it dispels! All those effects which contradict one another in the order of nature and in that of grace indicate no contradiction in the cause which produces them; on the contrary, they are so many evident proofs of the uniformity of God's conduct. All those ills which afflict us, all those disorders which appal us, all this accords easily with the wisdom, the goodness, the justice of Him who rules everything. I would have the wicked removed who live among the good, but I patiently await the consummation of time, the day of the harvest, that great day destined to render to all according to their deeds. God's work must be executed by ways which bear the character of His attributes. At present I admire the majestic course of general providence.

THEODORE. I see, Aristes, that you have closely and happily followed the principle which I have explained to you over these few days, for you still appear quite affected by it. But have you really understood it, have you really mastered it? That is what I still doubt, for in such a short time it is quite difficult to have meditated sufficiently to put yourself in full possession of it. Please, share some of your reflections with us, so that I might be delivered from my doubt and be at rest. For the more useful principles are, and the more fertile they are, the greater the danger of not really grasping them fully.

II. ARISTES. I think so too, Theodore. But what you have told us is so clear, your way of explaining providence agrees so perfectly with the idea of the infinitely perfect Being and with everything we see happen, that I know it is true. What joy I feel seeing myself delivered from the prejudice into which I see ordinary people and even many philosophers fall! When some evil befalls a wicked man or a man known to be such, everyone immediately judges of God's designs and decides outright that God willed to punish him. However, if it happens, as it only too frequently does, that someone treacherous, a blackguard, succeeds in his enterprises, or that a good man succumbs to the calumny of his enemies, is this because God wants to punish the one and reward the other? Not at all. Some say it is because God wants to test the virtue of this good man, and others say it is an evil He permitted but did not cause by design. I find that those people reason more soundly who derive glory from hating and scorning the poor, on the principle that God Himself hates and scorns the wretched because He leaves them in their misery. On what basis do we decide to judge God's plans? Should we not understand that we know nothing of them, since we constantly contradict ourselves?

THEODORE. Is this how you understand my principles, Aristes? Is this the use you make of them? I find that those whom you condemn are more right than you.

ARISTES. How so, Theodore! I think you jest or want to amuse yourself by contradicting me.

THEODORE. Not at all.

ARISTES. What! Do you approve, then, the impertinence of those impassioned historians who, after having recounted the death of a prince, judge God's plans for him according to their passion and the interests of their nation? Either the Spanish or the French writers must be wrong, or perhaps both, when they describe the death of Philip II. Must not kings die as well as we?

THEODORE. These historians are wrong, but you are not right. We must not judge that God designs to harm an enemy prince whom we hate. That is true. But we can and should believe that He plans to punish the wicked and reward the good. Those who judge God on the basis of the idea they have of the strict justice of the infinitely perfect Being, judge Him correctly; and those who attribute to Him plans which favor their disordered inclinations, judge Him very poorly.

III. ARISTES. True, but one of the results of the natural laws may be that particular people are crushed under the ruins of their house, and that there would have been no escape even for the best of people.

THEODORE. Who doubts it? But have you already forgotten that it is God who established these natural laws? The false idea of an imaginary nature still somewhat occupies your mind and prevents you from properly grasping the principle I have explained to you. Therefore, take note. Since it is God who established natural laws, He had to combine the physical and the moral in such a way that the effects of these laws would be the best possible, I mean, the most worthy of His justice and goodness as well as of His other attributes. Thus we are right to say that the terrible death of a brute or of someone impious is an effect of divine vengeance. For although this death is commonly only the result of the natural laws which God established, He established them only for the sake of effects like that. But if some misfortune befalls good people while they are about to do a good deed, we must not say that God willed to punish them, because God did not establish general laws with effects like that in view. We must say either that God permitted this misfortune, because it is a natural result of those laws He established for the best effects, or that He thereby had the plan to test these good people and to make them merit their reward. For among the motives God had in combining the physical and the moral in a particular way, we must surely take into account the great goods which God foresaw we would derive from our present miseries through the aid of His grace.

Thus, people are right to attribute the evils which befall the wicked to God's justice. But I believe they err in two ways. First, they pass these judgments only in the case of the extraordinary punishments which strike their mind. For if villains die of fever people do not ordinarily pronounce it a punishment of God. For this they must die from a bolt of lightning or at the executioner's hands. Second, they imagine that remarkable punishments are the effects of a particular volition of God. This is another false judgment, which deprives divine providence of its

simplicity and generality by effacing the character of infinite foreknowledge and immutability from it. For surely infinitely more wisdom is
required to combine the physical and the moral in such a way that
certain people are justly punished for their misdeeds as a consequence
of the series of causes, than is required to punish them by means of a
particular and miraculous providence.

ARISTES. I understand it in this way, Theodore. But what you are
saying does not justify the temerity of those who boldly judge of God's
plans in everything they see happen.

IV. THEODORE. Nor do I claim that they are always right. I am
simply saying that they are right when their judgments are exempt from
passion and interest and are based on the idea we all have of infinitely
perfect Being. Again, I am not claiming that they do well to say too
positively that God had some particular design. For example, it appears
certain to me that one motive for the establishment of general laws was a
good person's particular affliction, if God foresaw that this would be a
great reason for merit to that person. Thus, God willed this affliction
which, to those of us who do not foresee its effects, appears to be
inconsistent with His goodness. Those who decide, then, that God
simply permitted a particular evil to befall such a person, judge falsely.
But what do you want, Aristes? It is better to leave people, predisposed
as they are to their imaginary nature, the freedom to judge God's plans
too positively, than to criticize them for the contradiction in their
judgments concerning effects which appear to contradict the divine
attributes. What matter if minds contradict themselves and become
perplexed with their false ideas, provided that fundamentally we are not
mistaken in essential matters? Provided people do not attribute to God
plans which are contrary to His attributes, and do not have Him act to
sanction their passions, I believe we must listen to them quietly. Instead
of confusing them with contradictions which are inexplicable on their
principles, kindness dictates that we accept what they say in order to
strengthen them in the idea they have of providence, since they are not
in a position to have a better one. For it is better to attribute a human
providence to God, than to believe that everything happens by chance.
But they are, moreover, fundamentally right. When a wicked person
dies, we can say confidently that God planned to punish them. We
would be even more right to say that God willed to prevent them from

corrupting others, because through the general laws He established God in fact always wills to do all the good it is possible to do. A certain good man dies prematurely while going to assist someone in misery; even if he had been struck by lightning, we should not be afraid to judge that God willed to reward him. We can say of him what Scripture says of Enoch: "He was taken away lest wickedness should alter his understanding, or deceit beguile his soul."[1] Death removed him, lest the age corrupt his mind and heart. All these judgments conform to the idea we have of God's justice and goodness, and they accord sufficiently well with the plans He had when He established the general laws which govern the ordinary course of His providence. It is not that we are often mistaken in these judgments. For, apparently, a particular good man who died young would have acquired even greater merits and converted many sinners, had he lived longer in the circumstances in which he would have been as a consequence of the general laws of nature and grace. But these kinds of judgments, though a little rash or bold, do not have bad effects, and those who make them do not so much believe them to be true, as adore the wisdom and goodness of God in the governance of the world.

ARISTES. I understand you, Theodore. It is better that people speak badly of providence, than never speak of it.

THEODORE. No, Aristes. But it is better that people frequently speak of providence according to their feeble ideas, than never speak of it. It is better that people speak of God in a human way, than never say anything about Him. We must never speak badly either of God or of providence. That is true. But we are allowed to falter over such elevated matters, provided we do so according to the analogy of faith. For God is pleased by the efforts we make to recount His marvels. Believe me, Aristes; we can scarcely speak worse of providence, than never to say anything of it.

THEOTIMUS. Would you prefer, Aristes, that only philosophers speak of providence, and among philosophers only those who possess the idea you possess now?

V. ARISTES. Theotimus, I would like people never to speak of providence in a way apt to make simple folk believe that the wicked never succeed in their undertakings. For the prosperity of the impious

---

[1]   Wisdom 4: 11.

is so sure a fact that it can and often does foster mistrust in minds. If temporal goods and ills were fairly closely regulated according to merits and trust in God, the way we ordinarily speak of providence would not have bad effects. However, take note: the majority of people, and principally those who have the most piety, fall into very great misfortunes, because instead of employing the sound means which general providence furnishes them in their needs, they tempt God in the deceptive hope of a particular providence. If they have a trial, for example, they neglect to provide the documentation necessary to instruct the judges in the justice of their cause. If they have enemies or envious people who lay traps for them, then instead of watching them to discover their plans, they expect God will not fail to protect them. Women who have unpleasant husbands, instead of winning them over through patience and humility, will make complaints about them to every good person they know and commend the husbands to their prayers. In this way we do not always obtain what we desire and hope for, and yet we hardly fail to grumble against providence and to entertain views which offend the divine perfections. You know, Theotimus, the grievous effects which a poorly understood providence produces on the minds of simple people, and it is principally from this that superstition derives its origin, superstition which causes an infinity of ills in the world.

THEOTIMUS. I grant you, Aristes, it would be desirable for everyone to have an accurate idea of divine providence. But I maintain, with Theodore, that as this is impossible it is better that they speak as they do than say nothing at all about it. The idea they have of it, entirely false as it is, and even that natural inclination which carries minds toward superstition, is quite advantageous to them in their condition, for it prevents them from falling into a thousand disorders. Once you have thought about it, I think you will agree. Certain people lose their case for having ignored the natural ways to win it. What matter, Aristes? The loss of their goods will perhaps be the cause of their salvation. Surely, if laziness and negligence did not cause them to lose everything, but a blessed act of faith in God and the fear of entering into the quibbling spirit and pointlessly wasting their time; if that is it, they have won their case before God, although perhaps they have lost it before people. For more profit will be gained from a case lost in this manner, than will be won from another with costs, damages, and interest.

VI. We are Christians, Aristes, we have a right to the true goods; heaven is now open and Jesus Christ, our precursor and leader, has already entered it for us. Thus, God no longer as before rewards our faith in Him by an abundance of temporal goods. He has something better for His children adopted in Jesus Christ. That time is past with the law. The old covenant representing the new is now abrogated. If we were Jews, I mean carnal Jews, here below we would have a reward proportioned to our merits; again, I say the carnal Jews. For the Christian Jews shared in the cross of Jesus Christ before sharing in His glory. But we have better hopes than they, "a better and a lasting substance,"* founded on a better covenant and better sacrifices: "by so much is Jesus made a surety of a better testament ..."** "with better sacrifices than these." †The prosperity of the wicked should be no more surprising than the Christian Jews, than the Mohammedans, than those who do not know the difference between the two covenants, between the grace of the Old Testament and that of the New, between the temporal goods God distributed to the Jews through the ministry of angels and the true goods God gave His children through our leader and mediator Jesus Christ. We believe people ought to be wretched in proportion as they are criminal. It is true; but fundamentally we are right to believe it, for it will happen sooner or later. There is no Christian who does not know that the day will come when God will render to each according to his deeds. The prosperity of the wicked, then, can disturb only those who lack faith and recognize no other goods than those of the present life. Thus, Aristes, the confused and imperfect idea most people have of providence does not produce as many bad effects as you think in true Christians, although it troubles the mind and is extremely disquieting for ordinary people who often notice that it does not accord with experience. But it is better that they have this idea of it than none at all, which would gradually happen if they let it be effaced from their mind by a pernicious silence.

ARISTES. I grant you, Theotimus, that faith often prevents us from drawing impious consequences from the prosperity of the wicked and the afflictions of good people. However, as faith is not as tangible as the continual experience of these untoward events, it does not always prevent the mind from becoming unsettled and mistrusting providence. Moreover, Christians almost never follow the principles of their

* Hebrews 10: 34.   ** [Hebrews] 7: 22.   † [Hebrews] 9: 23.

religion; they speak of goods and evils like the carnal Jews. When a father exhorts his son to virtue, he is not afraid to tell him that if he is a good man all his enterprises will succeed. Do you believe his son is thinking of the true goods? Alas! Perhaps the father never thought of them himself. However, the freethinkers who carefully note the contradictions in all our unreflective discourse on providence do not fail to derive justifications for their impiety from it; and these justifications are so sense-based and tangible that it is enough to propose them in order to unsettle good people, and to subvert those whom faith does not sustain. "Or those eighteen upon whom the tower fell in Liloe, and slew them: think you," asks Jesus Christ, "that they also were debtors above all the men that dwelt in Jerusalem?" "No," He says, "but except you do penance, you shall all likewise perish."* In this way we must speak to people to teach them that in this life the most wretched are not thereby the most criminal, and that those who live amidst plenty, surrounded by pleasures and honors, are not thereby dearer to God, or protected by a more particular providence.

VII. THEOTIMUS. Yes, Aristes. But everyone is not always in a position to savor this truth. "This saying is hard."[2] Carnal people, those who still have the Jewish spirit, understand nothing of it. We must speak to people according to their capacity and accommodate ourselves to their weakness, in order to win them over gradually. We must carefully preserve in their mind such an idea of providence as they are capable of having. We must promise them a hundredfold, so that they understand as they are able, according to the dispositions of their heart. True, carnal people understand poorly; but it is better that they believe that virtue will be rewarded badly, than that it will not be rewarded at all. Indeed, according to their false ideas, it will be rewarded perfectly well. Some freethinker will tell them that vain promises are made to them. Granted. But perhaps that will serve to make them understand that they are deluding themselves, and that the goods they esteem so greatly are quite paltry, since God distributes them so badly to their liking and according to their prejudices. Surely, Aristes, we can hardly speak too much of providence, even when we know nothing about it. For it always awakens in the mind that thought which is the

---

[2] John 6: 61.
* Luke 13: 4.

foundation of all religions, that there is a God who rewards and punishes. The confused idea of providence is as useful for bringing ordinary people to virtue as the idea you have of it. It cannot explain the difficulties of the impious; we cannot defend it without falling into an infinite number of contradictions. That is true. But that is something which hardly troubles simple people. Faith sustains them; and their simplicity and humility provide shelter from the attacks of the freethinkers. Thus, I believe that in discourse directed at everyone we must speak of providence according to the most common idea, and what Theodore has taught us must be reserved to silence those supposed freethinkers and to reassure those who find themselves unsettled by the consideration of effects which appear to contradict the divine perfections. Still, we must suppose them capable of the attention necessary to follow our principles; for otherwise it would in fact be shorter, if they were Christians, to quiet them solely by the authority of Scripture.

ARISTES. I submit, Theotimus. We must address people according to their ideas, when they are not in a position to consider matters deeply. If we criticized the confused opinion they have of providence, we would perhaps be an element of their downfall. It would be easy to confuse them with the contradictions into which they fall. But it would be quite difficult to deliver them from their predicament. For too much application is required to recognize and follow the true principles of providence. I understand this, Theotimus, and I think it is mainly for this reason that Jesus Christ and the apostles have not formally taught the rational principles which theologians employ to support the truths of faith. They assumed that enlightened people would know these principles and that simple people, who submit solely to authority, would not need them and could even be shocked by them and take them badly, for want of application and intelligence. I am, then, quite resolved to allow people the freedom to speak of providence after their own fashion, provided they say nothing which overtly violates the divine attributes, provided they do not bestow unjust and bizarre designs upon God and do not make Him act to satisfy their ungoverned inclinations. As for philosophers, however, and above all certain supposed freethinkers, surely I will not suffer their impertinent mockery. I expect I will have my turn and I will deeply embarrass them. They have occasionally reduced me to silence, but I will soon oblige them to be silent. For I now have something to reply to all their most specious and their strongest objections against me.

VIII. THEODORE. Careful, Aristes, lest vanity and self-love animate your zeal somewhat. Do not seek adversaries for the glory and pleasure of vanquishing them. It is the truth that must be made to triumph over those who have fought it. If you claim to confound them you will not win them over, and perhaps they will even confound you. For I believe you have the wherewithal to force them into silence, but that is assuming they are willing to listen to reason, which assuredly they will not be when they sense you are seeking to prevail. If they mock you, they will have laughter on their side. If they frighten you, they will spread fear in minds. You will be alone with your principles, of which no one will understand anything. I advise you, then, Aristes, to take these people in particular whom you have in mind and propose your opinion to them as if to learn from them what you should believe about it. To answer you they will have to work to examine it, and perhaps the evidence will convince them. Above all be careful they do not think you are playing with them. Speak as a disciple in good faith, so that they do not recognize your charitable dissimulation. But once you have seen that the truth has sunk into them, then combat it without fear of their abandoning it. They will look at it as a good which belongs to them and which they have acquired through their application and work. They will take interest in its defense, perhaps not because they truly love it, but because their self-love will have a stake in it. Thus, you will engage them on behalf of the truth; and between them and the truth you will form ties of interest not easily broken. Most people view the truth as quite a useless piece of furnishing, or rather as a quite troublesome and inconvenient piece of furnishing. But when it is of their own doing, and when they see it as a good we want to confiscate from them, they attach themselves to it so strongly and consider it so attentively that they can no longer forget it.

ARISTES. You are right, Theodore: to win people over securely, we must find the way to appease their self-love. That is the test. I shall try to follow your charitable advice exactly. But do you think I possess your principles sufficiently well to convince others of them, and to reply to all their difficulties?

THEODORE. If you are indeed resolved to assume the air and

manner of a disciple among your people, you need not know these principles more exactly. They will teach them to you as well as I.

ARISTES. How will they teach as well as you, Theodore?

THEODORE. Better than I, Aristes; you will see this through experience. Simply recall the principal truths I explained to you, and to which you should refer all the questions you ask them.

Remember that God can act only according to what He is, only in a way which bears the character of His attributes; that thus He does not form His plans independently of the ways of executing them, but chooses the work and the ways which all together express the perfections, which He glories in possessing, better than any other work in any other way. That, Aristes, is the most general and most fertile principle.

Recall that the more simplicity, uniformity, and generality there is in providence, other things being equal, the more it bears the character of the divinity. Thus God governs the world by general laws, to make His wisdom shine through in the series of causes.

But recall that creatures do not act upon each other by their own efficacy, and that God communicates His power to them only because He established their modalities as occasional causes which determine the efficacy of the general laws He prescribed. Everything depends on this principle.

IX. Here, Aristes, are the general laws according to which God regulates the ordinary course of His providence.

1. The general laws of the communication of motion, of which laws the impact of bodies is the occasional or natural cause. It is through the establishment of these laws that God communicated to the sun the power to illumine, and to fire the power to burn, and likewise for the other powers which bodies have of acting on one another; and it is by obeying His own laws that God does everything secondary causes do.

2. The laws of the union of the soul and body, the modalities of which are reciprocally the occasional causes of their changes. It is by these laws that I have the power to speak, to walk, to sense, to imagine, and so on, and that through my organs objects have the power to touch and affect me. By these laws God unites me to all His works.

3. The laws of the union of the soul with God, with the intelligible substance of universal Reason, for the laws of which our attention is the occasional cause. It is by the establishment of these laws that the mind

has the power to think what it wills, and to discover the truth. There are only these three general laws which Reason and experience teach us, but the authority of Scripture informs us of two others as well, namely:

4. The general laws which give good and evil angels power over bodies, which are substances inferior to their nature.* It is through the efficacy of these laws that angels governed the Jewish people, that they punished and rewarded them by means of temporal goods and ills, according to the order they received from God. It is through the efficacy of these laws that demons still have the power to tempt us and that our guardian angels have the power to defend us. The occasional causes of these laws are their practical desires, for it is a contradiction that something other than the creator of bodies could be their mover.

5. Finally, the laws by which Jesus Christ received sovereign power in heaven and on earth, not only over bodies but over minds; not simply to distribute temporal goods, as the angels in the synagogue, but to spread into hearts the inner grace which renders us children of God and which gives us the right to eternal goods.** The occasional causes of these laws are the various movements of the blessed soul of Jesus. For our mediator and sovereign priest constantly intercedes, and His intercession is always and immediately fulfilled.

These, Aristes, are the most general laws of nature and grace which God follows in the ordinary course of His providence. By these laws He executes His plans in a way which admirably bears the character of His infinite foreknowledge, of His nature as seer into hearts, of His immutability and other attributes. It is by these laws that He communicates His power to creatures and gives them a share in the glory of the work He executes through their ministry. Indeed, it is through this communication of His power and glory that He renders the most honor to His attributes. For an infinite wisdom is required to employ free causes as readily as necessary causes in the execution of His designs.

But although God prescribed Himself these general laws and also some others of which it is unnecessary to speak, like those by which the fire in hell has the power to torment demons, the baptismal waters have the power to purify us, and in the past the extremely bitter waters of

---

* Cf. the last *Eclaircissement* of the *Traité de la Nature et de la Grace* [*OC* V 197–206] and the *Réponse à la Dissertation de M. Arnauld* against that *Eclaircissement* [*OC* VII 535–46].
** Cf. *Traité de la Nature et de la Grace* II [*OC* V 65–99].

jealousy had the power to punish the infidelity of women,[*] and so on; although, I say, God prescribed Himself these laws and does not depart from the generality of His conduct without good reasons, remember still that when He receives more glory by departing from it than by following it, then He never fails to abandon it. For to reconcile the contradictions which appear in the effects of providence it suffices to recall that God acts and must act ordinarily through general laws. Hold on to these principles, then, and ask your questions in such a way that they tend to make those, whom you hope to convert, simply think about the principles.

ARISTES. I shall do this, Theodore, and I hope I shall succeed in my plan. For all these principles appear so evident to me, so well connected with one another, and in such accord with what we see happen, that provided that prejudices and passions do not present too great an obstacle to the impression they should make on our mind, it will be difficult for people to resist them. I thank you for the warning you gave me to appease their self-love, for I see very well I would ruin everything if I behaved as I wanted to behave. However, Theodore, assuming I succeed in my plan and have indeed convinced them of the truth of our principles, how can I oblige them to recognize the authority of the church, for they are born into heresy, and I would quite like to lead them away from it.

THEODORE. Truly, Aristes, that is quite another matter. Perhaps you think that providing good proofs of the infallibility of the church is enough to convert heretics. It is necessary, Aristes, for heaven to intervene. For a spirit of partisanship daily forms so many secret ties in the heart of those who are unfortunately engaged in it, that it blinds them and closes them to the truth. If people exhorted you to become a Huguenot, surely you would not willingly listen to them. Be aware, then, that they are perhaps more ardent than we are, because in the condition they are in they are each exhorted to show signs of their resolve. Thus, having an infinity of obligations, ties, prejudices, and selfish reasons which keep them in their sect, what skill is needed to oblige them to consider without prejudice the proofs we can give them that they are in error?

ARISTES. I know, Theodore, that their sensitivity on the matter of religion is extreme, and that however carefully one touches that spot, all

[*] Cf. Numbers 6. [The correct reference is Numbers 5: 17–29.]

their passions rebel. But do not fear. For aside from the fact that those of whom I am speaking are not as sensitive as many others, I shall assume the demeanor of a very submissive disciple so well that to answer me I shall oblige them to examine the doubts I shall be raising for them. Just give me some proofs of the infallibility of the church, in conformity with the idea you have given me of providence.

X. THEODORE. It is certain from Scripture, which the heretics dare not reject, that God "will have all men to be saved, and to come to the knowledge of the truth."* Thus, in the order of providence we must find sound means of making all people come to the knowledge of the truth.

ARISTES. I deny this conclusion. God wills that all people be saved, but He does not will to do everything necessary to save all of them. If He willed this, all would be saved; the Chinese and so many other peoples would not be deprived of the knowledge of the true God and His Son Jesus Christ, in which eternal life consists.

THEODORE. I am not telling you, Aristes, that God wills to do everything necessary to save all people. He does not will to perform miracles every moment. He does not will to infuse overpowering grace into every heart. His conduct must bear the character of His attributes, and He must not depart from the generality of His providence without good reasons. His wisdom does not always allow Him to proportion His assistance to the present need of the wicked and the foreseen negligence of the just. Everyone would be saved if He acted in this way toward us. I claim only that in providence we must find the general ways corresponding to God's volition that everyone come to the knowledge of the truth. Now, we can arrive at this knowledge only in two ways, either through examination or through authority.

ARISTES. I understand you, Theodore. The way of examination corresponds, perhaps, to the volition God has to save the learned; but God wills to save the poor, the simple, the ignorant, and those who cannot read as well as men of rank who are critics. Still I do not see that the Grotiuses, the Kochs, the Saumaises, the Buxtorfs,[3] have arrived at

---

[3]   Hugo Grotius (1583–1645), Johannes Koch (1603–69), and Johannes Buxtorf (1564–1629). The reference to "the Saumaises" is most likely to Claude de Saumaise (1588–1653), but may also include his father, Bénigne de Saumaise (1560–1640).

*   1 Timothy 2: 4.

this knowledge of the truth at which God wills we should all arrive. Perhaps Grotius was near it when death overtook him. What! Does providence provide only for the salvation of those who have enough life, as well as mind and knowledge, to discern truth from error? Surely that is not likely. The way of examination is completely inadequate. Now that our reason is weakened, we must be led by the way of authority. This way is sensible, sure, general, it corresponds perfectly to the will God has that everyone come to the knowledge of the truth. But where shall we find this infallible authority, this safe path we could follow without fear of error? Heretics claim it is found only in the sacred books.

XI. THEODORE. It is found in the sacred books, but it is by the authority of the church that we know it. St. Augustine was right to say that without the church He would not believe in the Gospel. How can simple people be certain that our four Gospels have an infallible authority? Ignorant people have no proof that they are by the authors who bear their names, and that they have not been corrupted in essential matters; nor do I know if the learned have very sure proofs of this. But even if we were certain that the Gospel of St. Matthew, for example, is by that apostle, and that it is today such as he composed it, surely if we do not have infallible authority which teaches us that this evangelist was divinely inspired, we cannot base our faith on his words as on those of God Himself. There are those who claim that the divinity of the sacred books is so palpable that we cannot read them without perceiving it. But on what is this claim based? Something more than conjecture and prejudice is needed to attribute infallibility to them. The Holy Spirit must reveal it either to each person individually or to the church for all individuals. Now the latter is much more simple, more general, more worthy of providence than the former.

Still, I grant that all those who read Scripture know by a particular revelation that the Gospel is a divine book which has not been corrupted through the malice and negligence of copyists; who will give us understanding of it? For reason is not always sufficient to glean its true meaning. The Socinians are as rational as other people, and they find there that the Son is not consubstantial with the Father. The Calvinists are people just like the Lutherans, and they claim that those words,

"Take ye, and eat. This is my body"[4] signify, in the context in which they are found, that what Jesus Christ gives His apostles is only the representation of His body. Who will disabuse either of them? Who will lead them to the knowledge of the truth, where God wills we should all arrive. At every moment each individual person would require the assistance of the Holy Spirit, which the heretics deny the entire church when it is assembled to form its decisions. What extravagance, what blindness, what pride! It is imagined that we understand Scripture better than the universal church which preserves the blessed storehouse of tradition and which, somewhat more than any individual, deserves that Jesus Christ, who is its leader, undertake to defend it against the powers of hell.

XII. Most people are persuaded that God leads them by a particular providence, or rather that He so leads those for whom they have great esteem. They are disposed to believe that particular people are cherished by God in such a way that He will neither permit them to fall into error, nor allow people to involve them in it. They attribute a kind of infallibility to them, and they willingly rest on this chimerical authority which they have erected for themselves by a number of reflections on the great and excellent qualities of these persons, in order to free themselves from the inconvenient task of examination. These are the blind who follow other blind people, and who will fall into the precipice with them. For everyone is subject to error: "Every man is a liar."[5] It is true that we require a visible authority now that we cannot easily enter into ourselves to consult Reason, and that there are truths necessary for salvation which we can learn only through revelation. But that authority on which we are to support ourselves must be general and it must be the effect of a general providence. God does not ordinarily act in minds through particular volitions to prevent them from erring. That does not agree with the idea we should have of providence, which must bear the character of the divine attributes. God charged our mediator with the task of our salvation. But in making nature serve grace and in choosing general means for the execution of His work, Jesus Christ Himself imitates the conduct of His Father as much as possible. He sent His apostles throughout the world to announce the truths of the Gospel to

---

[4]   Matthew 26: 26.   [5]   Psalm 115: 11.

people. He gave His church bishops, priests, doctors, a visible leader to govern it. He established sacraments to diffuse His grace into hearts. These are certain signs that He constructs His work by ways which are general and furnished to Him by the laws of nature. No doubt Jesus Christ can inwardly enlighten minds without the assistance of preaching, but He certainly does not do so. He can restore us without baptism, but He does not wish to render His sacraments useless. He will never act in a certain person in a particular manner without some particular reason, without some kind of necessity. But where is the necessity that He specifically enlighten particular critics, in order that they properly grasp the sense of a passage from Scripture? The authority of the church suffices to prevent us from going astray; why will we not submit to it? It suffices for Jesus Christ to preserve the infallibility of His church, in order at the same time to preserve the faith of all humble and obedient children in their mother. Woe to the foolhardy and presumptuous who, contrary to Reason and the order of His conduct which He regulates on the basis of immutable order, expect Jesus Christ to enlighten them especially. Jesus Christ never fails to assist the just in their needs. He never refuses them the grace necessary to vanquish temptation. He opens their mind in reading the sacred books. He often rewards their faith by the gift of understanding. For it is in conformity with order, and it is necessary for their instruction and the edification of people. But to preserve our faith in settled matters, we have the authority of the church. This is sufficient: He wills that we submit to it. It is from Him alone that we can receive the assistance necessary to vanquish temptation. That is why He constantly intercedes to preserve our love in us. But He does not constantly intercede for the presumptuous not to fall into error in reading Scripture, having given us an infallible authority on which we must rely, that of the church of the living God, the pillar and firm support of the truth, "the pillar and ground of the truth."[*]

ARISTES. What you are telling me, Theodore, accords perfectly with the idea of providence you have given me. God has His general laws and our mediator and leader has His rules which He follows inviolably as God follows His laws, unless immutable order, which is the primary law of all intellects, requires exceptions. It is infinitely more simple and consistent with Reason for Jesus Christ to assist His church

[*] 1 Timothy 3: 15.

to prevent it from falling into error, than to assist each particular individual and principally those who have the temerity to bring settled matters into doubt and thereby accuse the savior either of having abandoned His bride or of having been unable to defend it; for heretics can refuse to believe the decisions of the church only on the principle that it teaches error and that therefore Jesus Christ cannot or will not lead it. Thus they believe that, contrary to His promise, Jesus Christ abandons His cherished bride and consequently all Catholics, rather than they themselves. Now we need an infallible authority. Providence has provided it, in a manner which appears to me worthy of the divine attributes and of the qualities of our savior Jesus Christ, in a manner which corresponds perfectly to that volition of God that all people be saved and come to the knowledge of the truth.

THEODORE. True, Aristes. For the apostolic and Roman church is visible and recognizable. It is perpetual through all time and universal in all places; at least, it is the society most exposed to the eyes of all the earth, and most venerable for its antiquity. No particular sect bears any character of truth, any mark of divinity. Those which now appear to have some luster began long after the church. Everyone knows this, even those who allow themselves to be dazzled by that dull luster which scarcely extends beyond the borders of their country. Thus, insofar as His general laws allowed Him, God provided all people with an easy and sure way of arriving at the knowledge of the truth

THEOTIMUS. I do not understand, Aristes, on what basis we can doubt the infallibility of the church of Jesus Christ. Is it because the heretics do not believe that it was divinely established and that it is divinely governed, that they doubt it is divinely inspired? To believe it to be subject to error in the decisions it makes for the instruction of its children, we cannot have any idea at all of the church of Jesus Christ, and we must look at it like other societies. Yes, Aristes, there is no one, unless strangely prejudiced, who does not see from the start that since Jesus Christ is the leader of the church whose spouse He is, whose protector He is, it is impossible that the gates of hell prevail against it, and that it teach error. Provided we have the idea of Jesus Christ which we should have of Him, we cannot conceive of His church becoming the mistress of error. We need not undertake a great examination to see that; it is a truth which strikes the simplest and most unsophisticated people as obvious. In all societies an authority is necessary. Of this everyone is convinced. Even the heretics will that those of their sect submit to the decisions of their synods. In effect, a society without authority is a many-headed monster. Now, the church is a society divinely established to lead people to the knowledge of the truth. Thus, it is evident that its authority must be infallible, so that we can achieve what God wills us all to attain, without being obliged to follow the perilous and inadequate path of examination.

THEODORE. Let us even assume that Jesus Christ is neither the leader nor the spouse of the church, that He does not watch over it, that He is not in its midst until the fullness of time to defend it against the powers of hell. It would no longer have that divine infallibility which is the unshakable foundation of our faith. Nevertheless, it appears evident to me that we must have lost our mind or be prejudiced by a prodigious stubbornness, to prefer the opinions of heretics to the decisions of its councils. Let us take an example. We are at pains to know whether it is the body of Jesus Christ or the symbol of His body that is in the Eucharist. We all agree that the apostles knew very well what it was. We agree that they taught what had to be believed about this in all the churches they founded. What do we do to clarify the issue we are contesting? We convene the most general assemblies possible. We bring together in one place the best witnesses there can be of what people believe in various countries. Bishops know well whether or not people in the church where they preside believe that the body of Jesus Christ is in the Eucharist. We ask them, then, what they think about this. They declare that it is an article of their faith that the bread is changed into the body of Jesus Christ. They pronounce anathema against those who maintain the contrary. The bishops of other churches, who were unable to be at the assembly, positively approve the decision; or if they have no dealings with those of the council, they are silent and by their silence give sufficient testimony that they are of the same opinion. Otherwise they would not fail to condemn it, for the Greeks do not spare the Latins. This being the case, I maintain that even on the assumption that Jesus Christ has abandoned His church, one must have renounced common sense to prefer the opinion of Calvin or Zwingli to that of all these witnesses, who attest a fact which it is impossible for them not to know.

ARISTES. That is conclusive evidence. But you will be told that these bishops who cannot fail to know what is at present believed in their churches concerning the fact of the Eucharist, could be ignorant of what was believed about it a thousand years ago; and that it could be the case that all these particular churches have unwittingly fallen into error.

THEODORE. In supposing that Jesus Christ does not govern His church, I agree it can happen that all the churches generally fall into error. But that they all fall into the same error is morally impossible. That they fall into it without history leaving glaring marks of their disputes is another moral impossibility. Finally, that they fall into an error similar to that which the Calvinists attribute to us is an absolute impossibility. For what has the church decided? That the body of a man exists in an infinity of places at the same time; that the body of a man exists in as small a place as the Eucharist occupies; that after the priest has spoken some words, the bread changes into the body of Jesus Christ, and the wine into His blood. What! Speaking as a heretic, will this folly, this extravagance, be put into the minds of Christians of all churches? It seems to me one must be demented to maintain it. The same error is never generally approved unless it generally conforms to the dispositions of the mind. All peoples were able to worship the sun. Why? Because generally this star dazzles all people. But if one insane people worshipped mice, another will have worshipped cats. If Jesus Christ abandoned His church all Christians could indeed gradually lapse into the heresy of Calvin concerning the Eucharist, because in fact this error offends neither reason nor the senses. But to maintain that all Christian churches have entered into an opinion which outrages the imagination, shocks the senses, astonishes reason, and have done this so imperceptibly that we are unaware of it, once again we need to have renounced common sense; we cannot have any knowledge of human beings nor have ever reflected on their inner dispositions.

However, Aristes, I do grant that if God abandoned His church, it would be possible for all Christians to fall into the same error, an error that is shocking and entirely contrary to the dispositions of the human mind, and this without their even being aware of it. Notwithstanding this supposition I still claim that we cannot refuse to submit to the decisions of the church without ridiculous prejudice. On our supposition it is possible that the church is mistaken. True. But without supposing anything, it can happen much more naturally that a particular person falls into error. It does not have to do with a truth which depends on some principles of metaphysics, but with a fact; it has to do with what, for example, Jesus Christ intended to say by those words, "This is my body," which can best be known only through the testimony of those who succeeded the apostles. What the council decided is contrary to what was once believed? Very well. This is, then, because all the bishops together did not know the tradition as well as Calvin. But where are the ancient authors who say to the peoples, as they would have had to say: "Be careful; these words, 'This is my body,' do not mean that it is the body of Jesus Christ, but only the symbol of Jesus Christ?" Why do they confirm them in the thought which these words, which are so clear, naturally give rise to in the mind – so naturally that, although nothing appears more incredible than the meaning they contain, all churches believed themselves obliged to accept it? As the same thing can be both symbol and reality in different respects, I admit there are Church Fathers who spoke of the Eucharist as a symbol. For in fact the sacrifice of the mass symbolizes or represents that of the cross. But they would not have been content to emphasize the symbol; they would have carefully rejected the reality. Yet we observe the complete opposite. They are afraid of our faith wavering on the difficulty there is in believing the reality, and they frequently reassure us by the authority of Jesus Christ and by the knowledge we have of the divine power.

Even if we insist upon saying that the decision of the council is contrary to reason and good sense, still I maintain that the more it appears to offend reason, the more certain it is that it conforms to the truth. For, after all, were not people of centuries past made like those of today? Our imagination rebels when it is said to us that the body of Jesus Christ is in heaven and on our altars at the same time. But do we seriously think that there was a time when people were not outraged by such a frightening thought? Yet this extraordinary mystery was believed in all Christian churches. The fact is established by the testimony of those best able to know it, I mean, through the suffrage of the bishops. Thus people were instructed by a superior authority, by an authority which they believed to be infallible and which we at once see is infallible, without any examination, when we have the idea we should have of Jesus Christ and His church. Thus, let us suppose what we will, we have only to consider what we should believe when on the one side we see the decision of the council, and on the other the dogmas of a particular person or a particular assembly which the church does not approve.

ARISTES. I understand, Theodore, through the reasons you give me here, that those who divest the church of Jesus Christ of the infallibility essential to it, do not thereby deliver themselves from the obligation to submit to its decisions. To be free and clear of that obligation, they must renounce common sense. Nonetheless, we so frequently observe that the most common opinions are not the truest that we are easily led to believe that whatever some learned person advances is much more certain than what we hear everybody say.

THEODORE. You put your finger, Aristes, on one of the principal causes of the prejudice and obstinacy of the heretics. They do not sufficiently distinguish between the dogmas of faith and the truths we can discover only through the labor of attention. Since anything which depends on an abstract principle is not accessible to everyone, good sense would have us distrust what the multitude thinks about such things. It is infinitely more likely that people who seriously apply themselves to the search for the truth will come across it, than a million others who do not give it any thought. It is true, then, and we often note, that the most common opinions are not the truest. But in matters of faith it is entirely the contrary. The more witnesses there are who attest a fact, the more certainty that fact possesses. The dogmas of religion are not learned by speculation; it is by authority, by the testimony of those who preserve the sacred storehouse of tradition. What everyone believes, what we have always believed, is what must be eternally believed. For in matters of faith, of revealed truths, of decided dogma, common opinions are the true ones. But the desire to be different causes us to cast doubt on what everyone believes and to consider indubitable what ordinarily passes for quite uncertain. Self-love is not satisfied when we do not excel beyond others, and when we know only what everyone knows. Instead of building solidly on the foundations of faith, and through humility elevating ourselves to the understanding of the sublime truths to which it leads; instead of thereby deserving a true and solid glory both before God and before fair-minded people, we derive an evil pleasure and an opportunity for vanity from unsettling these sacred foundations, and we foolishly smash upon that terrible rock which crushes all those who have the insolence to strike it.

ARISTES. In this, Theodore, I have more than I need to question my people and lead them to where I have long hoped to lead them. If the church is divinely governed it must indeed be divinely inspired. If

Jesus Christ is its leader it cannot become the teacher of error. As God wills all people to come to the knowledge of the truth, He could not have left the way which leads to the truth to a debate of the human mind. His providence had to find a sure and easy path for the simple as well as for the learned. The particular revelations made to all those who read Scripture are completely inconsistent with the idea we should have of divine providence. Experience teaches us that all people explain it according to their prejudices. After all, even on the assumption that Jesus Christ does not govern His church, we cannot, without a prejudice contrary to good sense, prefer the particular opinions of some sect or other to the decision of a council. All this, Theodore, appears evident to me. Now I fear only the stubbornness of my friends, and seek only good ways of appeasing their self-love. For I am quite afraid of not having the proper ways of releasing them from obligations of all kinds under which I shall perhaps find them.

THEODORE. You have everything you need for this, Aristes. Courage. You know only too well how people are managed, what makes them rebel, what make them bolt. We must hope that grace will break what might restrain them, namely, those hidden ties you cannot undo. While you are speaking to their ears, perhaps God will open their mind and touch their heart by His goodness.

Dialogue XIV

Continuation of the same subject. The incomprehensibility of our mysteries is a certain proof of their truth. The way to clarify the dogmas of faith. Of the incarnation of Jesus Christ. Proof of His divinity against the Socinians. No creatures, not even angels, can worship God except through Him. How faith in Jesus Christ renders us pleasing to God.

I. ARISTES. Ah, Theodore! How can I open my heart to you? How can I express my joy? How can I make you feel the happy state into which you have put me? I now resemble a person who has escaped shipwreck, or who finds calm after a storm. I have often felt myself unsettled by dangerous stirrings when faced with our incomprehensible mysteries. Their profundity frightened me, their obscurity troubled me, and although my heart yielded to the force of authority, it was not without difficulty on the part of the mind. For as you know, the mind is naturally fearful in the dark. But now I find everything is in harmony in me: mind follows heart. What am I saying! The mind leads, the mind transports the heart. For – what a paradox! – the more obscure our mysteries are, the more credible they now appear to me. Yes, Theodore, even in the obscurity of our mysteries, received now as they are by so many different nations, I find an invincible proof of their truth.

How, for instance, do we reconcile unity with the Trinity, a society of three different persons in the perfect simplicity of the divine nature? This is surely incomprehensible, but it is not incredible. True, it is beyond us. But a little good sense and we will believe it, at least if we wish to share the same religion as the apostles. For, after all, assuming they did not know this ineffable mystery or did not teach it to their successors, I maintain that it is impossible that such an extraordinary opinion could have found in minds that universal credence which it receives in every church and among so many different nations. The more monstrous – in the expression of the enemies of faith – this adorable mystery appears, the more it shocks human reason, the more it taxes the imagination, the more obscure, incomprehensible, and impenetrable it is, the less believable it is that it naturally insinuated itself into the minds and hearts of Catholics in so many countries so far apart. I understand, Theodore; the same errors are never universally disseminated everywhere, particularly those kinds of errors which in some strange way disgust the imagination, which contain nothing sensible, and which seem to contradict the simplest and most common notions.

If Jesus Christ did not watch over His church, the number of Unitarians would soon surpass the number of true Catholics. I understand that. For there is nothing in the opinions of these heretics which does not naturally occur to the mind. I can well conceive how opinions commensurate to our intellect can be established over time. I can even conceive how the most bizarre opinions can predominate among certain peoples of an entirely singular turn of imagination. But that a truth so sublime, so remote from the senses, so opposed to human reason, in a word so contrary to all nature as this great mystery of our faith; that a truth of this character, I say, should be able to be universally disseminated and triumph in every nation where the apostles preached the Gospel, assuming above all that those first preachers of our faith knew and said nothing of this mystery, is surely something inconceivable, however little knowledge one has of the human mind.

I am not at all surprised that there were heretics who were opposed to such a lofty dogma. I would think it strange had no one ever disputed it. This truth came very close to being suppressed. That may be. We will always find merit in attacking whatever seems to injure Reason. But it requires, it seems to me, only a little good sense to recognize that there is nothing less likely than that the mystery of the Trinity should have at last prevailed, that it was established everywhere where the religion of Jesus Christ is received, without its having been known and taught by the apostles, without a divine authority and force. For it is not even likely that a dogma so divine, so above reason, so remote from everything capable of striking the imagination and the senses, could naturally enter the mind of anyone.

II. THEODORE. Surely, Aristes, your mind should be quite at rest, since you know how to draw light from darkness itself and turn the impenetrable obscurity surrounding our mysteries into evident proof of them. Let the Socinians blaspheme against our holy religion, let them turn it to ridicule; the blasphemy and ridicule they would heap upon it inspire you with respect for it. What disturbs others can only strengthen you; how could you not enjoy a profound peace? For, after all, what can engender a certain fear and turmoil in us is not those plausible truths everyone believes without difficulty; it is the profundity and impenetrability of our mysteries. I understand, then, how you are in a great calm. Enjoy it, my dear Aristes. But please let us not judge the church of Jesus Christ as we judge purely human societies. It has a leader who will never permit it to become the teacher of error. Its infallibility is based on the divinity of Him who leads it. We must not judge solely by the rules of good sense that certain of our mysteries cannot be inventions of the human mind. We have a decisive authority, a way still shorter and surer than that kind of examination. Let us humbly follow that path, to honor the power, vigilance, goodness, and other qualities of the sovereign pastor of our souls, by our trust and submission. For to desire unconditionally proofs of the necessary truths of our salvation other than those derived from the authority of the church is in some way to blaspheme against the divinity of Jesus Christ, or at least against His love for His bride.

If you believe, Aristes, a particular article of our faith, because by examination you clearly recognize it to be of the apostolic tradition, by your faith you honor the mission and apostolate of Jesus Christ. For your faith expresses that judgment you make that God sent Jesus Christ into the world to instruct it in the truth. But if you believe only for this reason, without regard for the infallible authority of the church, you do not honor the wisdom and generality of providence which furnishes simple and ignorant people with a very sure and natural way of being instructed in the truths necessary for salvation. You do not honor the power or at least the vigilance of Jesus Christ over His church. It seems you would be suspecting Him of willing to abandon it to the spirit of error, so that the faith of those who humbly submit to the authority of the church renders much more honor to God and to Jesus Christ than your faith, since it more exactly expresses the divine attributes and the qualities of our mediator. Add to this that it accords perfectly with the judgment we should make about the weakness and limitation of our mind; and that if on the one hand it expresses our trust in God and in the love of Jesus Christ, on the other hand it indicates clearly that we have a just and salutary mistrust of ourselves. Thus, you can well see that the faith of one who submits to the authority of the church is quite pleasing to God, since however we consider it, it expresses the judgments which God wills we make about His own attributes, the qualities of Jesus Christ, and the limitation of the human mind.

III. Nonetheless, Aristes, remember that the humble and submissive faith of those who bow to authority is neither blind nor imprudent: it is founded in reason. Surely infallibility is contained in the idea of a divine religion, of a society which has a nature subsisting in eternal wisdom for its leader, of a society established for the salvation of the simple and the ignorant. Good sense would have us believe the church to be infallible. We must, then, blindly submit to its authority. But it is Reason which makes us see that there is no danger in submitting to it, and that Christians who refuse to do so, by their refusal belie the judgment they ought to make concerning the qualities of Jesus Christ.

Our faith is perfectly rational in its source. It does not owe its establishment to prejudice but to right reason. For Jesus Christ proved His mission and His qualities in an invincible manner. His glorious resurrection is so well attested that, to cast doubt on it, we would have to renounce common sense. Today the truth hardly ever makes itself respected by the luster and majesty of miracles. For it is supported by the authority of Jesus Christ, whom we recognize as infallible and who has promised His all-powerful assistance and His vigilance, which is full of tenderness, to the divine society of which He is leader. Let the church's faith be attacked by the various heresies of particular sects; this needs to happen in order to manifest the fidelity of good people. The vessel where Jesus Christ reposes may be battered by the tempest, but it runs no risk. To fear the storm is to lack faith. The winds must howl and the sea must swell before calm descends. Without this we are incapable of coming to appreciate the power we have of commanding them. But if the Lord permits the powers of hell . . .

THEOTIMUS. Allow me to interrupt you, Theodore. You know we can spend no more time with you than the rest of the day. We have already spent too much on the church's infallibility. Aristes is convinced of it. Please, give us some principles capable of leading us to the understanding of the truths we believe, which can augment in us the profound respect we should have for religion and Christian morality, or provide us with some idea of the method you employ in such a sublime matter.

IV. THEODORE. I do not have any particular method for this. I judge things only on the basis of the ideas representing them, depending on the facts known to me. That is my whole method. The principles of my knowledge are found in my ideas, and the rules of my conduct in relation to religion lie in the truths of faith. My entire method reduces to a serious attention to what enlightens and guides me.

ARISTES. I do not know if Theotimus understands what you are telling us. But as for me, I understand nothing of it. It is too general.

THEODORE. I believe Theotimus understands me well. But further explanation is necessary. I always carefully distinguish the dogmas of faith from the proofs and explanations we can give of them. Concerning dogmas, I look for them in tradition and in the consent of the universal church, and I find they are better indicated in the definitions of the councils than anywhere else. I think you will agree with this, since because the church is infallible we must adhere to what it has decided.

ARISTES. But do you not also look for them in the holy Scripture?

THEODORE. I believe, Aristes, that the surest and shortest method is to seek them in the holy Scripture, but Scripture as explained by tradition, that is, by the general councils, or as they are generally received everywhere, as explained by the same spirit which dictated them. I am well aware that Scripture is a divine book and the rule of our faith. But I do not separate it from tradition, because I have no doubt that the councils interpret it better than I do. Take what I am telling you fairly. The councils do not reject Scripture. They accept it with respect, and indeed they thereby authorize it for the faithful, who could well confound it with the apocryphal books. But beyond this they teach us several truths which the apostles entrusted to the church and which were attacked. These truths are not easily discerned in the canonical writings, for how many heretics find the complete contrary there? In a word, Aristes, I try to be very sure of the dogmas on which I wish to meditate, in order to have some understanding of them. And I then use my mind in the same way as those who study physics. With all the attention of which I am capable I consult the idea I have of my subject, such as faith presents it to me. I always come back to what appears most simple and general to me, in order to find some light. When I find it I contemplate it. But I follow it only insofar as it invincibly draws me by the force of its evidence. The least obscurity makes me fall back on dogma, which in my fear of error is and will always inviolably be my rule in questions concerning faith.

Those who study physics never reason against experience. But nor do they ever decide against Reason through experience. They hesitate, not seeing the means to pass from one to the other. They hesitate, I say, neither over the certainty of experience nor over the evidence of Reason, but over the way to reconcile the one with the other. The facts of religion or established dogmas are my experiences in matters of theology. I shall never bring them into doubt. That is what governs me and leads me to understanding. But when, believing myself to be following them, I feel myself collide against Reason, I pull up short, well aware that the dogmas of faith and the principles of Reason must be in harmony in the truth, whatever their opposition in my mind. I remain, therefore, subject to authority, full of respect for Reason, convinced only of the weakness of my mind and in perpetual mistrust of myself. Finally, if the ardor for the truth is rekindled, I begin my investigations anew and by directing my attention alternatively to the ideas which enlighten me and to the dogmas which support and guide me, without any other special method I discover the means of passing from faith to understanding. But, ordinarily fatigued by my efforts, I leave an investigation of which I do not believe myself capable to people more enlightened or more industrious than I; and all the reward I derive from my work is that I am continually more aware of the smallness of my mind, the profundity of our mysteries, and the extreme need we all have of an authority to guide us. Very well, Aristes, are you satisfied?

ARISTES. Not quite. Everything you are saying here is still so general that it seems to me you are teaching me nothing. Examples, if you please. Reveal some truth to me, that I might just see how you attain it.

THEODORE. What truth?

ARISTES. The fundamental truth of our religion.

THEODORE. But that truth is already known to you, and I believe you have properly demonstrated it.

ARISTES. No matter. Let us see. It cannot be proved too much. It is from there that we must begin.

THEOTIMUS. True. But that will be where we finish. For soon we shall have to part.

ARISTES. I also hope it will not be long before we meet again.

V. THEODORE. That is what I do not know, for I hope for it so strongly that I fear it will not happen. But let us not discourse about the future. Let us profit from the present. Be attentive to what I am going to tell you.

To discover by reason from among all religions which one God established, we must attentively consult the notion we have of God or of infinitely perfect Being. For it is evident that whatever causes bring about must necessarily have some relation to them. Let us then consult, Aristes, that notion of infinitely perfect Being, and reexamine in our mind everything we know of the divine attributes, since it is from there that we must draw the light we need to discover what we seek.

ARISTES. Very well. And assuming this?

THEODORE. Slowly, slowly, please. God knows perfectly those attributes which I assume you have present to your mind. He glories in possessing them, He takes infinite gratification in them. He can act, therefore, only according to what He is, only in a manner which bears the character of these same attributes. Take careful note of that. For it is the great principle we must follow if we claim to know what God does or does not do. People do not always act according to what they are. But that is because they are ashamed of themselves. I know a miser whom you would take for the most generous man in the world. Therefore do not be deceived by this. By their actions, and still less by their words, people do not always reveal the judgment they pass on themselves, since they are not what they should be. But it is not the same with God. The infinitely perfect Being cannot but act according to what He is. When He acts He necessarily manifests outwardly the eternal and immutable judgment He passes on His attributes, because He delights in them and glories in possessing them.

ARISTES. That is evident. But I do not see where all these generalities are leading.

VI. THEODORE. To this, Aristes: God indicates perfectly the

judgment He passes on Himself only through the incarnation of His Son, only through the consecration of His pontiff, only through the establishment of the religion we possess, in which alone He is able to find the worship and adoration which express His divine perfections, and which agree with the judgment He passes on them. When God drew chaos from nothingness, He declared: I am the almighty. When He formed the universe from it, He revelled in His wisdom. When He created us free and capable of good and evil, He expressed the judgment He makes on His justice and goodness. But when He unites His Word to His work, He declares that He is infinite in all His attributes, that this great universe is nothing in relation to Him, that all is profane in relation to His sanctity, to His excellence, to His sovereign majesty. In a word, He speaks as God, He acts according to what He is and according to all that He is. Compare, Aristes, our religion with that of the Jews, the Mohammedans, and all the others you know; and judge which one most distinctly declares the judgment which God has and we must have of His attributes.

ARISTES. Ah, Theodore! I understand you.

VII. THEODORE. I suppose so. But take note of this. God is spirit and wills to be worshipped in spirit and in truth. True worship does not consist in outward appearances, in a particular position of our bodies, but in a particular position of our minds in the presence of the divine majesty; that is, it consists in the judgments and movements of the soul. Now, people who offer the Son to the Father, people who worship God through Jesus Christ, by their action pronounce a judgment similar to the one God makes of Himself. From all His judgments, I say, He declares the one which expresses the divine perfections most exactly, and above all that excellence or infinite sanctity which separates the divinity from everything else or which elevates Him infinitely above all creatures. Thus, faith in Jesus Christ is the true religion, access to God through Jesus Christ is the sole true worship, the sole way to place our minds in a position to worship God, consequently the sole way of attracting signs of kindness and good will from the author of the felicity for which we hope.

People who give part of their goods to the poor or who risk their life to save their homeland, even people who, knowing well that God is powerful enough to reward their sacrifice of their life, generously lose it in order not to commit an injustice, through that action truly evince a judgment which honors divine justice and renders it favorable to them. However, this action, as completely meritorious as it is, does not worship God perfectly if those whom I am here assuming capable of undertaking it refuse to believe in Jesus Christ and claim to have access to God without His mediation. As the judgment to count for something in relation to God, which these people pass on themselves by their refusal, is directly opposed to the one which God demonstrates through His mission and the consecration of His pontiff, this presumptuous judgment renders such an otherwise meritorious action useless for their eternal salvation. This is because to merit the possession of an infinite good fairly, it is not enough to express God's justice through some good deeds of moral virtue; we must divinely declare, through faith in Jesus Christ, a judgment which honors God according to all that He is. For it is only through the merit of this faith that our good works receive that supernatural excellence which grants us the right to the heritage of the children of God. Indeed it is only through the merit of this faith that we can obtain the power to vanquish our dominant passion and to sacrifice our life by a pure love of justice. In fact our actions derive their morality from the relation they have to the immutable order, and they derive their merit from the judgments we exhibit through them concerning the divine power and justice. But they derive their supernatural worth and as it were their infinity and divinity only through Jesus Christ, whose incarnation, sacrifice, and priesthood, which clearly reveal that there is no relation between creator and creature, thereby set in place so great a relation that God delights and glories in His work. Do you understand very distinctly, Aristes, what I am able to express to you only quite imperfectly?

VIII. ARISTES. It seems to me that I understand it. There is no relation between the finite and the infinite. This can pass for a common notion. Compared to God the universe is nothing and must be counted as nothing. But it is only Christians, only those who believe in the divinity of Jesus Christ, who truly count their own being, and this vast universe we admire, as nothing. Perhaps philosophers pass this judgment. But they do not declare it. On the contrary they belie this judgment by their actions. They dare to approach God as if they no longer knew that the distance from Him to us is infinite. They imagine

God to delight in the profane worship they render to Him. They have the insolence or, if you will, the presumption to worship Him. Let them be silent. Their respectful silence will declare, better than their words, the speculative judgment they form concerning what they are in relation to God. It is only Christians who may open their mouths to praise the Lord divinely. It is only they who gain access to His sovereign majesty. For they truly count themselves for nothing, themselves and all the rest of the universe in relation to God, when they profess that it is only through Jesus Christ that they claim to have any relation to Him. This annihilation to which their faith reduces them gives them a genuine reality before God. That judgment they pronounce in agreement with God Himself bestows an infinite worth upon all their worship. All is profane in relation to God, and must be consecrated through the divinity of the Son in order to be worthy of the sanctity of the Father, to merit His satisfaction and good will. This is the unshakable foundation of our sacred religion.

IX. THEODORE. Surely, Aristes, you definitely understand my thought. From the finite to the infinite and, what is more, from the profound nothingness to which sin has reduced us to the divine sanctity, to the right hand of the most high, the distance is infinite. By nature we are but children of wrath: "by nature children of wrath."[*] We are as *Atheists* in this world,[**] without God, without benefactor: "without God in this world."[†] But through Jesus Christ we are already risen, we have been raised up and are seated in the highest heavens: God "hath quickened us together in Christ ... and hath raised us up together, and hath made us sit together in the heavenly places, through Jesus Christ."[‡] At present we are unaware of our adoption in Jesus Christ, our divinity: "partakers of the divine nature."[§] But that is because our life is hidden in God with Jesus Christ. When Jesus Christ appears again, then shall we appear with Him in glory: "We know, that, when he shall appear, we shall be like to him."[¶] "Your life," says St. Paul, "is hid with Christ in God. When Christ shall appear, who is your life, then you also shall appear with him in glory."[||] Between us and the divinity there is no longer this infinite distance that separated us. "But now in Christ Jesus, you, who some

[*] Ephesians 2: 3. [**] Ἄθεοι. [†] [Ephesians 2:] 12. [‡] [Ephesians 2:] 5–6.
[§] 2 Peter [1:] 4. [¶] 1 John 3: 2. [||] Colossians 3: 3[–4].

time were afar off, are made nigh by the blood of Christ. For he is our peace . . ."* For through Jesus Christ we all gain access to the Father. "For by him we have access both in one Spirit to the Father."** Therefore, listen again to the apostle's conclusion: "Now therefore you are no more strangers and foreigners; but you are fellow citizens with the saints, and the domestics of God, built upon the foundation of the apostles and prophets, Jesus Christ himself being the chief corner-stone: in whom all the building, being framed together, groweth up into an holy temple in the Lord. In whom you also are built together into an habitation of God in the Spirit."† Weigh all these words, Aristes, and principally these: "in whom all the building, being framed together, groweth up into a holy temple in the Lord."‡

ARISTES. It is only the Man–God, Theodore, who can join creature to creator, who can sanctify the profane, construct a temple where God can live in honor. I now understand the sense of those words: "God indeed was in Christ, reconciling the world to himself."§ It is a common notion that there is no relation between the finite and the infinite. Everything depends on this incontestable principle. Any worship that belies this principle offends Reason and dishonors the divinity. The eternal wisdom cannot be its author. It is only pride, only ignorance, or at least simply the stupidity of the human mind which can now approve it. For it is only the religion of Jesus Christ that declares the judgment which God passes and which we must ourselves form on the limitation of creatures and on the sovereign majesty of the creator.

THEODORE. What do you say then, Aristes, of the Socinians and Arians, of all those false Christians who deny the divinity of Jesus Christ and who nonetheless claim to have access to God through Him?

ARISTES. These are people who find some relation between the infinite and the finite, and who count themselves something compared to God.

THEOTIMUS. Not at all, Aristes, since they recognize that it is only through Jesus Christ that they gain access to God.

ARISTES. Yes, but their Jesus is pure creature only. They find then some relation between the finite and the infinite, and they pronounce this false judgment, this judgment which is insulting to the divinity,

---

* Ephesians 2: 13[–14].   ** [Ephesians 2:] 18.   † Ephesians 2: 19[–22].
‡ Ephesians 2: 21.   § 2 Corinthians 5: 19.

when they worship God through Jesus Christ. How will the Jesus of the heretics give them access to the divine majesty, to Him who is infinitely remote from them? How will He establish the worship which makes us pass that judgment which God passes on Himself, which expresses the sanctity, the divinity, the infinity of His essence? All worship founded on such a Jesus assumes, Theotimus, some relation between the finite and the infinite, and infinitely debases the divine majesty. It is a false worship, insulting to God, incapable of reconciling Him with people. The only true religion can be that which is founded on the only Son of the Father, on that Man–God who joins heaven and earth, the finite and the infinite, through the incomprehensible agreement between the two natures which render Him at once equal to His Father and similar to us. This appears evident to me.

X. THEOTIMUS. It is clear, I grant you. But what shall we say of angels? Did they wait to glorify God, until Jesus Christ was at their head?

ARISTES. Let us not abandon what appears evident to us, Theotimus, whatever difficulty we have in reconciling it with certain things we hardly know. Please answer for me, Theodore.

THEODORE. The angels did not wait for Jesus Christ, for Jesus Christ is before them. He is the first born of all creatures, "the firstborn of every creature."* It is only two thousand years since He was born in Bethlehem, but six thousand since He was sacrificed: "the lamb, which was slain from the beginning of the world."** How so? It is because of the first of God's plans, the incarnation of His Son, because it is only in Him that God receives the adoration of the angels, suffered the sacrifices of the Jews, and receives and will eternally receive our praises: "Jesus Christ, yesterday, and today; and the same for ever."† Everything expresses and represents Jesus Christ. Everything is related to Him after its manner, from the most noble of intellects down to the most contemptible insects. When Jesus Christ is born in Bethlehem, then do the angels glorify the Lord. They all sing in shared harmony, "Glory to God in the highest."‡ They all declare that it is through Jesus Christ that heaven is full of glory. But it is to us they declare it, to us to whom the future is not present. Before Him who is immutable in His designs

* Colossians 1: 15.   ** Apocalypse 13: 8.   † Hebrews 13: 8.
‡ Luke 2: 14.

and who sees His works before they are executed, they always urged the need for a pontiff to worship Him divinely. They recognized the savior of people as their leader, even before His temporal birth. They always considered themselves nothing in relation to God, excluding perhaps those proud angels who were cast into hell because of their pride.

ARISTES. You remind me, Theodore, of what the church sings when we are about to offer sacrifice to God: "It is through him that thy majesty is praised by angels, adored by dominations, feared by powers," and so on.[1] The priest raises his voice to lift up our spirits to heaven, "Let us lift up our hearts;"[2] to teach us that it is through Jesus Christ that the angels themselves worship the divine majesty, and to bring us to join them under this divine leader in order to form but a single choir of praises and to be able to say to God, "Holy, holy, holy art thou, Lord God of hosts. Thy glory fills all heaven and earth."[3] Heaven and earth are full of God's glory, but through Jesus Christ, the pontiff of the most high. It is only through Him that creatures, however excellent they may be, can worship God, pray to Him, render to Him acts of grace for His blessings.

THEOTIMUS. Surely it is in Jesus Christ that everything subsists, since without Him heaven itself is not worthy of the majesty of the creator. By themselves the angels cannot have relation, access, or society with the infinite Being. Jesus Christ must intervene and pacify heaven as well as earth, in a word, generally reconcile all things with God. It is true He is not the savior of angels in the same sense that He is the savior of people. He did not deliver them from their sins as He delivered us; but He delivered them from the natural incapacity of creatures to have any relation with God, to be able to honor Him divinely. Thus He is their leader as well as ours, their mediator, their savior, since it is only through Him that they subsist and approach the infinite majesty of God, that they are able to impart, in agreement with God Himself, the judgment they pass on His sanctity. It seems to me that St. Paul had this truth in mind when he wrote all these divine words to the Colossians: "Who hath delivered us from the power of darkness, and hath translated us into the kingdom of the Son of his love, in whom we

---

[1] Order of the Low Mass, The Common Preface, in *The Missal in Latin and English* (New York: Sheed & Ward, 1949), p. 724.

[2] Order of the Low Mass, Preface to the Canon, ibid., p. 723.

[3] Order of the Low Mass, The Common Preface, ibid., p. 724.

have redemption through his blood, the remission of sins; who is the image of the invisible God, *the firstborn of every creature*: for in him were all things created in heaven and on earth, visible and invisible, whether thrones, or dominations, or principalities, or powers: all things were created by him and in him. *And he is before all, and by him all things consist. And he is the head of the body, the church*, who is the beginning, the firstborn from the dead; *that in all things he may hold the primacy*: because in him, it hath well pleased the Father, that all fulness should dwell; and through him to reconcile *all* things unto himself, making peace through the blood of his cross, both as to the things that are on earth, and the things that *are in heaven*."[4] How excellent these words are, and how nobly they express the great idea we should have of our sacred religion!

XI. ARISTES. It is true, Theotimus, that this passage from St. Paul, and perhaps some others too, agree perfectly well with what we have just said. But in good faith we must grant that the great reason Scripture gives God for the incarnation of His Son is His goodness toward men. "For God so loved the world," says St. John, "as to give his only begotten Son."[*] There are a number of other passages you know better than I, which teach us this truth.

THEOTIMUS. Who doubts that the Son of God was made man through goodness toward people, to deliver them from their sins? But who can also doubt that He delivers us from our sins in order to consecrate us a living temple to the glory of His Father, in order that we and the angels themselves should divinely honor the sovereign majesty through Him? These two motives are not contrary; they are subordinate to one another. And since God loves all things to the extent that they are lovable, since He loves Himself infinitely more than us, it is clear that the greater of the two motives, to which all others are related, is that His attributes be divinely glorified by all His creatures in Jesus Christ our savior.

As Scripture is not written for angels, it was not necessary that it continually reiterate that Jesus Christ came to be their leader as well as ours, and that with them we make but a single church and a single concert of praises. Scripture, written for people and for people who are

---

[4]   Colossians 1: 13–20 (Malebranche's italics).
[*]   John 3: 16.

sinners, had to speak as it did and constantly propose to us the motive most capable of exciting an ardent love of our liberator in us. It had to represent our unworthiness to us and the absolute necessity of a mediator to gain access to God, a necessity founded much more on the nothingness and abomination of sin than on the natural incapacity of all created beings. No mere creatures are able to honor God divinely by themselves, but nor do they dishonor Him as the sinner does. God does not set His store in them, but nor does He hold them in horror like He holds sin and him who commits it. Thus, Scripture had to speak as it did of the incarnation of Jesus Christ, to make people feel their wretchedness and the mercy of God, in order that the feeling of our wretchedness would hold us in humility, and God's mercy would fill us with trust and love.

THEODORE. You are right, Theotimus. Holy Scripture speaks to us according to the plans of God, which are to humble creatures, to relate them to Jesus Christ and through Jesus Christ to Himself. If God left all people enveloped in sin, in order to extend them mercy in Jesus Christ, this was in order to humble their pride and enhance the power and worthiness of His pontiff. He willed that we should owe our divine leader all that we are, in order to tie us more closely to Him. He allowed the corruption of His work so that the Father of the future world, the author of the celestial Jerusalem, would labor on the nothingness not of being but of sanctity and justice, and that through a grace which cannot be merited we would become a new creature in and through Him. Filled with the divinity whose plenitude lives in Him substantially, through Jesus Christ alone we would be able to render divine honors to God. Read the Epistles of St. Paul reflectively, and there you will find what I am telling you. What do we not owe Him who raises us to the dignity of God's children, after having pulled us from a state worse than nothingness itself, and who, to draw us from that state, annihilates Himself to the point of rendering Himself like us in order to be the victim of our sins? Why then would Scripture, which is not written for the angels, which is written not so much for philosophers as for simple people, which is written only to make us love God and relate us to Jesus Christ and through Jesus Christ to God; why, I say, would Scripture explain to us the plans of the incarnation in relation to the angels? Why would it rest on the unworthiness natural to all creatures, the unworthiness of sin being infinitely more tangible, and the sight of this unworthiness being much more capable of humbling and annihilating us before God?

The angels who are in heaven have never offended God. Yet St. Paul teaches us that Jesus Christ pacifies what is in heaven as well as what is on earth: "making peace through the blood of his cross, both as to the things that are on earth, and the things that are in heaven."* God reestablishes us, maintains or, according to the Greek,** reunites all things under a single leader, what is in heaven and on earth: "he hath purposed in him ... to re-establish all things in Christ, that are in heaven and on earth, in him."† In brief, Jesus Christ is the leader of the entire church: "he ... hath made him head over all the church."‡ Does this not suffice to make us understand that it is only through Jesus Christ that the angels themselves worship God divinely; and that they have society, access, and relation with Him only through this well-beloved Son in whom the Father is singularly pleased, through whom He delights perfectly in Himself? "My beloved in whom my soul hath been well pleased."§

ARISTES. That appears evident to me. There are not two different churches, two holy Sions. "But you are come," says St. Paul, "to mount Sion, and to the city of the living God, the heavenly Jerusalem, and to the spirits of the just made perfect."¶ And since God established Jesus Christ over the entire church, I believe it is only through Him that the angels themselves render their duties to God, and are and have always been favorably received by Him. However, I have an objection to put to you against the principle you established at the outset.

XII. You told us, Theodore, that God wills to be worshipped in spirit and in truth, that is, by judgments and movements of the soul; and that our worship and even our good works draw their moral goodness from the judgments they declare, which judgments are in conformity with the divine attributes or the immutable order of the divine perfections. You understand me well. However, I ask you, do you think that ordinary people understand so much subtlety? Do you think they form these judgments which worship God in spirit and in truth? Yet if people generally do not pass the judgment they ought to pass on the divine attributes or perfections, they will not signify those judgments by their actions. Thus they will not do good deeds. They will not worship both in spirit and in truth through their faith in Jesus Christ unless they actually

---

*   Colossians 1 [: 20].   ** Ἀνακεφαλαιώσασθαι.   † Ephesians 1: 10.
‡   [Ephesians 1:] 22.   § Matthew 12: 18.   ¶ Hebrews 12: 22.

know that to offer the Son to the Father is to declare that creatures and sinners cannot stand in direct relation to God. And it seems to me that it is about this that many Christians do not think. They are good Christians, however, whom I do not believe you would dare condemn.

THEODORE. Take careful note, Aristes. To do a good act it is not absolutely necessary to know distinctly that we are thereby evincing a judgment which honors the divine attributes or conforms to the immutable order of the perfections which the divine essence contains. But in order for our actions to be good, they must necessarily entail such judgments by themselves; and people who act must possess the idea of order at least confusedly, and love it, though they might not really know what it is. I shall explain. When people give alms, it can happen that at the time they are not thinking that God is just. Far indeed from making the judgment that they are rendering the divine justice honor through their alms and are rendering it favorable, it can happen that they are not thinking of reward. It can also happen that they do not know that God contains in Himself this immutable order whose beauty actually moves them, nor that it is the conformity which their action has to this order that renders them essentially good and pleasing to Him whose inviolable law is but this very order. Yet it is true to say that people who give alms demonstrate, by their liberality, the judgment that God is just; and it is true to say that they demonstrate it more distinctly to the extent that the good of which they deprive themselves by their charity is more necessary to satisfy their passions; and finally it is true to say that the more distinctly they demonstrate it, all the more honor they bestow upon the divine justice, all the more they oblige it to reward them, all the greater the merit they acquire before God. Likewise, although they do not precisely know what the immutable order is, nor that the goodness of their act consists in the conformity it has to that same order, it is nonetheless true that it is and can be just only through this conformity.

Since the first sin our ideas are so confused and the natural law is so dim, that we need a written law to teach us in a tangible way what we must do or not do. As most people do not enter into themselves, they do not hear that inner voice which cries to them, "Thou shalt not covet."[5] This voice had to be sounded from without and had to enter

---

[5] Romans 7: 7.

their mind through their senses. Nonetheless they were never able to efface completely the idea of order, that general idea corresponding to the words 'we must,' 'we ought,' 'it is just to.' For the least sign reveals this indelible idea even in children still at their mother's breast. Without it people would be completely incorrigible, or rather absolutely incapable of good or evil. Now, provided we act by depending on this confused and general idea of order, and what we do is otherwise in perfect conformity with it, it is certain that the movement of the heart is regulated, though the mind is not quite enlightened. It is true that it is obedience to divine authority that produces faithful and good people. But as God can command only according to His inviolable law, the immutable order, only according to the eternal and invariable judgment He passes upon Himself and the perfections He contains in His essence, it is clear that all our deeds are essentially good only because they express and so to speak declare that judgment. Let us come now to the objection of those good Christians who worship God in the simplicity of their faith.

XIII. It is evident that the incarnation of Jesus Christ declares from without, as it were, that judgment God makes of Himself, that nothing finite can be related to Him. People who recognize the necessity of a mediator judge of their own unworthiness; and if at the same time they believe that this mediator cannot simply be a creature, however excellent we might suppose it to be, they enhance the divine majesty infinitely. In itself their faith is, then, in conformity with the judgment God passes on us and on His divine perfections. Thus, it worships God perfectly, since by these judgments which are true and conform to those which God passes on Himself, it places the mind in the most respectful position in which it can be in the presence of His infinite majesty. However, you say, most Christians do not understand so much subtlety. They go to God in quite a simple way. They are simply unaware that they are in such a respectful position. This I grant you. They do not all know it in the way you know it. But they do not cease being there. And God sees quite well that they are there, at least in the disposition of their heart. They leave it to Jesus Christ, who is their head and who as it were is their spokesman in presenting them to God in the condition which suits them. And Jesus Christ, who regards them as His people, as the members of His own body, as united to Him through their love and their faith, does not fail to speak for them and to declare openly what they cannot express. Thus, in the simplicity of their faith and the readiness of their heart, all Christians, with a very perfect adoration which is very pleasing to God, forever worship all His divine attributes through Jesus Christ. It is not necessary, Aristes, that we know exactly the reasons for our faith, I mean the reasons with which metaphysics can furnish us. But it is absolutely necessary that we profess it, just as it is not necessary that we distinctly conceive what constitutes the morality of our deeds, although it is absolutely necessary that we do good deeds. I do not believe, however, that those who deal in philosophy can employ their time more usefully than by attempting to obtain some understanding of the truths which faith teaches us.

ARISTES. Surely, Theodore, there is no more sensible pleasure, or at least no more solid joy, than that which the understanding of the truths of faith produces in us.

THEOTIMUS. Yes, in those who have considerable love for religion, and whose heart is not corrupted. For there are people for whom light is painful. They become angry when they see what perhaps they would like not to be there.

THEODORE. There are few of these people, Theotimus. But there are many who are afraid, and rightfully so, of falling into some error and dragging others down with them. They would be glad if one explained matters and defended religion. But as we naturally mistrust those whom we do not know, we become fearful, frightened, excited, and consequently pass judgments of passion, always unjust and contrary to charity. This silences many people who should perhaps speak and from whom I would have learned better principles than those I have proposed to you. But often that does not oblige those heedless and reckless authors to be silent, who loudly broadcast everything that comes into their mind. As for me, when people have as a principle to submit only to evidence and to authority, when I perceive them working only to seek good proofs of received dogmas, I am not afraid of their being able to go dangerously astray. Perhaps they will fall into some error. But what do you want? This is entailed by our wretched condition. It would be to banish reason from the world if we had to be infallible in order to have the right to reason.

ARISTES. I must in good faith confess my prejudice to you, Theodore. Before our discussion I was of the opinion that it was absolutely necessary to banish reason from religion, as being capable only of disrupting it. But I now recognize that if we leave it to the enemies of faith, we shall soon be pushed to the limit and decried as brutes. Those with Reason on their side have very powerful arms to render themselves masters of minds. For after all we are all rational, and essentially rational. And to claim to divest oneself of Reason as one casts off a ceremonial robe is to make oneself ridiculous and vainly to attempt the impossible. Thus, at the time I decided we must never reason in theology I actually felt that I was demanding something of the theologians that they would never grant to me. I now understand, Theodore, that I lapsed into an excess which was very dangerous and did not do much honor to our sacred religion, founded by sovereign Reason which is accommodated to us in order to render us more rational. It is better to adhere to the attitude you have adopted, to found dogmas on the authority of the church and to seek the proofs of these dogmas in the simple and clearest principles with which Reason furnishes us. Thus, we must make metaphysics serve religion (for of all the parts of philosophy there is scarcely any other that could be of use to it) and shed onto the truths of faith that light which serves to reassure the mind and place it in genuine harmony with the heart. In this way we shall preserve our rational nature, notwithstanding our obedience and submission to the authority of the church.

THEODORE. Remain firm in this thought, Aristes, always submissive to the authority of the church, always prepared to yield to Reason. But do not take the opinions of certain doctors, of certain communities, and even of an entire nation, for certain truths. And do not condemn them too lightly. As for the opinions of the philosophers, yield to them completely only when evidence obliges and forces you to do so. I am giving you this advice to cure any evil I may have caused; and if I have had the misfortune of proposing to you opinions which are hardly certain as if they were true, you should be able to recognize their falsehood by following this good advice, this advice which is so necessary and which I strongly fear having often neglected.

Index

Cambridge texts in the history of philosophy

Titles published in the series thus far

Antoine Arnauld and Pierre Nicole *Logic or the Art of Thinking* (edited by Jill Vance Buroker)

Boyle *A Free Enquiry into the Vulgarly Received Notion of Nature* (edited by Edward B. Davis and Michael Hunter)

Conway *The Principles of the Most Ancient and Modern Philosophy* (edited by Allison P. Coudert and Taylor Corse)

Cudworth *A Treatise Concerning Eternal and Immutable Morality* with *A Treatise of Freewill* (edited by Sarah Hutton)

Descartes *Meditations on First Philosophy*, with selections from the *Objections and Replies* (edited with an introduction by John Cottingham)

Kant *The Metaphysics of Morals* (edited by Mary Gregor with an introduction by Roger Sullivan)

Kant *Prolegomena to any Future Metaphysics* (edited by Gary Hatfield)

La Mettrie *Machine Man and Other Writings* (edited by Ann Thomson)

Leibniz *New Essays on Human Understanding* (edited by Peter Remnant and Jonathan Bennett)

Malebranche *Dialogues on Metaphysics and on Religion* (edited by Nicholas Jolley and David Scott)

Malebranche *The Search after Truth* (edited by Thomas M. Lennon and Paul J. Olscamp)

Mendelssohn *Philosophical Writings* (edited by Daniel O. Dahlstrom)

Nietzsche *Human, All Too Human* (translated by R. J. Hollingdale with an introduction by Richard Schacht)

Schleiermacher *On Religion: Speeches to its Cultured Despisers* (edited by Richard Crouter)